Phonics for Teachers

Self-Instruction, Methods, and Activities

Second Edition

J. Lloyd Eldredge
Brigham Young University

PEARSON

Merrill
Prentice Hall

Upper Saddle River, New Jersey
Columbus, Ohio

Library of Congress Cataloging in Publication Data

Eldredge, J. Lloyd (Joseph Lloyd)
Phonics for teachers : self-instruction, methods, and activities / J. Lloyd Eldredge.—2nd ed.
p. cm.
Includes bibliographical references and index.
ISBN 0-13-111524-3
1. Reading—Phonetic method. 2. Reading—Phonetic method—Problems, exercises, etc. 3.
Education, Elementary—Activity programs. I. Title.
LB1573.3.E427 2004
372.46'5—dc21

2003048641

Vice President and Executive Publisher: Jeffery W. Johnston
Senior Editor: Linda Ashe Montgomery
Editorial Assistant: Laura Weaver
Production Editor: Mary M. Irvin
Production Coordination: WordCrafters Editorial Services, Inc.
Design Coordinator: Diane C. Lorenzo
Cover Designer: Tom Borah
Cover Image: Getty Images
Production Manager: Pamela D. Bennett
Director of Marketing: Ann Castel Davis
Marketing Manager: Darcy Betts Prybella
Marketing Coordinator: Tyra Poole

This book was set in Palatino by Carlisle Communications, Ltd. It was printed and bound by R. R.
Donnelley & Sons Company. The cover was printed by Phoenix Color Corp.

Pearson Education Ltd.
Pearson Education Singapore Pte. Ltd.
Pearson Education Canada, Ltd.
Pearson Education—Japan

Pearson Education Australia Pty. Limited
Pearson Education North Asia Ltd.
Pearson Educación de Mexico, S.A. de C.V.
Pearson Education Malaysia Pte. Ltd.

10 9 8 7 6 5 4 3 2 1
ISBN: 0-13-111524-3

Preface

Reading and writing are complex processes requiring a variety of knowledge sources and thinking abilities. For effective reading and writing, individuals need a working knowledge of encoding/decoding, vocabulary, syntax, anaphora, prosody, and text structure. They need to have experiences with the world in which they live—experiences stored in the brain and used as they construct meaning during the reading and writing process.

Reading involves the ability to translate written language into spoken language (decoding), and writing involves the ability to represent spoken language with the symbols designated for that purpose (encoding). Writers select appropriate words (vocabulary/schemata), use appropriate punctuation (prosodic features of print), use appropriate sentence patterns (syntax), organize their sentences in some cohesive fashion (anaphora), and organize the entire text in some meaningful way (text structure) to communicate their ideas to readers. Readers use their schemata, vocabulary, prosody, syntax, anaphora, and text structure knowledge to help them understand what writers are trying to communicate. In other words, writers need specific knowledge sources to be able to connect important ideas between sentences *and* larger units of text, and readers need those same knowledge sources to be able to perceive those idea relationships.

Furthermore, both readers and writers must be able to think. Effective writers use their thinking abilities to entertain, teach, and create visual images from written words. Effective readers use their thinking abilities to read between the lines, perceive relationships among ideas, create their own visual images, and critically evaluate the messages writers create.

Reading is a process involving much more than decoding. However, without the ability to translate the written language into spoken language, readers could not "read." Without the ability to decode, individuals could not access the knowledge sources and thinking abilities needed to construct meaning from written text. In short, the knowledge sources used by readers to engage in literal, inferential, and critical reading are dependent on their ability to decode. Decoding knowledge, therefore, is a critical component in the reading process.

The focus of this text is decoding. The major portion of this book is organized as a self-instruction text to help you understand phonics and its role in the enhancement of decoding processes and overall reading growth. Phonics knowledge is needed for the identification of words both by analogy and context. It is also necessary for "sounding out" both single-syllable and multisyllabic words, and for identifying words by morphemic analysis. Furthermore, existing research reveals that phonics knowledge is needed for extensive word recognition. Since word recognition is necessary for reading fluency, and reading fluency is essential for reading comprehension, phonics knowledge is extremely important.

The latter portion of this book is devoted to phonics teaching. In this portion of the book, you will be introduced to teaching activities that direct children's attention toward written words so they can discover how speech sounds are mapped onto print. These activities are designed to help children learn strategies for identifying written words they don't recognize and, in the process, enhance their word recognition abilities.

This text can be used in college courses, in-service workshops, and independently by individuals who wish to improve their understanding and use of phonics.

Acknowledgments

We would like to thank the reviewers of the manuscript for their insightful comments: Patricia P. Fritchie, Troy State University–Dothan; Edward W. Holmes, Towson State University; Nancy B. Keller, State University of New York–Oneonta; William S. O'Bruba, Bloomsburg University; and Nancy H. Phillips, Lynchburg College.

About the Author ■■■■■■■■■

J. Lloyd Eldredge is a professor in the College of Education at the Brigham Young University, where he teaches both graduate and undergraduate literacy courses.

Dr. Eldredge is a former elementary school teacher, school principal, and school superintendent. He has also served as the Utah Director of Chapter I, the Utah Director of Early Childhood Education, and the Utah Director of Elementary Education.

During the past 18 years his research has been focused on phonemic awareness, phonics, a reconceptualization of decoding instruction in the early years of schooling, whole language, oral reading, and the effects of various forms of "assisted reading" strategies (dyad reading, group assisted reading, and taped assisted reading) on young and "at risk" readers. His work is published in such journals as *Journal of Educational Research, Reading Research and Instruction, Journal of Reading, The Reading Teacher, Journal of Literacy Research*, and *Reading Research Quarterly*. He is the author of two books on phonics and decoding: *Decoding Strategies* and *Teaching Decoding in Holistic Classrooms*.

Discover the Companion Website Accompanying This Book

THE PRENTICE HALL COMPANION WEBSITE: A VIRTUAL LEARNING ENVIRONMENT

Technology is a constantly growing and changing aspect of our field that is creating a need for content and resources. To address this emerging need, Prentice Hall has developed an online learning environment for students and professors alike—Companion Websites—to support our textbooks.

In creating a Companion Website, our goal is to build on and enhance what the textbook already offers. For this reason, the content for each user-friendly website is organized by topic and provides the professor and student with a variety of meaningful resources. Common features of a Companion Website include:

FOR THE PROFESSOR—

Every Companion Website integrates **Syllabus Manager** ™, an online syllabus creation and management utility.

- **Syllabus Manager** ™ provides you, the instructor, with an easy, step-by-step process to create and revise syllabi, with direct links into Companion Website and other online content without having to learn HTML.
- Students may logon to your syllabus during any study session. All they need to know is the web address for the Companion Website and the password you've assigned to your syllabus.
- After you have created a syllabus using **Syllabus Manager** ™, students may enter the syllabus for their course section from any point in the Companion Website.
- Clicking on a date, the student is shown the list of activities for the assignment. The activities for each assignment are linked directly to actual content, saving time for students.
- Adding assignments consists of clicking on the desired due date, then filling in the details of the assignment—name of the assignment, instructions, and whether or not it is a one-time or repeating assignment.
- In addition, links to other activities can be created easily. If the activity is online, a URL can be entered in the space provided, and it will be linked automatically in the final syllabus.
- Your completed syllabus is hosted on our servers, allowing convenient updates from any computer on the Internet. Changes you make to your syllabus are immediately available to your students at their next logon.

FOR THE STUDENT—

- **Topic Overviews—** Outline key concepts in topic areas.
- **Strategies—** These websites provide suggestions and information on how to implement instructional strategies and activities for each topic. The Assessment topic also contains Practice Case Studies as well.

- **Web Links—** A wide range of websites that allow the students to access current information on everything from rationales for specific types of instruction, to research on related topics, to compilations of useful articles, and more.
- **Electronic Bluebook—** Send homework or essays directly to your instructor's email with this paperless form.
- **Message Board—** Virtual bulletin board to post or respond to questions or comments from a national audience.
- **Chat—** Real-time chat with anyone who is using the text anywhere in the country—ideal for discussion and study groups, class projects, etc.

To take advantage of these and other resources, please visit the *Phonics for Teachers: Self-Instruction, Methods, and Activities,* Second Edition, Companion Website at

www.prenhall.com/Eldredge

Contents

ONE　　　**PHONICS SELF-INSTRUCTION**　　**1**

Self-Evaluation: A Pretest　　2

Chapter 1　Phonics and Phonemic Awareness Research　　**8**
Phonemic Awareness and Phonics Knowledge Defined, 8
Importance of Phonemic Awareness, 8
Importance of Phonics Knowledge, 9
Phonemic Awareness and Phonics Knowledge—Necessary, But Not Sufficient, 9
Research Findings on Teaching Reading, 10
Phonics and Literacy Development, 11
Review 1, 19

Chapter 2　Consonants　　**21**
Review 2, 26
Consonant Phonemes, 26
Review 3, 30
Single-Letter Consonant Graphemes (b, c, d, f, g), 31
Review 4, 36
Single-Letter Consonant Graphemes (h, j, k, l, m), 37
Review 5, 40
Single-Letter Consonant Graphemes (n, p, q, r, s), 41
Review 6, 45
Single-Letter Consonant Graphemes (t, v, w, x, y, z), 46
Review 7, 49
Consonant Digraphs, 50
Review 8, 55
Consonant Blends, 55
Review 9, 59

Chapter 3　Vowels　　**60**
Review 10, 64
Vowel Phonemes, 65
Review 11, 69
Long Vowel Phonemes and Graphemes, 69
Review 12, 73

Short Vowel Phonemes and Graphemes, 73
Review 13, 80
Vowel Teams, 80
Review 14, 90
A Review of Phonemes and the Graphemes Most Frequently
    Representing Them, 91

Chapter 4   Onsets and Rimes   92
Review 15, 96

Chapter 5   Syllabication and Accent   98
The Syllable, 98
Accented and Unaccented Syllables and the Schwa Phoneme, 102
Accent Placement Clues, 104
Review 16, 107
Syllable Division Clues, 108
Review 17, 114

Self-Evaluation: A Posttest   115

TWO   CLASSROOM PHONICS ACTIVITIES   121

Chapter 6   Teaching Phonics to Children   122
Phonics Knowledge, 122
Phonics Instruction, 123

Chapter 7   Developmental Stages of Decoding   127

Chapter 8   Early Experiences with Written Text   130
Reading Books with Children, 130
Using Books to Develop Word Awareness, 132
Using Books to Develop Awareness of Rhyme, 139
Developing Phonemic Awareness and Simple Phonics Knowledge, 142
Early Writing Activities, 168

Chapter 9   Learning to Read and Write
Single-Syllable Words   177
Developmental Spelling Stages, 178
Important Phonics Knowledge, 180
Discovering Syllable Patterns, 182
Syllable Pattern Activity with Single Consonants, 183

Discovering Consonant Digraphs, 187
Syllable Pattern Activity with Beginning Consonant Digraphs, 188
Discovering Consonant Blends, 190
Activities with Consonant Blends, 191
Syllable Pattern Activity with Beginning Consonant Blends, 192
Discovering Vowel Team Patterns, 195
Syllable Pattern Activity Involving Open, Closed, VCe, and Vowel Team
    Syllables, 196

*Chapter 10   Learning to Read and Write Words of More Than One
Syllable   199*
Important Phonics and Structural Analysis Knowledge, 200
Morphemic Analysis, 202
Syllabication and Phonics, 209
Making Words with Syllables, 213

Answers to Reviews and Self-Evaluation Tests   217

Appendix: Common Rime Word List,   222

References   227

Index   233

Educator Learning Center: An InvaluableOnline Resource

Merrill Education and the Association for Supervision and Curriculum Development (ASCD) invite you to take advantage of a new online resource, one that provides access to the top research and proven strategies associated with ASCD and Merrill—the Educator Learning Center. At **www.EducatorLearningCenter.com** you will find resources that will enhance your students' understanding of course topics and of current educational issues, in addition to being invaluable for further research.

HOW THE EDUCATOR LEARNING CENTER WILL HELP YOUR STUDENTS BECOME BETTER TEACHERS

With the combined resources of Merrill Education and ASCD, you and your students will find a wealth of tools and materials to better prepare them for the classroom.

Research

- More than 600 articles from the ASCD journal *Educational Leadership* discuss everyday issues faced by practicing teachers.
- A direct link on the site to Research Navigator™ gives students access to many of the leading education journals, as well as extensive content detailing the research process.
- Excerpts from Merrill Education texts give your students insights on important topics of instructional methods, diverse populations, assessment, classroom management, technology, and refining classroom practice.

Classroom Practice

- Hundreds of lesson plans and teaching strategies are categorized by content area and age range.
- Case studies and classroom video footage provide virtual field experience for student reflection.
- Computer simulations and other electronic tools keep your students abreast of today's classrooms and current technologies.

LOOK INTO THE VALUE OF EDUCATOR LEARNING CENTER YOURSELF

Preview the value of this educational environment by visiting **www.EducatorLearningCenter.com** and clicking on "Demo." For a free 4-month subscription to the Educator Learning Center in conjunction with this text, simply contact your Merrill/Prentice Hall sales representative.

Part One

Phonics Self-Instruction

Self-Evaluation: A Pretest

This is a test to give you an indication of your present knowledge of phonics and issues related to it. Read each item carefully, including all of the choices. Circle the letter (a, b, c, d, or e) to indicate your best answer. Be sure to respond to all test items.

I. Multiple Choice. Select the best answer.

1. How many phonemes are in the word *stretch?*

    a. one   **b.** two   **c.** five   **d.** six   **e.** seven

2. How many graphemes are in the word *stretch?*

    a. one   **b.** two   **c.** five   **d.** six   **e.** seven

3. Which of the following most adequately completes the sentence? The meanings young readers acquire from reading are largely based on

    a. written context.
    b. prosody.
    c. decoding.
    d. their knowledge of spoken words.
    e. phonics.

4. Which of the following most adequately completes the sentence? The written language is

    a. difficult to understand.
    b. as easy to acquire as the oral language.
    c. used more often in schools than the oral language.
    d. a representation of the oral language.
    e. a primary language form.

5. Which of the following most adequately completes the sentence? Language can be

    a. either associative or communicative.
    b. either expressive or receptive.
    c. either oral or written.
    d. All of the above.
    e. Both b and c.

6. Which of the following most adequately completes the sentence? The major reason we study phonics is to

    a. learn about consonant and vowel sounds.
    b. learn how to "sound out" words.
    c. learn how the spoken language relates to the written language.
    d. become phonemically aware.
    e. Both b and c.

7. Which of the following most adequately completes the sentence? The differences in the meanings that we associate with spoken words are affected mostly by

   a. graphemes.
   b. phonemes.
   c. syllables.
   d. phonological awareness.
   e. syntax.

8. Which of the following most adequately completes the sentence? If we didn't have a written language, there would be little reason to

   a. learn about syntax.
   b. study phonics.
   c. develop phonemic awareness.
   d. learn about text structure.
   e. Both b and c.

9. Which of the following statement/s are correct?

   a. A phoneme is the written representation of a grapheme.
   b. A grapheme is the written representation of a phoneme.
   c. A phoneme is the smallest unit of sound in a word.
   d. *Grapheme* and *letter* are synonymous terms.
   e. Statements b and c are correct.

10. Which of the following statement/s are correct?

    a. The letter *x* has no sound of its own.
    b. The letter *c* has no sound of its own.
    c. The letter *y* and *w* are used to represent both consonant and vowel phonemes.
    d. The letter *q* has no sound of its own.
    e. All of the statements above are correct.

11. The letter *y* is most likely to be a consonant when

    a. it is the first letter in a word or syllable.
    b. it is the final letter in a word or syllable.
    c. it occurs in the middle of a syllable.
    d. it follows the letter *a* in a word or syllable.
    e. None of the above.

12. Which of the following most adequately completes the sentence? Most of the consonant speech sounds are predictably represented by

    a. 18 consonant letters and 5 consonant digraphs.
    b. 21 consonant letters.
    c. single-letter consonants and consonant blends.
    d. 21 consonant phonemes.
    e. The written form of the American English language is too irregular for any safe predictions.

13. The consonant digraph is illustrated by

  a. the *ai* in *rain.*
  b. the *sh* in *wish.*
  c. the *str* in *strap.*
  d. the *nd* in *bend.*
  e. the *gh* in *brought.*

14. The voiced equivalent of the consonant sound represented by the *p* in *pie* is

  a. the consonant sound represented by the *d* in *dog.*
  b. the consonant sound represented by the *b* in *bug.*
  c. the consonant sound represented by the *g* in *go.*
  d. the consonant sound represented by the *v* in *van.*
  e. the consonant sound represented by the *z* in *zoo.*

15. The voiceless equivalent of the consonant sound represented by the *j* in *job* is

  a. the consonant sound represented by the *f* in *fun.*
  b. the consonant sound represented by the *s* in *sit.*
  c. the consonant sound represented by the *ch* in *chin.*
  d. the consonant sound represented by the *t* in *top.*
  e. the consonant sound represented by the *c* in *can.*

16. Which of the following most adequately completes the sentence? Consonant phonemes and graphemes are

  a. used in the middle of syllables.
  b. used at the beginning and ending of syllables.
  c. more important than vowel phonemes and graphemes.
  d. Both a and b.
  e. None of the above.

17. Which of the following most adequately completes the sentence? The consonant letter *q* is not really needed to represent consonant phonemes because

  a. it never occurs in words without the letter *u* after it.
  b. other letters represent the sound/s it represents.
  c. it looks too much like the letter *g.*
  d. Both a and b.
  e. All of the above.

18. The consonant letter *s* most frequently represents the sound/s heard in

  a. *shall.* **b.** *zipper.* **c.** *sure.* **d.** *sun.* **e.** Both b and d

19. The word *stuff* ends with the same sound as the sound represented by

  a. the *f* in *of.*
  b. the *ph* in *graph.*
  c. the *gh* in *caught.*
  d. the *gh* in *ghost.*
  e. Both a and b.

20. The consonant letter *c* followed by an *e* is most likely to represent the same sound represented by

    a. the letter *c* in *cello.*
    b. the letter *s* in *sit.*
    c. the letter *c* when followed by *o.*
    d. the letter *c* when followed by *i.*
    e. Both b and d.

21. The consonant letter *g* followed by a *u* is most likely to represent the same sound represented by

    a. the *j* in *just.*
    b. the *gh* in *ghetto.*
    c. the *g* in *sing.*
    d. the letter *g* followed by *i.*
    e. Both a and d.

22. The open syllable in the nonsense word *pabel* would most likely rhyme with

    a. *crab.*
    b. *stay.*
    c. *fell.*
    d. *babe.*
    e. *rub.*

23. A vowel diphthong is best illustrated by the vowels representing the sound of

    a. *oo* as in *book.*
    b. *ou* as in *out.*
    c. *ai* as in *plaid.*
    d. *oy* as in *boy.*
    e. Both b and d.

24. The schwa sound is represented by

    a. the *o* in *lemon.*
    b. the *ay* in *day.*
    c. the *e* in *the.*
    d. the *e* in *wished.*
    e. Both a and c.

25. An example of a closed syllable is found in which of the following words?

    a. *bone*
    b. *go*
    c. *stand*
    d. *high*
    e. *see*

26. Which of the following has an incorrect diacritical mark?

    a. *wăll*   **b.** *sŏft*   **c.** *ŭs*   **d.** *bĕd*   **e.** *bĭg*

27. Which of the following has an incorrect diacritical mark?

    a. *ūse*   **b.** *ēve*   **c.** *dīme*   **d.** *glōve*   **e.** *pāge.*

28. When the single vowel *u* is followed by a single consonant and a final *e*, the *u* would most likely have the sound of

  a. the *u* in *rude.*
  b. the *ew* in *few.*
  c. the *u* in *guest.*
  d. the *oo* in *moon.*
  e. Both a and d.

29. If the vowel *o* was the only and final vowel in a syllable, the *o* would most likely represent the same sound as

  a. the *o* in *other.*
  b. the *a* in *water.*
  c. the *o* in *to.*
  d. the *ough* in *dough.*
  e. None of the above.

30. If the single vowel *a* was in a syllable ending with one or more consonants, the *a* would most likely represent the same sound as

  a. the *ea* in *steak.*
  b. the *ai* in *said.*
  c. the *a* in *fall.*
  d. the *au* in *laugh.*
  e. None of the above.

31. The word containing a murmur diphthong is

  a. *trout.*
  b. *boy.*
  c. *first.*
  d. *cow.*
  e. *coin.*

32. When the letters *ai* appear together in a syllable, they usually represent the same sound as

  a. the *a* in *bag.*
  b. the *i* in *rib.*
  c. the *aw* in *saw.*
  d. the *eigh* in *sleigh.*
  e. the *a* in *was.*

33. An example of a vowel team syllable is

  a. *bone.*   **b.** *go.*   **c.** *stand.*   **d.** *diet.*   **e.** *herd.*

II. Multiple Choice. Select the word in each row in which the primary accent is correctly placed.

34. *sympathetic*   **a.** *sym'pathetic*   **b.** *sympa'thetic*   **c.** *sympathet'ic*   **d.** *sympathetic'*
35. *convulsion*   **a.** *con'vulsion*   **b.** *convul'sion*   **c.** *convulsion'*
36. *geography*   **a.** *ge'ography*   **b.** *geog'raphy*   **c.** *geogra'phy*   **d.** *geography'*
37. *impeccable*   **a.** *im'peccable*   **b.** *impec'cable*   **c.** *impecca'ble*   **d.** *impeccable'*

III. Multiple Choice. Select the word in each row that is incorrectly syllabicated.

38. **a.** *ti ger*   **b.** *pi lot*   **c.** *ba con*   **d.** *ca bin*   **e.** *fe ver*
39. **a.** *win dow*   **b.** *bot tle*   **c.** *ham ster*   **d.** *hat chet*   **e.** *vic tim*
40. **a.** *merch ant*   **b.** *ath lete*   **c.** *e ther*   **d.** *watch ful*   **e.** *dis charge*
41. **a.** *re gion*   **b.** *pi rate*   **c.** *gi ant*   **d.** *page ant*   **e.** *as sas si nate*
42. **a.** *var i ous*   **b.** *an i mal*   **c.** *si mi lar*   **d.** *av er age*   **e.** *A mer i ca*

IV. Multiple Choice. Select the words in each item (a, b, c) that contain a sound that the letter or group of letters at the left might represent. If none of the words contain a sound represented by the letter or group of letters, mark e. If all of the words contain a sound represented by the letter or group of letters, mark d.

43. *ti*   **a.** *chin*   **b.** *shop*   **c.** *sure*   **d.** All   **e.** None
44. *ci*   **a.** *shoot*   **b.** *sit*   **c.** *sugar*   **d.** All   **e.** None
45. *ge*   **a.** *guest*   **b.** *jet*   **c.** *soldier*   **d.** All   **e.** None
46. *ce*   **a.** *sign*   **b.** *cat*   **c.** *keep*   **d.** All   **e.** None

V. Multiple Choice. Select the word in each item (a, b, c) that contains the same sound as that represented by the underlined part of the word at the left. If none of the words contain that sound, mark e. If all of the words contain that sound, mark d.

47. <u>h</u>orse   **a.** *honest*   **b.** *who*   **c.** *fight*   **d.** All   **e.** None
48. m<u>oo</u>n   **a.** *grew*   **b.** *blue*   **c.** *do*   **d.** All   **e.** None
49. <u>w</u>atch   **a.** *show*   **b.** *whom*   **c.** *one*   **d.** All   **e.** None
50. si<u>ng</u>   **a.** *stranger*   **b.** *bank*   **c.** *get*   **d.** All   **e.** None

See page 221 for answers to Self-Evaluation: A Pretest.
Number correct _____

Chapter 1

Phonics and Phonemic Awareness Research

PHONEMIC AWARENESS AND PHONICS KNOWLEDGE DEFINED

Phonemic awareness and phonics knowledge refer to different, but related, abilities. A phoneme is one of the 45 individual sound units used to produce spoken words. Therefore, phonemic awareness refers to an individual's ability (awareness) to perceive the individual phonemes in spoken words. Phonics knowledge, on the other hand, refers to a person's ability to associate the appropriate letter, or letter combination, with each phoneme.

IMPORTANCE OF PHONEMIC AWARENESS

In order for children to learn to write and read, they need to develop an understanding of how spoken language maps onto written language. Phonemic awareness helps them develop this understanding (Ball & Blachman, 1991). Furthermore, phonemic awareness appears to be necessary for children if they are to benefit from any type of phonics instruction (Juel, Griffith, & Gough, 1986). This finding makes sense. If children cannot hear the sounds in spoken words that letters in written words represent, phonics instruction will probably be of little benefit. Furthermore, phonemic awareness also seems to be necessary for spelling development since children must assign letters to represent sounds in the words they spell (Beers & Henderson, 1977; Juel, Griffith, & Gough, 1986; Lundberg, Frost, & Peterson, 1988; Morris, 1983; Read, 1971).

The phonemic awareness skill generally referred to as segmentation seems to be of critical importance to beginning readers and writers. This skill is demonstrated when children are able to isolate the individual phonemes in a word, such as *man* (/m/ . . . /a/ . . . /n/). The findings of several reports suggest that preschool, kindergarten, and first grade children with the poorest phonemic segmentation skills are likely to be our poorest readers and spellers (Ball & Blachman, 1991; Juel, 1988; Tangel & Blachman, 1992).

Various studies conducted in both the United States and abroad suggest that children's phonemic awareness abilities are significantly related to their success in word recognition and spelling (Blachman, 1983, 1984, 1989; Blachman & James, 1985; Bradley & Bryant, 1983, 1985; Calfee, Lindamood, & Lindamood, 1973; Fox & Routh, 1975, 1980; Helfgott, 1976; Juel, 1988; Juel, Griffith, & Gough, 1986; Liberman, 1973; Liberman, Shankweiler, Fischer, & Carter, 1974; Lomax & McGee, 1987; Lundberg, Olofsson, & Wall, 1980; Mann & Liberman, 1984; Rohl & Tunmer, 1988;

Share, Jorm, Maclean, & Mathews, 1984; Stanovich, Cunningham, & Cramer, 1984; Tunmer & Nesdale, 1985; Wagner, 1986; Wagner & Torgesen, 1987; Williams, 1986).

Phonemic awareness seems to be a more powerful predictor of children's reading achievement than I.Q. measures or general language proficiency. In fact, experts suggest that phonemic awareness is the best predictor of reading achievement presently existing (Adams, 1990; Blachman, 1989; Fox & Routh, 1984; Golinkoff, 1978; Lundberg, Olofsson, & Wall, 1980; Mann, 1984; Stanovich, 1985; Vellutino & Scanlon, 1987).

IMPORTANCE OF PHONICS KNOWLEDGE

The evidence supporting the relationship of phonics knowledge to the acquisition of basic reading skills seems to be substantial (Backman, Bruck, Herbert, & Seidenberg, 1984; Hoover & Gough, 1990; Jorm, Share, Maclean, & Matthews, 1984; Juel, 1988; Juel, Griffith, & Gough, 1986; Manis & Morrison, 1985; Perfetti & Hogaboam, 1975; Snowling, 1980, 1981; Stanovich, Cunningham, & Freeman, 1984; Thompson, 1986; Tunmer, 1989; Tunmer, Herriman, & Nesdale, 1988; Tunmer & Nesdale, 1985). Phonics knowledge seems to provide a system for the development of word recognition abilities (Ehri & Wilce, 1983, 1985), and fluent, automatic word recognition seems to be a necessary condition for good reading comprehension (Adams, 1990; Anderson, Hiebert, Scott, & Wilkinson, 1985; Barr, 1972; Cohen, 1974-75; Eldredge, Quinn, & Butterfield, 1990; Johnson & Bauman, 1984, p. 595; Nathan & Stanovich, 1991, p. 176).

Poor word recognition seems to make reading comprehension difficult since the inability to recognize words quickly and accurately creates a "working memory" bottleneck that interferes with reading comprehension (LaBerge & Samuels, 1974; Liberman & Shankweiler, 1979; Perfetti, 1985, 1986). These findings are supported by studies reporting strong correlations between speed and accuracy of context-free word recognition and reading comprehension, especially among children in the lower grades (see Lesgold, Resnick, & Hammond, 1985; Perfetti, 1985).

PHONEMIC AWARENESS AND PHONICS KNOWLEDGE— NECESSARY, BUT NOT SUFFICIENT

The development of phonemic awareness and phonics knowledge is necessary, but not sufficient, for emerging readers and writers. The causal chain seems to be as follows: phonemic awareness is necessary for the optimal development of phonics knowledge; phonics knowledge is necessary for the optimal development of word recognition; word recognition is necessary for the optimal development of reading fluency; and reading fluency is necessary for the optimal development of reading comprehension.

While phonemic awareness, phonics knowledge, word recognition, and reading fluency are necessary for reading, *they are not sufficient!* The ability to read and write is also strongly affected by an individual's language and thinking abilities. Such things as vocabulary knowledge, knowledge of prosody, parsing, language structures and conventions, the ability to visualize images from print, inferencing, critical thinking, and so on, also contribute to one's ability to read. The development of these, and other, language and thinking abilities is influenced by a host of other important factors, including, but not limited to, culture, schemata, self-confidence, and motivation. The caveat appropriate here is that while phonemic awareness and phonics knowledge are important for emerging readers, instructional programs designed for young children must address other equally important issues as well.

RESEARCH FINDINGS ON TEACHING READING

Among the important meta-analyses of reading instruction are Chall's *Learning to Read: The Great Debate* (1967) and Adams's *Beginning to Read: Thinking and Learning About Print* (1990). One of Chall's conclusions, based on an analysis of some 22 programs, reviews of published studies, and classroom observations, was that children who received code-emphasis instruction (emphasis on phonics and decoding) achieved better in the first three grades than children who received meaning-emphasis instruction (emphasis on word identification through context). Her findings regarding the importance of phonics in reading were substantiated in later reports (1983, 1996).

Adams (1990), after reviewing research reports on reading, reaffirmed Chall's position, arguing that phonics approaches were more successful than nonphonics approaches in teaching children to read. She also offered an explanation for why there had been so much resistance to the direct teaching of decoding, and suggested that both "holistic" and "skills" instruction should be integral components of an effective instructional program.

In the late 1990s, the National Research Council (NRC), the research arm of the National Academy of Sciences, reviewed research reports to develop a set of recommendations to reduce young children's reading difficulties (Snow, Burns, & Griffin, 1998). Among other investigations, they reviewed research on family literacy, parental influences on children's cognitive and social development, preschools, teacher preparation, and reading. Their report reemphasized the importance of phonemic awareness and phonics knowledge for young children learning to read. Furthermore, they warned everyone that children's failure to master word recognition hinders their text comprehension.

In 1997 Congress asked the National Institute for Child Health and Human Development and the Department of Education to establish a National Reading Panel. One of the assignments given to this panel was to examine applying reading research to classroom practice. The National Reading Panel (NRP) studied, among other things, computer technology in reading, fluency, comprehension, phonemic awareness, and phonics. They set rigid guidelines for the research studies accepted in their meta-analyses of these topics so only the best of the existing research was involved.

The NRP (2000) decided that there was not enough quality research to make valid conclusions in some of the areas they studied. However, they did have the research needed to draw conclusions about the impact of phonemic awareness and phonics instruction on children's reading growth. First, they concluded that phonemic awareness instruction helps all children learn to read. Normally developing readers, children at risk, disabled readers, preschoolers, kindergartners, first graders, and children in the second through sixth grades, across various SES levels, all benefit from phonemic awareness instruction. Second, they concluded that systematic phonics instruction helps children at all SES levels learn to read more effectively than nonsystematic phonics instruction or instruction teaching no phonics. They also noted that phonics instruction produces the largest impact on children's reading growth when it is introduced in kindergarten or first grade.

The question regarding the importance of phonics instruction has been debated over and over again for nearly two centuries. P. David Pearson (2000), in his report *Reading in the Twentieth Century,* discussed a major shift from the popular qualitative research studies of the 1980s and early 1990s back to the quantitative research studies emphasizing reliable, replicable research of the mid-1990s. Not all reading educators were supportive of that shift for a variety of reasons. One of them, of course, is the fact that qualitative and quantitative researchers are not always interested in the same research agenda.

Each time the phonics debate has been revisited by quantitative researchers, however, the conclusion is always the same: phonics knowledge is essential for becoming a proficient reader, and instructional procedures teaching phonics explicitly seem to be more effective than those that do not (Rayner et al., 2001). Some educators (Rayner et al., 2002) asked, "If researchers are so convinced about the need for phonics instruction, why does the debate continue?" It continues for a myriad of reasons. Perhaps the most important one involves the ideological and philosophical differences among educators that seem to be difficult to bridge, including, but not limited to, research.

PHONICS AND LITERACY DEVELOPMENT

When the word *phonics* is mentioned, many individuals visualize children grunting and groaning as they attempt to "sound out" unfamiliar written words. Some visualize children involved in time-wasting workbook activities and long hours of meaningless skill exercises. Unfortunately, there are still educators today who place little value on phonics instruction. Yet strong data reveal that if phonics is correctly understood and applied in classrooms, it can play a very powerful role in the literacy development of children.

We have reviewed the strong research base revealing that phonics knowledge is causally related to successful reading and writing, and that phonics knowledge is necessary for the development of sight word recognition, reading fluency, and even reading comprehension.

What are the phonics patterns, phonics elements, and literacy processes involving phonics that children can be taught to help them become better readers and writers? To help you answer this question, this book includes a pretest and a posttest. Do not look at the posttest now. You may even wish to remove it from the book and file it away until you complete your study of this text.

Turn to page 2 and take the pretest now. Correct it. At your next sitting, turn back to this section and continue reading.

Your success with this text will depend on two factors: your desire to learn about phonics and your willingness to follow the directions as you proceed through the program.

This text is arranged in frames. In each frame you will be asked to provide missing information or make other types of responses. The left portion of the frame provides the answers. *It is essential that you write your responses before you see the correct answers.* To avoid looking at the left column while you read the text, cut the mask from the back cover of this book or use heavy paper to make one similar to it. Place the mask over the left-hand column to conceal the correct answers as you read the text.

When you have written your responses to the first frame, move the mask down to reveal the answers for that frame. Compare your answers with those provided. Since this is a teaching text (not a test) and is designed to guide you to the correct answers, you will more than likely find that you have responded correctly. However, even if your answers are wrong, you will learn something by following the instructions in the text. If you respond incorrectly, reread the frame and respond again. Equivalent answers should be considered correct, but make sure they are equivalent.

You will find much repetition and many opportunities for review. This will help you fix the important information in your mind. At times it may seem that you are asked to make simple, obvious answers. You may be tempted not to write them and instead respond mentally or look at the answers while you are reading the frame. PLEASE DO NOT DO ANY OF THESE THINGS. IT IS ESSENTIAL THAT YOU WRITE YOUR RESPONSES BEFORE YOU LOOK AT THE ANSWERS!

It is also suggested that you not work too long at one sitting. Several short periods a day will produce better results than one long period.

You are now ready to begin the program.

---

	1. We use language so we can communicate with each other. In this communication process we either "send" messages or "receive" them. Therefore, language can be either *expressive* or *receptive*. When we speak we express ourselves to others, so we say that speech is a(n)
expressive	_____ process. When we listen we are the recipients (expressive, receptive)
	of someone else's speech, so we call listening a(n)
receptive	_____ process. (expressive, receptive)

sound sounds communicating	**2.** Speech, our primary language, is based on *sounds.* When we hear a spoken word, we associate the _____ we hear with something meaningful to us. Because word meanings are based on _____, (sounds, print) and because we learn to speak and listen before we learn to read and write, we say that the spoken language is our primary means of _____ with each other. (associating, communicating)
writing	**3.** We represent speech, our primary language, by _____. We use a written language so we can (writing, speaking) communicate with people who cannot hear us speak—people who are not near us or people yet unborn.
spoken alphabet	**4.** The written language uses a system of symbols, called a *code,* to represent the _____ language. In English, the code we <div align="center">(written, spoken)</div> use is comprised of 26 alphabetic letters. We call the written code used to represent the spoken language the _____ code. <div align="right">(written, alphabet)</div>
code phonics	**5.** An essential step in the reading process is called *decoding.* Decoding is translating the written _____ into spoken language. This <div align="center">(code, sounds)</div> decoding process can either be a fast process we call word *recognition,* or it can be a slower process we refer to as word *identification.* Both of these processes are founded on a knowledge of _____. <div align="right">(phonics, word shape)</div>

necessary decoding	**6.** Although decoding is not a sufficient condition, by itself, for reading comprehension, it is nevertheless a(n) _____ (necessary, unnecessary) component of reading. Without _____ there would be (questions, decoding) no comprehension.
expressive receptive	**7.** In the written language, writing is a(n) _____ process, (expressive, receptive) while reading is a(n) (expressive, receptive) process.
written receptive	**8.** Language can be classified as being either spoken and _____, or expressive and _____.
written letters	**9.** We study phonics so we can learn how the spoken language relates to the (oral, written) language. *Phonics* is a term we use to describe the relationship that exists between the sounds of speech and the (letters, shapes) used to represent those sounds.
three graphemes	***Phonemes and Graphemes*** **10.** In our written language we use "smaller than syllable" word sounds called *phonemes* and represent.them by *graphemes* (letters or letter combinations). For example, the word *man* has (How many?) phonemes. When we write the word *man,* we use the letters *m, a, n,* respectively, to represent its three phonemes. The letters that are used to represent phonemes are called _____.

	### *Phoneme*
phoneme	**11.** The *eme* suffix means "a structural element of language." The root *phon* means "sound." Therefore, the smallest sound unit in a word is called a _____. A phoneme is the smallest unit of
	(phon + eme)
sound	_____ that distinguishes one word from another.
	(print, sound)
four	**12.** Say the words *last* and *fast.* Each word has _____
	(How many)
	phonemes. The beginning phoneme in the word *last* and the beginning
sound	phoneme in the word *fast* are the smallest units of _____
	(print, sound)
	distinguishing the words from each other.
	Differences in word meanings are determined by
phonemes	_____.
	(graphemes, phonemes)
	13. Because a single phoneme can affect the meaning of a word,
phonemes	a word's unique sequence of _____ sets it apart
	(phonemes, graphemes)
	from all other words (homophones excepted). Therefore, each spoken word in the language is recognized by its unique sequence of
phonemes	_____. Furthermore, the meanings we have attached
	(graphemes, phonemes)
	to words are based on each word's unique sound—its coarticulated
phonemes	(or blended) _____.
	(phonemes, graphemes)

phonemes writing	**14.** If we didn't have a written language, there would be little reason for our learning about phonemes since we speak and listen with little or no conscious awareness of phonemes. However, since we use letters to write words, and since those letters represent each word's _____, an awareness of phonemes is very important (graphemes, phonemes) for successful reading and _____.
spoken phonemic awareness	**15.** In order for individuals to successfully learn to read and write, they must learn how _____ language maps onto written language. Phonemic awareness helps them grasp this concept. It is no surprise, therefore, to learn that the level of a child's _____when entering school (vocabulary knowledge, phonemic awareness) is the best predictor of his/her success in reading and writing.
grapheme graphemes	### Grapheme **16.** The *eme* suffix means "a structural element of language." The root *graph* means "drawn, written, recorded." Therefore, the _____ is the written representation of the phoneme. Therefore, (graph + eme) letters that represents phonemes are called _____. (print, graphemes) A grapheme is the the written representation of the phoneme.

phoneme
 	
grapheme
 	
phonics
	17. In summary, then, the _____ is the smallest sound
	                    (grapheme, phoneme)
	
	unit in the spoken language, and the _____ is the unit
	                        (grapheme, phoneme)
	
	in the written system that represents the phoneme. The relationship that exists between graphemes and phonemes is called _____.
	    (phonics, reading)

graphemes	**18.** Technically speaking, we cannot write sounds (phonemes). Instead we write _____ that represent phonemes. (graphemes, words) In order for you to know when I am speaking about the sound represented by a grapheme instead of the grapheme itself, I will use the symbol / /. So when you see /p/, I am talking about the
sound represented by the letter *p*	_____. (letter *p*, sound represented by the letter *p*) The symbol / / refers to the sound represented by a grapheme.

three
 	
 four   three
 	
 w
 i
 sh
	19. A grapheme and a letter are not synonymous. A grapheme will always consist of at least one letter, but graphemes may also consist of more than one letter. In the word *fish* there are _____
	                            (How many?)
	
	 phonemes and _____ letters. There are _____
	         (How many?) (How many?)
	
	 graphemes in the word *fish*. The phoneme /w/ is represented by the grapheme _____, the phoneme /i/ is represented by the grapheme _____, and the phoneme /sh/ is represented by the grapheme _____.

/th/ /n/ *th* *n*	**20.** Say the words *with* and *win*. The phonemes that differentiate these two words are _____ and _____. The letters that represent these graphemes are _____ and _____, respectively.
phonemes graphemes	**21.** In our language there are 45 separate sounds (or _____) used to create spoken words. These 45 (graphemes, phonemes) separate sounds are represented by various_____ in (graphemes, phonemes) written words.

26	**22.** In summary, then, there are _____ letters in our alphabet
	(How many?)
	that we use either separately or in combination with other letters to
45	represent the _____ phonemes used in spoken words.
	(How many?)
phonemes	**23.** Some of the alphabet letters are used with other letters to
	represent _____. For example, the letters
	(graphemes, phonemes)
ch	_____ represent the phoneme /ch/ in such words as *chop,*
	peach, and *church.*
phoneme *a*	**24.** Some of the alphabet letters are used to represent more than one
	_____. For example, the letter _____ represents
	(grapheme, phoneme)
	three different phonemes in the following words: *can, cane, call.*
grapheme	**25.** Often when a letter represents more than one phoneme, there are
	clues within the written word to indicate which sound the
	_____ represents. This text will help you learn these
	(grapheme, phoneme)
	clues so you can teach children to recognize and use them.
w	**26.** Sometimes letters used in written words do not represent any
	sound. For example, in the word *sword,* the letter
k	_____ does not represent a phoneme, and in the word
silent	*know,* the letter _____ does not represent a phoneme. Letters
	such as these are often referred to as _____ letters.

graphemes

graphemes

27. Although the phoneme/grapheme relationships existing between spoken and written words are not simple, once you understand these relationships properly, you will realize that phonics and spelling are not as inconsistent and unreliable as many people claim. We will begin our study with the consonant _____ (graphemes, phonemes),

because the phonemes associated with these graphemes appear to be more consistent* than those associated with the vowel _____. (graphemes, phonemes)

(*Note: The phonemes associated with the vowel letters are predictably consistent with the written pattern of the syllable; however, to those unfamiliar with phonics, the vowel letters appear to be more inconsistent than consonants. Once you recognize how the vowel sounds in written words are related to syllable patterns, however, consonant letters do not appear to be more consistent than vowels. Syllable patterns will be discussed in Chapter 3.

The reviews will give you important feedback regarding the effectiveness of your study. They will also help you determine whether you need to review the material presented in a particular section. Write your answers to the reviews on a separate sheet of paper. Correct your answers and analyze the results. After a few days, recheck yourself by answering the review questions again. Keep track of your scores so you will know where additional study and review are needed.

 Review 1

1. Language is either expressive or _____. It is either oral or _____.

2. We represent speech, our primary language, by writing. The written representation of the smallest sound unit in words is called a _____.

3. We encode words when we write, and we decode them when we read. Decoding is the process of _____.

4. A phoneme is _____.

5. Is a grapheme just another term for the word *letter*?

6. Practically speaking, American-English words use (How many?) _____ phonemes.

7. How many phonemes are there in the word *athlete*?

8. How many graphemes are there in the word *athlete*?

Turn to the Answers section, page 217, and check your answers. You should have answered all of the questions correctly. If you succeeded, congratulations! If you did not succeed, review this section again.

Chapter 2

Consonants

Place the mask over the left-hand column. As you work through this section, it will be necessary for you to say some sounds out loud. Be sure that you are seated where this is possible. Remember, study the entire frame and write your responses before you look at the answers in the left-hand column.

vowels consonants, *y* *w* *r*	**1.** There are 26 letters in the alphabet. Five of these letters are called _____ and 21 are called _____ . Three (consonants, vowels) (consonants, vowels) of the letters used to represent consonant phonemes are also used in the representation of vowel phonemes. These letters are _____, _____, and _____.
vowel	**2.** The letter *y* always represents a consonant phoneme when used to begin words or syllables; for example: *yellow, canyon.* When the letter *y* is not used to begin words or syllables, it represents a _____ phoneme. (vowel, consonant)
consonant graphemes	**3.** The grapheme *w* always represents a consonant phoneme when used to begin words or syllables; for example: *water, reward.* In the words *highway* and *with*, the grapheme *w* represents a _____ phoneme because it is used to begin a syllable (consonant, vowel) and a word. When the letter *w* is used with either an *a, e,* or *o* to form the vowel _____ *aw, ew,* or *ow* (*saw, few,* and *cow*), *w* is a part (phonemes, graphemes) of a vowel team. (Vowel teams are explained in Chapter 3.)

consonant	**4.** The grapheme *r* always represents a consonant phoneme when used to begin words or syllables; for example: *run, around.* In the words *rabbit* and *bathrobe,* the grapheme *r* represents a _____ phoneme because it is used to begin a word and a (consonant, vowel) syllable. When the letter *r* follows a vowel, however, it is a "semivowel," and the vowel/*r* combination (*ir, er, ur, ar, or,* etc.) is known as a murmur dipthong. (Murmur diphthongs are explained in Chapter 3.)
21	**5.** There are only _____ consonant letters, but there are 25 (How many?) consonant phonemes. Furthermore, 3 of the 21 consonant letters (*c, x,* and *q*) are superfluous in a sense because other letters of the alphabet represent the sounds those letters represent.
grapheme *k* *c* *s*	### The Consonant Letter C **6.** Say the phonemes in the word *cat.* The phoneme represented by the _____ *c* in the word *cat* is the same phoneme (phoneme, grapheme) represented by the grapheme _____ in the word *keep.* Say the phonemes in the word *cent.* The phoneme represented by the grapheme _____ in the word *cent* is the same phoneme represented by the grapheme _____ in the word *soap.*
c	**7.** Because the phonemes /k/ and /s/ are predictably represented by the consonant letters *k* and *s,* we say that the consonant letter _____ has no sound of its own.

grapheme	### *The Consonant Letter* X **8.** Say the phonemes in the word *box*. The phonemes represented by the _____ *x* in the word *box* are /k/ and /s/ blended (phoneme, grapheme) together. These sounds are the same sounds as those represented by
k *s*	the letters _____ and _____ in the word *books*.
/g/ /z/	Say the phonemes in the word *exam*. The phonemes represented by the grapheme *x* are _____ and _____ blended together. These sounds are the same sounds as those represented by the letters
g *z*	_____ and _____.
x	**9.** Because the phonemes represented by the grapheme *x* are represented by other consonant letters, we say that the consonant letter _____ has no sound of its own.
	### *The Consonant Letter* Q **10.** The letter *q* does not occur in English words without a *u* after it: *quiet, queen, antique, opaque, quay*. Say all of the phonemes in the word *quit*. The phonemes represented
/k/ /w/	by the letters *qu* represent the phonemes _____ and
k *w* /k/	_____ blended together. These phonemes are usually represented by the letters _____ and _____. Sometimes the grapheme *qu (technique)* represents the phoneme _____ and
/k/ /w/	at other times it represents the phonemes _____ and _____ *(quiet)* blended together, but the letter *q* has no sound of its own.
18	**11.** When we subtract the three consonant letters that have no sounds of their own from the 21 consonant letters available, we have only _____ consonant letters that represent unique phonemes. Those consonant letters are *b, d, f, g, h, j, k, l, m, n, p, r, s, t, v, w, y,* and *z*.

12. The sounds predictably represented by these 18 consonant letters are listed below:

b The consonant grapheme _____ represents /b/ as in *bat*.

d The consonant grapheme _____ represents /d/ as in *dog*.

f The consonant grapheme _____ represents /f/ as in *fish*.

g The consonant grapheme _____ represents /g/ as in *go*.

h The consonant grapheme _____ represents /h/ as in *had*.

j The consonant grapheme _____ represents /j/ as in *jump*.

k The consonant grapheme _____ represents /k/ as in *kiss*.

l The consonant grapheme _____ represents /l/ as in *lamp*.

m The consonant grapheme _____ represents /m/ as in *man*.

n The consonant grapheme _____ represents /n/ as in *no*.

p The consonant grapheme _____ represents /p/ as in *pan*.

r The consonant grapheme _____ represents /r/ as in *run*.

s The consonant grapheme _____ represents /s/ as in *sun*.

t The consonant grapheme _____ represents /t/ as in *teeth*.

v The consonant grapheme _____ represents /v/ as in *voice*.

w The consonant grapheme _____ represents /w/ as in *watch*.

y The consonant grapheme _____ represents /y/ as in *yes*.

z The consonant grapheme _____ represents /z/ as in *zoo*.

13. If 18 consonant letters predictably represent 18 of the 25 consonant phonemes, there are graphemes for _____ consonant

7

(How many?)

phonemes that we have yet to discuss.

14. Six of the seven remaining consonant phonemes are represented by two-letter graphemes called consonant digraphs. The prefix *di* means "two"; and the root *graph* means "written." Therefore, a consonant digraph is a two-letter grapheme representing one phoneme.

ch The consonant digraph _____ represents /ch/ as in **church.**

sh The consonant digraph _____ represents /sh/ as in **shoe.**

ng The consonant digraph _____ represents /ng/ as in **sing.**

th The consonant digraph _____ represents /th/ as in **thing.**

th The consonant digraph _____ represents /<u>th</u>/ as in **the.**

wh The consonant digraph _____ represents /hw/ as in **white.**

si *s* *z*	**15.** The consonant phoneme we have yet to discuss is the /zh/ phoneme heard in such words as *division* and *treasure.* In the word *vision* the letters _____ represent the /zh/ phoneme, in the word *measure* the letter _____ represents the /zh/ phoneme, and in the word *azure* the letter _____ represents the /zh/ phoneme.
25 18 (see frame 12) 5 (*sh, ch, ng, th, wh*) *th*	**16.** In summary, then, there are _____ consonant phonemes. <center>(How many?)</center>All of these phonemes except /zh/ are represented by _____ <center>(How many?)</center>single-letter graphemes and _____ two-letter graphemes; one <center>(How many?)</center>of those two-letter graphemes, the _____ , represents two consonant phonemes, /th/ as in *thing* and /<u>th</u>/ as in **the.**
graphemes graphemes 24 /zh/	**17.** When we refer to the "regular" consonant grapheme/phoneme relationships, we are referring to the phonemes associated with the 18 single-letter _____ presented in frame 12, and the phonemes associated with the 5 two-letter _____ presented in frame 14. These 23 graphemes represent _____ of our 25 consonant <center>(How many?)</center>phonemes. The consonant phoneme _____ is *not* predictably represented by any one grapheme.
/s/ /z/	**18.** Even though we use the word *regular* to describe the consonant grapheme/phoneme relationships discussed so far, many of the graphemes discussed also represent other phonemes. For example, in the word *rats,* the grapheme *s* represents the _____ phoneme, but in the word *dogs* it represents the _____ phoneme.
t *ed*	**19.** Furthermore, in some instances phonemes are represented by different graphemes than those expected. For example, in the word *fat,* the grapheme _____ represents the phoneme /t/, but in the word *wished,* the grapheme _____ represents that phoneme. We study phonics so we can understand when and why graphemes represent the phonemes they represent.

 **Review 2**

1. Which two letters are used to represent both consonant and vowel phonemes?

2. The letters *y* and *w* always represent consonant phonemes when

_____.

3. Explain why the consonant letters *c, x,* and *q* are said to be superfluous.

4. There are 25 consonant phonemes used in spoken words. Eighteen of these phonemes are predictably represented by 18 of our 21 consonant letters (all of the consonant letters except *c, x,* and *q*). The /zh/ phoneme is represented by the graphemes *s, z,* and *si.* Write the 5 two-letter graphemes that represent the remaining six consonant phonemes.

5. A consonant digraph is _____.

Turn to the Answers section, page 217, and check your answers. You should have answered all of the questions correctly. If you succeeded, congratulations! If you did not succeed, review this section again.

Consonant Phonemes

vocal	1. Consonant phonemes are produced by the speech organs: the lips, tongue, teeth, gums, roof of the mouth (also called the palate), and the _____ cords.
speech	2. Consonant phonemes are sometimes referred to as speech gestures because they are formed by moving those body parts used for producing _____.
voiced	3. Some consonant phonemes, or gestures, are voiced and some are voiceless. When we produce consonant phonemes that are _____ , we vibrate our vocal cords. The vocal cords are (voiceless, voiced) comprised of two bands of elastic tissue that are positioned across the air pipe.

lips voiceless voiced	**4.** Say the words *pat* and *bat*. Notice what your mouth is doing when you make the phonemes /p/ and /b/. Both phonemes are made by using the _____ . However, the consonant phoneme /p/ is (teeth, lips) _____ , while the consonant phoneme /b/ is (voiceless, voiced) _____ . Voiced consonant phonemes are produced by (voiceless, voiced) vibrating the vocal cords.
vocal cords voiceless voiced /b/	**5.** The only difference between the phonemes /p/ and /b/ is that one is formed by vibrating the _____ _____ , while the other is produced by blowing air through the lips. The phoneme /p/ is _____ , while the phoneme /b/ is _____ . (voiceless, voiced) (voiceless, voiced) Therefore, the phoneme /p/ is the voiceless equivalent of the voiced phoneme _____ .
identically voiced voiceless /f/	**6.** Say the words *fan* and *van*. Pay attention to your teeth and lips as you say the beginning phoneme in both words. When saying the phonemes /f/ and /v/, the teeth and tongue are positioned _____ . However, the phoneme /v/ is _____ , (identically, differently) (voiceless, voiced) while the phoneme /f/ is _____ . The phoneme /v/ is (voiceless, voiced) the voiced equivalent of the voiceless phoneme _____ .
/z/ /s/	**7.** Say the words *zip* and *sip*. Notice that the phonemes /z/ and /s/ are both formed by placing your tongue near your gums and closing your mouth so your teeth almost touch. The phoneme _____ is the voiced equivalent of the voiceless phoneme _____ .

equivalent voiceless voiced	**8.** Say the words *tent* and *dent*. The phonemes /t/ and /d/ are _____ phonemes. However, the phoneme /t/ is (equivalent, nonequivalent) _____ , and the phoneme /d/ is _____ . (voiceless, voiced) (voiceless, voiced)
equivalent voiceless voiced	**9.** Say the words *gill* and *kill*. The phonemes /g/ and /k/ are _____ phonemes. However, the phoneme /k/ is (equivalent, nonequivalent) _____ , and the phoneme /g/ is _____ . (voiceless, voiced) (voiceless, voiced)
voiced voiceless	**10.** Say the words *that* and *thing*. The phoneme /<u>th</u>/ in the word *that* is _____ , while the phoneme /th/ in the word *thing* is (voiceless, voiced) _____ . (voiceless, voiced)
voiceless voiced	**11.** Say the words *ship* and *measure*. The phoneme /sh/ in the word *ship* is _____ , while the phoneme /zh/ in the word (voiceless, voiced) *measure* is _____ . (voiceless, voiced)
voiced voiceless voiceless voiced	**12.** Say the words *wait* and *white*. The phoneme /w/ in the word *wait* is _____ , while the phoneme /hw/ in the word *white* is (voiceless, voiced) _____ . Say the words *chump* and *jump*. The phoneme (voiceless, voiced) /ch/ in the word *chump* is _____ , while the phoneme (voiceless, voiced) /j/ in the word *jump* is _____ . (voiceless, voiced)

nine
 	
voiced
	13. There are _____ pairs of equivalent consonant phonemes.
	          (How many?)
	All of the _____ phonemes are produced by vibrating our
	        (voiceless, voiced)
	vocal cords.

/b/ /f/ /z/ /d/ /k/ /th/ /w/ /sh/ /ch/	**14.** The voiced equivalent for /p/ is _____. The voiceless equivalent for /v/ is _____. The voiced equivalent for /s/ is _____. The voiced equivalent for /t/ is _____. The voiceless equivalent for /g/ is _____. The voiceless equivalent for /<u>th</u>/ is _____. The voiced equivalent for /hw/ is _____. The voiceless equivalent for /zh/ is _____. The voiceless equivalent for /j/ is _____.
/d/	**15.** Many of the voiced consonant phonemes are difficult to say in isolation. For example, when isolating the phonemes /b/, /v/, /g/, /w/, /r/, /l/, /j/, /y/, and _____, we usually say "buh," "vuh," "guh," "wuh," and so on. The "uh" sound we add to these voiced consonants is like the /u/ sound you hear at the beginning of the word *up*.
      eliminated	**16.** We distort many of the voiced consonant phonemes when we try to "sound out" words letter by letter. For example, we usually say /du/. . . /i/. . . /g/ when sounding out the word *dig,* instead of /d/. . . /i/. . . /g/. These isolated sounds when blended together are /du-ig/, which is a distorted version of /dig/. However, if consonant phonemes in the initial position of words and syllables are coarticulated with the vowels following them, this distortion is _____ . (eliminated, increased)

syllables	**17.** Consonant phonemes (and the graphemes that represent them) are used at the beginning and ending of words or _____ . (A
	(phrases, syllables)
vowel	syllable is the smallest part of a word containing one _____
	(vowel, consonant)
	sound.) Consonant graphemes and phonemes are never used in the middle position of words or syllables. This position is reserved for
vowel	_____ graphemes and phonemes.

beginning	**18.** In the word *stretch,* the consonant phonemes represented by *str* are found at the _____ of the word, and the consonant phoneme
	(beginning, end)
end	represented by *tch* is found at the _____ of the word. In the
	(beginning, end)
	word *accept,* the first *c* represents the phoneme /k/, which
ends	_____ the first syllable of the word, and the second *c*
	(begins, ends)
begins	represents the phoneme /s/, which _____ the second
	(begins, ends)
	syllable of the word. The consonant cluster _____ is used at
pt	the end the word *accept.* Consonant phonemes and graphemes are
syllables	used at the beginning and ending of words or _____ .

Review 3

1. Name the speech organs used for producing consonant phonemes.
2. Consonant phonemes are voiced and _____ .
3. Voiced consonant phonemes are produced by _____ .
4. When any two consonant phonemes are produced by the same speech organs, except one is voiced and the other is voiceless, they are said to be _____ phonemes.
5. Write the nine pairs of equivalent consonant phonemes. List the voiced phoneme in each pair first.
6. In syllables and single-syllable words containing three or more phonemes, there are, generally speaking, three phoneme positions. These positions are (a) initial, (b) medial, and (c) final. In which positions do we find the consonant phonemes and graphemes?

Turn to the Answers section, page 217, and check your answers. You should have answered all of the questions correctly. If you succeeded, congratulations! If you did not succeed, analyze your study procedure. Are you writing responses before you look at the answers? Are you summarizing to yourself what you have learned as you finish a page? Review this section again if you did not have a perfect score.

Single-Letter Consonant Graphemes (b, c, d, f, g)

phonemes	**1.** A study of phonics is a study of the relationships existing between graphemes and _____ . In this section of the book, we (phonemes, letters) will study the phonemes represented by the 21 single-letter consonant
graphemes	_____ used in our written language. We will begin our (sounds, graphemes) study with the first five consonant graphemes of the alphabet: *b, c, d, f,*
letter	and *g.* Remember, a grapheme is not always a single _____ , (sound, letter) like those we are studying in this section.
phoneme	**2.** The grapheme *b* predictably represents the _____ /b/ as (letter, phoneme) in *bat*. Because of this consistent letter/sound relationship, we say that the grapheme *b* is a "consistent" grapheme. Occasionally, *b* is silent,
phoneme	meaning that it doesn't represent a _____ . In the words (phoneme, grapheme)
silent *m t*	*lamb, comb, debtor,* and *doubt,* the letter *b* is _____. When *b* is silent, it either has a(n) _____ before it or a(n) _____ after it.
silent	**3.** In the words *climb, subtle, thumb,* and *bomb,* the letter *b* is _____. The letter *b* is not a silent letter in words very often. In the 5,000 most frequently used words of our language, only eight of them contain a silent *b,* and three of them have the same root (*climb, climbed, climbing*). *Note:* The 5,000 most frequently used words in our language comprise over 99% of the running words used in text materials written for use in the public schools.

/s/ /k/	**4.** The grapheme *c* has no sound of its own. However, it represents two different phonemes in written words. In the word *cinder*, *c* represents the phoneme _____, and in the word *cat*, *c* represents the phoneme _____.
/s/ /s/	**5.** In the words *cent, center, city, cider, cyclone*, and *bicycle*, *c* represents the phomeme _____. When *c* is followed by the vowels *e, i,* or *y*, it represents the phoneme _____. When the grapheme *c* is followed by an *e, i,* or *y*, it represents the phoneme /s/. When the *c* is not followed by an *e, i,* or *y*, it represents the phoneme /k/.
/s/ an *e* follows *c* silent /k/ *c* is not followed by an *e, i,* or *y*	**6.** In the words *scene, fence, cellar, cement,* and *dance, c* represents the phoneme _____ because _____. Notice that when the grapheme *ce* occurs at the end of words, the letter *e* is _____. The letter *e* after the *c*, however, tells the reader that *c* represents the /s/ phoneme. In the words *climb, cat, cut, copy,* and *clock*, the *c* represents the phoneme _____ because _____.
/sh/	**7.** In very rare situations, a *ce* in a multisyllabic word will represent the phoneme /sh/. In the word *ocean*, for example, the *ce* grapheme represents _____. However, in the 5,000 most frequently used words in the language only two such incidents are found: *ocean* and *oceans*.
/sh/	**8.** Occasionally, a *ci* in a multisyllabic word will also represent the phoneme /sh/. In the words *social* and *especially*, the *ci* grapheme represents _____. However, in the 5,000 most frequently used words only 12 such words were found: *official, officials, especially, ancient, social, precious, commercial, associated, sufficient, delicious, glaciers,* and *artificial*.

/k/ /s/	**9.** In the words *climb, crop, car, caterpillar, cupcake,* and *corn,* the *c* grapheme represents the phoneme _____ because it is not followed by an *e, i,* or *y.* In the words *space, fancy, icy, scientist, cypress, cinnamon,* and *citizen,* the *c* grapheme represents _____ because in each word the *c* is followed by an *e, i,* or *y.* About 76% of the time, the grapheme *c* represents the /k/ phoneme in words; about 23% of the time, it represents the /s/ phoneme; and about 1% of the time, it represents other phonemes.
/d/ phoneme	**10.** The grapheme *d* predictably represents the phoneme _____ as in *dog.* Occasionally the letter *d* occurs twice in a word such as in *add* and *odd,* and in these cases the grapheme *dd* represents the _____ /d/.
/j/ /d/	**11.** In very rare situations, the grapheme *d* represents the phoneme _____ as seen in the words *education* and *soldier.* However, 99% of the time, the grapheme *d* represents the phoneme _____.
/f/ /f/	**12.** The grapheme *f* reliably represents the phoneme _____ as in *fish.* Occasionally, the letter *f* occurs twice in a word such as in *off* and *stuff,* and in these cases the grapheme *ff* represents the phoneme _____.
/v/	**13.** The grapheme *f* represents a phoneme other than /f/ in only one high-frequency word. That word is *of.* In the word *of, f* represents the voiced phoneme _____.
/g/ /j/	**14.** The grapheme *g* represents the phoneme _____ in the word *go.* However, it also represents the phoneme _____ in such words as *giant* and *gentle.*

/j/ *e, i,* or *y*	**15.** In the words *magic, gypsy, germ,* and *rage, g* represents the phoneme _____. When the *g* represents /j/, it is followed by the vowels _____ or _____ or _____. However, when the *g* is followed by an *e, i,* or *y,* it does not always represent /j/; sometimes it represents its own sound (*get, give, gynecologist*).
/g/	**16.** When the grapheme *g* is not followed by an *e, i,* or *y,* however, it generally represents its own sound (/g/). In the words *gun, got, gas,* and *glass, g* represents _____ because it is not followed by an *e, i,* or *y.*
e, i, or *y* /j/ /j/	**17.** Most of the time, *g* represents /j/ when it is followed by the vowels _____ or _____ or _____, and whenever *ge* occurs at the end of a word (*large, page, huge*), the letter *g* predictably represents the phoneme _____. In these situations, however, the *e* is silent and is only used to tell the reader that the *g* represents the _____ phoneme.
guess *ghost gnat* *dough night* *cough*	*gnat guess ghost cough dough night* **18.** In the words above, *g* represents /g/ in the words _____ and _____. The letter *g* is silent in the word _____. The letters *gh* are silent in the words _____ and _____, and the letters *gh* represent /f/ in the word _____.
silent	**19.** When the letter *g* is followed by the letter *n* (*sign, gnaw, campaign, gnarl*), the letter *g* is _____.
/g/	**20.** When words begin with *gu* followed by a vowel (*guitar, guard, guide*), *g* represents _____ and the letter *u* is silent.
h	**21.** When words begin with *gh* (*ghost, ghastly, ghetto*), *g* represents /g/ and the letter _____ is silent.

silent /f/	**22.** When the letters *gh* follow vowel letters (*caught, eight, sight*), *gh* is usually _____. However, occasionally *gh* preceded by vowel letters (*rough, laugh*) represents the _____ phoneme. Even though *gh* occasionally represents /f/ when it follows vowel letters (5% of the time), 95% of the time *gh* is silent when preceded by vowel letters.
/ng/ digraph	**23.** Remember that when the letters *ng* occur in words, *ng* represents the consonant phoneme _____ heard in such words as *rang, long,* and *sing*. The *ng* grapheme is a two-letter consonant grapheme that we call a consonant _____. (digraph, trigraph)

/g/
 	
/j/
 	
silent
	24. Let's summarize what we know about the letter *g*. The letter *g* represents its regular phoneme _____ when it is not followed by
	               (/j/, /g/)
	an *e, i,* or *y*. When the letter *g* is followed by an *e, i,* or *y*, it usually represents the phoneme _____ , but not always. When *g* is
	               (/j/, /g/)
	followed by an *n*, it is usually _____. The letter *g* represents /g/ in words about 70% of the time; it represents /j/ about 29% of the time, and it is silent less than 1% of the time.

/g/ beginning silent	**25.** Let's continue our summary about the letter *g*. The letter *g* represents its regular phoneme _____ when it is followed by a *u* plus a vowel letter (*guest*), and when it is followed by an *h* at the _____ of words (*ghost*). When vowel letters occur before *gh* (*naughty*), the *gh* is _____.

g is not followed by an *e, i,* or *y*	**26.** The grapheme *g* represents /g/ in the word *glad* because _____.
g is followed by an *e, i,* or *y*	The grapheme *g* represents /j/ in the word *geology* because _____.
g is followed by *n*	The letter *g* is silent in the word *gnome* because _____.
g is followed by a *u* and a vowel	The grapheme *g* represents /g/ in the word *guess* because _____.
gh follows vowels	The letters *gh* are silent in the word *midnight* because _____, and the letter *g* in the word *ghastly* represents /g/, while the letter *h* is silent because
gh begins the word	_____.

Review 4

1. When we say that the letters *b, d,* and *f* are reliable graphemes, what do we mean?

2. Occasionally, the letter *b* is silent in words. When it is silent, it either has an _____ before it or a _____ after it.

3. State the generalization regarding when the letter *c* represents /s/ and when it represents /k/.

4. Most of the time, *c* represents the phoneme _____.

5. When the letters *ce* or *ci* are followed by a vowel letter, *ce* and *ci* represent the phoneme _____.

6. State the generalization regarding when the letter *g* represents its own sound and when it represents /j/.

7. Most of the time, *g* represents the phoneme _____.

8. Ninety-five percent of the time when the letters *gh* follow vowel letters, *gh* _____.

9. When the letters *gh* begin a word, *gh* _____.

10. Occasionally the letter *g* is followed by the letter *n*, and occasionally it is followed by a *u* and some vowel. When *g* is followed by the letter *n*, *g* _____, and when *g* is followed by the letter *u* and another vowel, *g* _____.

See the Answers section for the answers to Review 4.

Single-Letter Consonant Graphemes (*h, j, k, l, m*)

/h/ final silent	**1.** We continue our study of single-letter consonant graphemes with the second five consonant graphemes of the alphabet: *h, j, k, l,* and *m.* The grapheme *h* is quite consistent. It represents the phoneme _____ as in *had.* A distinctive characteristic of the letter *h* is that it never represents the _____ phoneme in a word or a (initial, final) syllable. In other words, the letter *h* is seldom found at the end of words, and when it does appear (*oh, yeah*), it is always _____.
no silent	**2.** Read the following words: *oh, hallelujah, ah, hurrah.* Do you hear /h/ at the end of these words? _____ The letter *h* is _____ (yes, no) when it is found at the end of a word or syllable.
silent	**3.** Sometimes *h* is silent when it appears as the first letter of a word. There are no clues to help us know when, however. The letter *h* is _____ in the words *heir, honest, honor, hour,* and their (heard, silent) derivatives *heiress, honestly, honorable, hourly,* but there is some disagreement among individuals in different areas of the country regarding whether the *h* is silent in the words *herb, humble,* and *homage.*
k *r* *g* beginning	**4.** *H* is also silent when it follows certain consonants. Read the following words: *khaki, khan, rhyme, rhine.* The letter *h* is silent when it follows the consonants _____ and _____. We have also learned that the letter *h* is silent when it follows the consonant _____ (*ghost, ghastly*) at the _____ of words. (beginning, ending)
consistent /h/	**5.** The grapheme *h* is very _____. In the 5,000 most (inconsistent, consistent) frequently used words of the language, over 99% of the time, *h* represents the phoneme _____, and less than 1% of the time, it is silent.

digraph *with, wish, phone, charge, that, white*	**6.** Remember that a two-letter grapheme representing one consonant phoneme is called a consonant _____ . Most of the consonant <center>(digraph, blend)</center>digraphs contain the letter *h* and should not be confused with the grapheme *h*. Underline the consonant digraphs in the following words: *with, wish, phone, charge, that, white.* (*Note:* A discussion of consonant digraphs follows this discussion of single-letter consonant graphemes.)
/j/ final *dge ge*	**7.** The grapheme *j* is quite consistent. It represents the phoneme _____ as in *jump*. A distinctive characteristic of the letter *j* is that it never represents the _____ phoneme in a word. The <center>(initial, final)</center>graphemes that represent the /j/ phoneme at the end of words (*badge, huge*) is either _____ or _____. In other words, the grapheme *j* is used at the beginning of words (*joke*) or syllables (*enjoy*), but never at the end of words.
dge *ge*	**8.** When the phoneme /j/ is heard at the end of single-syllable words containing a short vowel sound (*edge, fudge, dodge, badge, bridge*), /j/ is generally represented by the grapheme _____. Otherwise, the phoneme /j/ heard at the end of words (*large, huge, range, cabbage*) is represented by the grapheme _____.
/y/	**9.** In the 5,000 most frequently used words, the grapheme *j* represents the phoneme /j/ 100% of the time. In one low-frequency word, *hallelujah*, the grapheme *j* represents the phoneme _____.
/k/ *c* /k/	**10.** Except when silent, the grapheme *k* consistently represents the phoneme _____ as in the word *kiss*. Remember, the grapheme _____ (*cut, cat, coast*) also represents the phoneme /k/ when it is *not* followed by an *e, i,* or *y*. However, when you see the grapheme *k* in a word, you can be quite sure that it will represent the phoneme _____.

/k/ an *e*, *i*, or *y*	**11.** Read the following words: *cup, cute, catch, cape, cost, coat, clock.* In all of these words, the grapheme *c* represents the phoneme _____ because the grapheme *c* is not followed by _____.
k *i* or *e* Almost none	**12.** Since the grapheme *c* doesn't represent the phoneme /k/ when it is followed by the vowels *i* or *e*, the grapheme _____ is used to represent /k/ in these circumstances (*kitten, kite, kettle, kept*). In fact, most of the time the grapheme *k* is used in words, it is used to represent /k/ when /k/ is followed by the vowels _____. How many words can you think of in which the grapheme *k* is followed by the vowels *a*, *o*, or *u*? _____ (many, almost none)
n	**13.** Study the following words to see if you can discover when the grapheme *k* is silent: *know, knife, knee, unknown, knocked, knot.* The *k* is silent at the beginning of a word or syllable when it is followed by _____.
/k/ silent	**14.** The grapheme *k* is very consistent. It represents the phoneme _____ when used in written words, and it is _____ when it is followed by *n*. *Note:* In the 5,000 most frequently used words, the grapheme *k* represents /k/ 95.5% of the time, and it is silent 0.5% of the time.
/l/	**15.** The consonant grapheme *l* is another very consistent grapheme. It represents the phoneme _____ as in the word *lamp.*
<u>milk, held</u>	**16.** Sometimes the letter *l* is silent. Study the following words: *talk, milk, folks, walk, yolk, could, held.* Underline the words in which the grapheme *l* is *not* silent.

no	**17.** Sometimes *l* is silent when it precedes another consonant within a word or syllable. Is this a consistent pattern? _____ Rewrite the words below omitting silent consonants.
silk, woud, chak	silk _____ would _____ chalk _____
gold, bel, shoud	gold _____ bell _____ should _____
very consistent /m/ /m/	**18.** Next we turn our attention to the grapheme *m*. This grapheme is _____ . *M* represents the phoneme _____ as (very consistent, not very consistent) in the word *man*. When we see *m* in a word, we can be sure it represents _____ .

Review 5

1. What can you say about the reliability of the graphemes *h, j, k, l,* and *m*?

2. A distinctive characteristic of the letter *h* is that it never

_____ .

3. On rare occasions, *h* is silent. This usually happens when *h*

_____ .

4. The letter *h* should not be confused with the consonant digraphs

_____ .

5. A distinctive characteristic of the letter *j* is that it never

_____ .

6. On rare occasions, *k* is silent. This usually happens when *k*

_____ .

7. Sometimes the letter *l* is silent. Although not consistent, the *l* is often silent when _____ .

See the Answers section for the answers to Review 5.

Single-Letter Consonant Graphemes (*n, p, q, r, s*)

digraph /n/ /ng/	**1.** Our study of single-letter consonant graphemes continues with the third group: *n, p, q, r,* and *s.* The grapheme *n* should not be confused with the consonant _____ *ng.* The grapheme *n* represents (blend, digraph) _____ as in the word *no.* The consonant digraph *ng* represents the phoneme _____ as found in the word *sing.*
/n/	**2.** The grapheme *n* consistently represents the phoneme _____. Sometimes the letter *n* can be silent when followed by an *m* as in *autumn;* however, in the 5,000 most frequently used words of the language, this situation occurs only three times.
grapheme	**3.** It might be interesting for you to know that the phoneme /n/ occurs more frequently in words than any other consonant phoneme. Therefore, the grapheme *n* occurs more frequently in words than any other consonant _____ . (sound, grapheme)
ng /n/ consonant grapheme	**4.** The most important things to remember about the grapheme *n* is (a) it should not be confused with the consonant digraph _____; (b) it consistently represents the phoneme _____; and (c) it occurs in words more frequently than any other _____ .
/p/ digraph /f/	**5.** The grapheme *p* represents the phoneme _____ as in the word *pan.* It also is a very consistent grapheme. It should not be confused with the consonant _____ *ph* (**phone, graph**), (digraph, blend) which represents the phoneme _____.

	6. Sometimes the letter *p* is silent in words such as *psalm, psychology, ptomaine, pneumonia,* and *pneumatic.* However, these situations are rare and usually occur in low-frequency words. Rewrite the words above without the letter *p.*
salm, sychology, tomaine	_____ _____ _____
neumonia, neumatic	_____ _____
beginning	**7.** When the letter *p* is silent, it is found at the _____ of a
	(end, beginning)
s, t, or *n*	word and is followed by the letters _____, _____, or _____.
phoneme	**8.** There is not a unique _____ represented by the
	(phoneme, grapheme)
	letter *q* (*quit, quiet*). Furthermore, *q* does not occur in English words
u	without the letter _____ after it (*mosquito, bouquet, quit, quake*).
	Sometimes the grapheme *qu* (*bouquet*) represents the phoneme
/k/	_____ and sometimes it (*quake*) represents the phonemes
/k/ /w/	_____ and _____ blended together.
	9. Study the following words: *opaque, mosque, plaque, antique, technique, unique.* Notice that the letter _____ follows *qu* in all of these
e	
final	words. Also notice that the *qu* plus the *e* represents the _____
	(final, first)
	phoneme of the word. The grapheme *que* in these words represents
/k/	the phoneme _____.
	10. Study the following words: *quietly, require, question, square, equal, quarter.* Notice that the *qu* in all of these words represents the
first	_____ phonemes of words or syllables. The grapheme *qu* in
	(final, first)
/k/ /w/	these words represents the phonemes _____ and _____
	blended together.

/k/ /w/ /k/	**11.** Although there are a few exceptions to the following pattern, generally speaking, the grapheme *qu* represents the phonemes _____ and _____ when it is used at the beginning of words or syllables, and *que* represents the phoneme _____ at the end of words or syllables.
an exception follow the pattern	**12.** Do the words *mosquito* and *conquer* follow the general pattern or are they an exception? _____ Do the words *frequency* and *liquid* follow the pattern or are they an exception? _____
/r/	**13.** The grapheme *r* is another very consistent consonant grapheme. It represents the phoneme _____ as in *run*. It should not be confused with murmur diphthongs (*ir, er, ur, ar,* and *or*), which we will discuss in Chapter 3. Whenever you see a vowel before an *r* in a syllable, the *r* is a part of the vowel and is called a murmur diphthong. A murmur diphthong is one grapheme, representing one phoneme, and should not be confused with the single-letter grapheme *r*.
beginning /r/	**14.** Study the following words: *right, read, bedroom, brick, already.* Notice that the *r* in these words is used at the _____ of (beginning, end) words or syllables. When we see *r* at the beginning of a word or syllable, we can be sure it represents _____ as in *run*. The phoneme /r/ is the fifth most frequently used consonant phoneme in the English language.
/z/ /zh/, /sh/	**15.** The grapheme *s* represents the phoneme /s/ as in *sun*. However, this grapheme also represents other phonemes. In the word *was, s* represents _____; in the word *treasure, s* represents _____; and in the word *sugar, s* represents _____.

/s/ /z/ /zh/ /sh/	**16.** About 84% of the time, *s* represents the phoneme _____ as in *sun*. About 12% of the time, *s* represents the phoneme _____ as found in the word *dogs,* and about 4% of the time, *s* represents the phonemes _____ and _____ as found in the words *measure* and *sure.*
digraph /sh/	**17.** The grapheme *s* should not be confused with the consonant _____ *sh* (*shoot, wish*), which consistently represents the (digraph, blend) phoneme _____.
soon sun *has pans* *treasure leisure* *ensure sugar*	**18.** Study the following words: *ensure, soon, has, sun, sugar, treasure, pans, leisure.* The grapheme *s* represents /s/ in the words _____ and _____. *S* represents /z/ in the words _____ and _____. *S* represents /zh/ in the words _____ and _____. *S* represents /sh/ in the words _____ and _____.
/s/	**19.** In the initial position of words, *s* represents the phoneme _____ except in the words *sure* and *sugar* and their derivatives. In the 5,000 most frequently used words there are only three words (*sure, sugar,* and *surely*) in which *s* in the initial position does not represent /s/.
/z/ voiced /z/	**20.** In the final position of words (*cats, dogs*), *s* represents the phonemes /s/ and _____. See if you can determine when *s* represents /z/. Study the consonants before the *s* in each of these words: *jobs, birds, legs, hills, drums, plans, cars.* Are the consonants before the *s* in each of these words voiced or unvoiced? _____ What is the phoneme represented by *s* in these words? _____
unvoiced /s/	**21.** Study the consonants before *s* in each of these words: *topics, books, roofs, cups, boats.* Are the consonants before *s* in each of these words voiced or unvoiced? _____ What is the phoneme represented by *s* in these words? _____

/z/ /s/	**22.** When words end in *s*, and *s* follows voiced consonants, it represents the phoneme _____. When words end in *s*, and *s* follows voiceless consonants, it represents the phoneme _____.
/z/ /p/ /s/	**23.** When words end in *es* (*does, lives, poles, flies, tubes,* etc.) the *es* represents the phoneme _____, unless the consonant phoneme before the *es* is /k/, /t/, or _____ (*techniques, makes, plates, pirates, ropes, shapes*). If words end in *es*, and *es* follows the graphemes *k, t,* or *p,* the *es* represents the phoneme _____.

Review 6

1. What can you say about the reliability of the graphemes *n, p,* and *r*?
2. An important thing to remember about the grapheme *n* is that it _____ than any other consonant phoneme.
3. The letter *n* should not be confused with the consonant digraph _____, and the letter *p* should not be confused with the consonant digraph _____.
4. On rare occasions, the letter *p* is silent. This happens when _____.
5. The letter *r* consistently represents the consonant phoneme /r/ when it occurs _____.
6. When vowel letters precede the letter *r*, the *r* is _____.
7. The letter *q* never occurs in words without a _____ after it.
8. When *qu* is found at the beginning of words and syllables, it usually represents the blended phonemes _____, and when *que* occurs at the end of words, it represents the phoneme _____.
9. About 84% of the time, the grapheme *s* represents the phoneme _____.
10. When the grapheme *s* occurs _____, it represents both the /s/ and /z/ phonemes.
11. When the grapheme *s* at the end of a word follows voiced consonants, the *s* represents the phoneme _____. Otherwise, it represents the phoneme _____.
12. When the grapheme *es* at the end of a word follows vowels or voiced consonants, it represents the phoneme _____. Otherwise, it represents the phoneme _____.

See the Answers section for the answers to Review 6.

Single-Letter Consonant Graphemes (*t, v, w, x, y, z*)

/t/ /t/	**1.** In written words, the grapheme *t* represents the phoneme _____ as in *teeth* about 98% of the time. Occasionally the letter *t* occurs twice in a word such as *mitt* and *mutt*, and in these cases the grapheme *tt* also represents _____.
digraph /th/ /<u>th</u>/	**2.** The grapheme *t* is very consistent. However, it should not be confused with the consonant _____ *th* (*with, that*), which (digraph, blend) represents the phonemes _____ and _____.
/sh/ /un/ /ch/ /ch/	**3.** In multisyllabic words, we see *tion* frequently used (*action, motion, solution, condition*). When it is used, the letters *ti* most frequently represent the phoneme _____ and the letters *on* represent the (/ch/, /sh/) coarticulated phonemes _____. (/un/, /on/) In very rare situations, the letters *ti* in *tion* represent the phoneme _____ (*mention, question*). When we see *tur* in multisyllabic (/ch/, /sh/) words (*natural, capture, moisture*), the grapheme *t* also represents the phoneme _____ . (/ch/, /sh/)
silent	**4.** There are several common words that we have taken from the French (*debut, beret, bouquet*) in which the letter *t* is _____. Occasionally, the letter *t* is also silent in some multisyllabic words such as *often, soften, listen, fasten,* and *moisten.* However, these situations are very rare.
/v/ *e* ends	**5.** The grapheme *v* consistently represents the phoneme _____ as in *voice.* One of the most interesting things about the grapheme *v* (*live, leave, love, solve, twelve, observe, serve, native, curve*) is that it is never found at the end of words without an _____ after it. In other words, the grapheme *v* never _____ a word. (ends, begins)

begins a word or syllable *o*	**6.** Earlier in this text you learned that the grapheme *w* predictably represents its consonant phoneme /w/ as in the word *watch* when it _____ . However, if the grapheme (begins a word/syllable, follows a vowel) *w* follows the vowels *a, e,* or _____, it is part of a vowel team (*lawn, blew, town*).
/w/ syllables	**7.** Except for those instances in which the letter *w* is silent in words (*write, two, who*), it consistently represents the phoneme _____ when it is used to begin words or _____.
r	**8.** Analyze the following words: *write, wrote, wrong, writer, wrapped, wreck, wrist.* We can predictably say that when the letter *w* precedes the letter _____, the *w* is silent.
phoneme /ks/ /gz/ *taks egzist*	**9.** There is not a unique _____ represented by letter *x* (phoneme, grapheme) (*fox, exam*). However, it does represent the coarticulated phonemes _____ in such words as *tax*, and the coarticulated phonemes _____ in such words as *exist*. If we were to write *tax* and *exist* using the letters usually associated with the sounds *x* represents in these words, we would write them _____ and _____.
/z/ /eks/	**10.** Sometimes the letter *x* is used at the beginning of a word (*Xerox, xylophone, xenon*), and the phoneme represented by *x* is _____. However, in the word *X-ray*, *x* represents the coarticulated phonemes _____, which represents the pronunciation of its own name.
/ks/ /ks/ /gz/	**11.** Most of the time the grapheme *x* represents _____ as heard in the word *box*. In the 5,000 most frequently used words of the English language, the grapheme *x* is found in 95 words. In 82 of those words (86.3%), it represents _____ as in the word *mix*. In 11 words (11.6%), *x* represents _____ as heard in the word *exact*. In two words (*anxious* and *anxiously*), *xi* represents the coarticulated phonemes /ksh/ (2.1%).

begins a word/syllable vowel	**12.** Earlier in this text you learned that the grapheme *y* predictably represents its consonant phoneme /y/ as in the word *yes* when it _____ . However, if the grapheme (begins a word/syllable, follows a vowel) is not used to begin words or syllables, it represents a _____ (vowel, consonant) phoneme (*myth, dry, rhyme, copy*) or is part of a vowel phoneme (*play, toy*).
yes, yellow, yet, year, lawyer by, why, baby, happy say, boy	**13.** Study the following words: *yes, yellow, lawyer, yet, year, by, day, why, say, boy, baby, happy.* Write all of the words in which *y* represents a consonant phoneme: _____ _____ Write all of the words in which *y* represents a vowel phoneme: _____ Write all of the words in which *y* is part of a vowel phoneme: _____
vowel, consonant	**14.** The grapheme *y* occurs more frequently in words as a _____ than as a _____. (consonant, vowel) (consonant, vowel)
/z/	**15.** The grapheme *z* is consistently used to represent the phoneme _____ as in *zoo*. However, it may surprise you that the grapheme *s* represents /z/ more frequently in words than the grapheme *z*.
/z/ /s/ /zh/	**16.** The grapheme *z* is very reliable. In the 5,000 most frequently used words in the English language, *z* represents the phoneme _____ 100% of the time it occurs. However, in a few low-frequency words, *z* is used to represent the phoneme _____ as in the word *waltz*, or the phoneme _____ as in the word *seizure*.

 **Review 7**   **1.** The grapheme *t* reliably represents the phoneme /t/. However, it should not be confused with the digraph _____.

2. In words of more than one syllable, the *tion* suffix occurs frequently. It most often represents the phonemes _____, but in rare situations represents the phonemes _____.

3. On rare occasions, the letter *t* is _____.

4. The grapheme *v* is (not very reliable, very reliable).

5. One of the most interesting things about the grapheme *v* is that

_____.

6. The grapheme *w* reliably represents /w/ when it occurs at the beginning of words and syllables, unless it is followed by the letter _____. On these occasions, the *w* is silent.

7. The grapheme *w* is used to represent a vowel phoneme when

_____.

8. About 86% of the time, the grapheme *x* represents the phonemes _____, and about 12% of the time, it represents the phonemes

_____.

9. The grapheme *y* reliably represents /y/ when it occurs at the beginning of words and syllables. It represents vowel phonemes when

_____.

10. The grapheme *z* reliably represents /z/, but in a few low-frequency words it represents the phonemes _____ and

_____.

11. The grapheme _____ represents the phoneme /z/ in more words than the grapheme *z*.

See the Answers section for the answers to Review 7.

Consonant Digraphs

digraph	**1.** Earlier in this text you learned that a two-letter grapheme representing one phoneme is called a _____ . The consonant (digraph, blend)
ng	digraph in the word *sing* is _____. This digraph occurs more frequently in words than any of the other consonant digraphs. It is found
ing	often in the _____ inflectional ending of word variants. The *ng* (ang, ing)
/ng/	digraph in *ing* consistently represents the phoneme _____ as in *sing*. *Note:* A word variant contains a root word (*walk*) and an inflectional ending (*ed*): *walked.* Inflectional endings are used in word variants so we can communicate (a) present, past, or future tense (examples: *I walk to school every* day. *I walked to school yesterday. I will be walking to school tomorrow.*); (b) plurals (example: *girls*); (c) possession (example: *girl's*); (d) comparison (example: *smart, smarter, smartest*); and (e) first, second, or third person (examples: *I walk. You walk. She walks*).
	2. The *ng* digraph also occurs in single-syllable words (*long, sang, rung, ring*) and other multisyllabic words (*finger, single, hungry*). Study the following words: *longer, ingest, engulf.* Only one of these words contains
longer	the *ng* digraph. Write that word: _____. Sometimes we confuse multisyllabic words containing a prefix ending in *n* (*in, en*) and a root
ng	beginning with a *g* (*gest, gulf*) with words containing the _____ digraph.
	3. There are other occasions in which *ng* occurs in words but doesn't represent a digraph. For example, when the letters *ng* are followed by an *e* or *i* in words (*change, challenge, range, engine, changing*), the *n* and *ge* or *gi* are usually separate graphemes, each representing separate phonemes. Do you remember what you learned regarding the letter *g* when it is followed by an *e, i,* or *y*? When the letter *e* or *i* is used after a *g* to
/j/	indicate the phoneme _____, the letter *n* represents its own
/n/	phoneme, _____. Therefore, in the word *exchange*, the
/n/	grapheme *n* represents the phoneme _____ and the grapheme
g is followed by an *e*	*g* represents the phoneme /j/ because _____.

is is not /j/	**4.** Vowel-beginning suffixes or inflectional endings (*er, est*) added to root words containing the digraph *ng* (*strong* + *er* = *stronger*; *young* + *est* = *youngest*) should not be confused with root words ending with *nge* (*change, challenge*). In the words *stronger* and *youngest*, *ng* _____ a digraph even though there is an *e* after the *ng*. In the (is, is not) words *challenging* and *engineer*, *ng* _____ a digraph because (is, is not) the root words are *challenge* and *engine*, and the *ge* and *gi* in these words are used to tell the reader that *g* represents the phoneme _____ .
/ng/	**5.** Once you learn to recognize the *ng* digraph in words, you will also recognize that this digraph consistently represents the phoneme _____ as in *sing* (almost 100% of the time it occurs in words).
/ng/ *jung.gul long.ger* *ang.gul* /g/	**6.** Study the following words: *congress, jungle, longer, angle*. The digraph *ng* in all of these words represents the phoneme _____ . The two syllables of the word *congress* written phonemically would be *kong. gres.* *Note:* To write a word phonemically, we write, in the order in which they occur, the symbols that represent each phoneme in the word. Write each syllable in the words *jungle, longer,* and *angle* phonemically: _____ _____ Notice that the second syllable of each of these words begins with the phoneme _____ .
/g/ *g*	**7.** You can conclude that when the *ng* digraph occurs in multisyllabic words not ending in *ing* (*single, youngest, triangle, longest*), the syllable after /ng/ begins with the phoneme _____ (/gul/, /gest/, /gul/, /gest/) even though the written representation of the syllable does not contain the grapheme _____ (*sing.le, young.est, tri.ang.le, long.est*).

/th/ /th/ /th/ /th/	**8.** The second most frequently occurring consonant digraph in written words is *th*. This digraph consistently represents either the voiceless phoneme _____ as in *thing* or the voiced phoneme _____ as in *the*. About 59% of the time, *th* represents the phoneme _____ (*thing*), and about 41% of the time, it represents the phoneme _____ (*the*).
consonant letter	**9.** There is little to help you determine when *th* represents voiceless /th/ or voiced /th/. One pattern, however, does seem to emerge from a study of words containing *th*. Study the following words: *three, months, forth, threw, health, birth, depth, sixth, tenth, warmth, throne*. Whenever *th* is preceded by or follows a _____ in a single-syllable word, the *th* represents the voiceless phoneme /th/. An analysis of all the words containing *th* in the 5,000 most frequently used words reveals this to be a consistent pattern (100% of the time).
/ch/ /k/ /sh/	**10.** The next most frequently occurring consonant digraph found in written words is *ch*. This digraph represents the phoneme _____ as in *church* in most words (89%). In about 10% of the words in which *ch* is used, it represents the phoneme _____ as in *school, chemical, character,* or *stomach.* In about 1% of the words, *ch* is used to represent the phoneme _____ as in *machine, machinery, Michigan,* or *Chicago.*
peach, chase, porch *ache, orchestra, chorus,* *technical, echo, scheme* *machines*	**11.** Study the following words: *ache, peach, orchestra, machines, chorus, chase, technical, porch, echo,* and *scheme*. Write the words in which *ch* represents the /ch/ sound: _____ Write the words in which *ch* represents the /k/ sound: _____. _____. Write the word in which *ch* represents the /sh/ sound: _____.

end short end is not	**12.** Sometimes the phoneme /ch/ is written *tch*. Consider the following words: *catch, kitchen, match, stretch, witch, sketch, ditch, scratch.* The grapheme *tch* occurs at the _____ of each word (beginning, end) or syllable. The vowel sound in all of these words is _____ . (long, short) Consider the following words: *peach, couch, each, speech, coach, teach, reach.* The grapheme *tch* occurs at the _____ of each word. (beginning, end) The vowel sound in all of these words _____ short. (is, is not)
end 100, short	**13.** Whenever the grapheme *tch* occurs in words, it is found at the _____ of words or syllables. It represents the phoneme (beginning, end) /ch/ _____ % of the time. It follows _____ vowel (long, short) phonemes.
/sh/	**14.** The next most frequently occurring consonant digraph is *sh*, which represents the phoneme _____ as in *shoe*. It consistently represents this phoneme.
/hw/ /h/	**15.** The digraph *wh* represents the phoneme _____ as in *white* about 90% of the time. It represents the phoneme _____ as in *who, whole,* and *whom* about 10% of the time.
/ng + k/	**16.** The letters *nk* at the end of words or syllables (thi*nk*, *Thanksgiving, bank, monkey, blanket*) consistently represent (100% of the time) two phonemes blended together. Write those phonemes: _____.

/ng/ /th/ /<u>th</u>/ /ch/ /k/ /sh/ /ch/ /sh/ /hw/ /h/ /ng/ /k/	**17.** In summary, there are six consonant digraphs that represent various phonemes. The grapheme *ng* represents _____ as in *sing.* The grapheme *th* represents both _____ and _____ as in *thing* and *the.* The grapheme *ch* represents _____ as in *church* most of the time, but it also represents _____ as in *echo* and _____ as in *machine* occasionally. The grapheme *tch* represents _____ as in *witch.* The grapheme *sh* represents _____ as in *shoe.* The grapheme *wh* represents _____ as in *white,* but it also represents _____ as in *who* occasionally. In addition, the letters *nk* represent the phonemes _____ and _____ blended together as in *sank.*
gh *f* *ph* *f*	**18.** The consonant digraphs we have been discussing so far represent phonemes not generally represented by single-letter graphemes. However, there are two digraphs that represent phonemes that are generally represented by single-letter graphemes. The first one is _____ as in *laugh.* This digraph represents the same phoneme that is most frequently represented by the grapheme _____. The second one is _____ as in *phone.* This digraph also represents the phoneme that is most frequently represented by the grapheme _____.
100	**19.** The *gh* digraph represents /f/ only when it follows vowel letters and even then it does it only 5% of the time. However, the *ph* digraph consistently represents /f/ (_____ % of the time) when it occurs in written words.
tough, paragraph, phrase, *telephone, elephant,* *photograph, telegraph*	**20.** Say the following words: *might, high, eight, ought, tough; paragraph, phrase, telephone, elephant, photograph, telegraph.* Write all of the words containing a digraph that represents the phoneme /f/: _____ _____ _____ _____

 **Review 8**

1. The consonant digraph _____ occurs more frequently in words than any other consonant digraph and is almost 100% reliable.
2. Describe those situations when readers think they see the *ng* digraph when they really don't.
3. About 59% of the time, the digraph *th* represents the phoneme _____, and about 41% of the time, it represents the phoneme _____.
4. Describe the situation in which the /th/ voiceless phoneme can be predicted in written words.
5. The consonant digraph *ch* represents /ch/ about 89% of the time. About 10% of the time, it represents the phoneme _____, and about 1% of the time, it represents the phoneme _____.
6. The consonant trigraph *tch* occurs at the _____ of words and syllables. It represents /ch/ _____ % of the time, and it follows _____ vowel phonemes.
7. What can you say about the reliability of the digraph *sh*?
8. What can you say about the reliability of the digraph *wh*?
9. The letters *nk* at the ends of words or syllables reliably represent the phonemes _____.

See the Answers section for the answers to Review 8.

Consonant Blends

Eighteen	**1.** We have completed our discussion of the 25 consonant phonemes of the American English language. _____ of these phonemes (How many?) are predictably represented by single-letter graphemes. Six of the
digraphs	phonemes are predictably represented by the _____ *ng, th, ch,* <div align="center">(blends, digraphs)</div>
/zh/	*sh,* and *wh,* and one phoneme, _____, is represented by various graphemes: *si* (*division*), *s* (*treasure*), and *z* (*azure*).

24 graphemes	**2.** Even though 23 graphemes (18 single-letter graphemes plus 5 digraphs) predictably represent _____ consonant phonemes (How many?) (all of the consonant phonemes, excluding /zh/), you have also learned that some _____ (*rats, dogs*) occasionally (phonemes, graphemes) represent more than one phoneme, and therefore, some phonemes are occasionally represented by more than one grapheme (*fat,* **phone**).
phonemes	**3.** Now that you have learned about the basic consonant grapheme/phoneme relationships, let's turn our attention to how some of the consonant graphemes are clustered together in words. Consonant graphemes that are clustered with each other in written words represent consonant _____ that are blended (graphemes, phonemes) together in spoken words.
s *g* consonant	**4.** Read the following words: *sag, stag.* Both words begin with the consonant grapheme _____, and both words end with the consonant grapheme _____. The *s* in the first word is followed by a vowel grapheme, but the *s* in the second word is followed by another _____ grapheme. When you say the second (consonant, vowel) word, you blend the consonant phoneme /s/ with the consonant phoneme /t/ to get /st/, so we call *st* a *consonant blend.*
six *st nd cr mp* *sl, nt* end	**5.** Study the consonant blends in the following words: **stand, cramp, slant.** In the words *stand, cramp,* and *slant,* there are _____ (How many?) different consonant blends. In their order of appearance those blends are _____, _____, _____, _____, _____, and _____. Consonant blends can occur at the beginning or the _____ of words or syllables.

one blended	**6.** Consonant blends should not be confused with consonant digraphs. Digraphs are two consonant letters representing _____ consonant phoneme, but blends are two or more (How many?) consonant letters representing phonemes that are _____ (blended, written) together.
str *rap* *trap* *strap*	**7.** Consider the word **strap**. The consonant blend in this word is _____. Since consonant blends are separate graphemes blended together, they can also be separated from each other. For example, you can separate *st* from *r* in the word *strap*, and you have the word _____. You can add *t* to *rap* and you have the word _____. You can then add *s* to *trap* and you again have the word _____.
sh /h/	**8.** Since consonant digraphs represent one phoneme, they cannot be separated. For example, in the word *show*, the digraph is _____. If you separate the *s* from the *h* in the digraph *sh*, you no longer have a digraph. Once the *s* is removed from the *h*, you have two separate graphemes, *s* and *h*, which represent two different phonemes, /s/ and _____. Also notice that the word that is left in this situation (*how*) doesn't even sound like the word you started with (*show*).
<u>stop</u>, <u>skip</u>, <u>slap</u> <u>blue</u>, <u>plug</u>, <u>club</u>, <u>drop</u> <u>flag</u>, <u>snob</u>, <u>frog</u>, <u>glad</u>	**9.** Read the following words and underline those that contain consonant blends: *stop* *skip* *shop* *slap* *this* *blue* *plug* *why* *club* *drop* *flag* *snob* *frog* *glad* *chip*

thr, shr *th* *r* *sh r*	**10.** The 27 *beginning* consonant blends that follow are arranged according to their frequency of use in American English words: *st, pr, tr, gr, pl, cl, cr, str, br, dr, sp, fl, fr, bl, sl, sw, sm, sc, thr, sk, gl, tw, scr, spr, sn, spl, shr.* Write the two consonant blends that contain digraphs: _____. In the word *three,* the digraph _____ is blended with the single-letter grapheme _____. In the word *shrub,* the digraph _____ is blended with the grapheme _____.
nch *n* *ch* *nk* *ngth* *ng* *th*	**11.** The 15 ending consonant blends that follow are arranged according to their frequency of use in American English words: *nt, nd, ct, nce, nk, mp, lt, ft, nge, sk, pt, nch, nse, sp, ngth.* Write the consonant blend that contains one digraph: _____. In the word *lunch,* the single-letter grapheme _____ is blended with the digraph _____. Write the blend that represents the phoneme /ng/ blended with the phoneme /k/: _____. In the word *sink, nk* represents the blended phonemes /ng//k/. Write the blend that contains two digraphs blended together: _____. In the word *length,* the digraph _____ is blended with the digraph _____.
/k/ /w/ *quake, question, require, quit, equal, square*	**12.** You learned earlier in the text that the letter *q* is always followed by the letter *u* in words. You also learned that *qu* at the beginning of words or syllables (*quiet, inquire, quickly*) usually represents the phonemes _____ and _____ blended together. When this happens, *qu* can also be considered a consonant blend. From the following words, write those in which *qu* is a consonant blend: *quake, unique, plaque, question, require, quit, equal, square.* _____ _____

Review 9   **1.** Explain the difference between consonant digraphs and consonant blends.

2. Sometimes a consonant digraph is blended with a consonant grapheme. Write a word containing a digraph blended with a consonant phoneme.

See the Answers section for the answers to Review 9.

Chapter 3

Vowels

Place the mask over the left-hand column. Write your responses in the right-hand column. Do not pull the mask down until you have written your responses to the entire frame. Make sure that you are seated where you can say sounds out loud. In order to get the full impact of this text, you must be able to say words and phonemes and listen carefully to what you say.

vowels	**1.** The 26 letters of the alphabet are divided into two categories: consonants and _____.
45	**2.** These 26 letters are used either individually or in combination with other letters to represent the _____ phonemes that make up words.

Twenty-one
 	
5
a, e, i, o,
u
no
	3. _____ letters of the alphabet are used to represent the 25
	   (How many?)
	consonant phonemes. Twenty-six letters minus 21 leaves only
	_____ letters. These letters are our vowel letters. Our vowel
	letters are _____, _____, _____, _____, and
	_____. Are these the only letters that are used to represent the 20
	vowel phonemes? _____
	         (yes, no)

y
 	
it
 	
ice
 	
i
	4. Say the following words: *myth, rhyme, my.* The letter used to represent the vowel phonemes in these words is _____. The vowel phoneme in the word *myth* is the same vowel phoneme heard in the word _____. The vowel phoneme in the words *rhyme* and
	     (it, ice)
	my is the same vowel phoneme heard in the word _____. When
	          (it, ice)
	the letter *y* is used in single-syllable words to represent a vowel phoneme, it represents the same phonemes the letter _____ represents.

e eve	**5.** Say the following words: *city, party, slowly.* The vowel phoneme represented by the letter *y* in the last syllable of these three words is the same phoneme represented by the letter _____ in the word _____. (*eve, ice*) Say the following words: *deny, supply, decry.* The vowel phoneme represented by the letter *y* in the last syllable of these three words is
i ice	the same phoneme represented by the letter ____ in the word _____. (*eve, ice*)
e *i*	**6.** When the letter *y* is used by itself at the end of multisyllabic words to represent a vowel phoneme, it represents either the same phoneme that the letter _____ represents in the word *eve (baby)* or the letter _____ represents in the word *ice (deny).*
y digraph vowel	**7.** Say the following words: *hay, they, boy, buy.* The vowel phonemes in these words are represented by the letter _____ plus another vowel letter. However, the two letters in each word represent only one sound. When two letters represent one sound, we have a _____. (blend, digraph) Therefore, *ay, ey,* and *uy* are _____ digraphs. (consonant, vowel) *Note:* The vowel team *oy* represents a special gliding vowel sound we call a *diphthong.* More will be said about that later.
a *ape* *oi* *coin* *i* *ice* no	**8.** The vowel phoneme in the words *hay* and *they* is the same vowel phoneme represented by the letter _____ in the word _____. The vowel phoneme in the word *boy* is the same vowel (*ape, at*) phoneme represented by the letters _____ in the word _____. The vowel phoneme in the word *buy* is the same vowel (*gym, coin*) phoneme represented by the letter _____ in the word _____. Does the letter *y* represent any vowel phoneme not (*ice, up*) represented by some other letter? _____ (yes, no)

phoneme	**9.** You have learned that *y* represents a vowel _____, by itself, in (phoneme, grapheme) words. However, when it does, it represents the same phonemes the
i e	letters _____ and _____ represent. You have also learned that when *a, e, o,* or *u* are combined with the letter *y* (*ay, ey, oy, uy*), these
phonemes	vowel combinations represent vowel _____. All of the phonemes (graphemes, phonemes) the letter *y* represents by itself or with other letters are also represented by existing vowel letters. Because the letter *y* does not represent any
probably	vowel phoneme not represented by other letters, we could _____ (probably, probably not) get along without it if we wanted to change our spelling system.
vowel	**10.** The letter *w* is also used to represent _____ phonemes. (vowel, consonant blend)
does not	However, the letter *w* by itself _____ represent a vowel phoneme. (does, does not)
w	**11.** Say the following words: *few, law, show.* The vowel phonemes used in these words are represented by the letter _____ preceded by another vowel. However, the two letters in each word represent
digraph	only one vowel phoneme, so *w* is a part of a vowel _____. (blend, digraph)
	12. Match the words containing the same vowel phonemes: *few, law, show, cow, oak, fraud, use, out*
few use *law fraud* *show oak* *cow out*	*few* _____ *law* _____ *show* _____ *cow* _____
yes	Do you think we could get along without using the letter *w* to represent vowel phonemes if we wanted to change our spelling system? _____ (yes, no)

vowel	**13.** Say the following words: *first, fern, fur, fork, far, hair, care, there, bear, fire.* Notice that in each word you find the letter *r*, and you see at least one _____ letter before the *r*. Some people (vowel, consonant) believe that the *r* does not represent a part of the vowel phoneme in these words. This is a serious mistake! When you see the following letter combinations in words, they represent vowel phonemes: *ir, er, ur, or, ar, air, are, eer, ire, ear.* They are special vowel phonemes called *murmur diphthongs.*
does not diphthong	**14.** When the letter *r* begins words or syllables (*run, three, around, country*) it _____ represent a vowel phoneme. However, if the (does, does not) letter *r* is preceded by a vowel letter, the vowel letter (or letters) and the *r* comprise a special vowel team called a murmur _____. (diphthong, digraph)
no	**15.** Are the vowel phonemes represented by murmur diphthongs represented by other vowel letters? _____ (yes, no)
igh *i ice* *i*	**16.** Say the words *high, light, slight, fight.* The vowel phoneme in these words is represented by the letters _____. One could say that *gh* in these words is silent, which of course is true. They certainly do not represent any other sound. However, the *igh* grapheme pattern consistently represents the same vowel phoneme as the letter _____ in the word _____. It will be shown shortly that (it, ice) vowel phonemes can be predicted by letter and syllable patterns. Therefore, a good case could be made that *igh* is a pattern of letters consistently representing the vowel phoneme _____.

no	**17.** The answer to the question, "Are the vowel letters the only alphabetic letters used to represent the 20 vowel phonemes?" is _____. In addition to the five vowel letters used to represent (yes, no)
y w r *gh y*	vowel phonemes, the letters _____, _____, _____, and _____ are also used. The letter _____ is used by itself to represent a vowel phoneme. However, it is also used with other vowels as a vowel digraph (*ay, ey, uy*), and it is used with the vowel *o* (*oy*) to represent a vowel diphthong. (A diphthong is a gliding vowel sound that we will discuss shortly.)
w	**18.** The letter _____ is used with the vowels *a* and *e* (*aw, ew*) to form vowel digraphs, and with the vowel *o* (*ow*) to form either a vowel digraph (*show*) or to represent a vowel diphthong phoneme (*cow*).
gh	**19.** The letters _____ are used with the letter *i* (*fight*) to represent the vowel phoneme heard in the word *ice*.
murmur diphthongs	**20.** The letter *r* represents a vowel when other vowels precede it (*burn, first*) and the phonemes represented by the *r* vowels are called _____ _____. Now that we have discussed the letters involved in the graphemes representing vowel phonemes, we next turn to the vowel phonemes themselves.

A B C Review 10

1. Besides the five vowel letters, what other letters are used to represent vowel phonemes?
2. When the letter *y* is used by itself in single-syllable words to represent a vowel phoneme, it represents _____.
3. When the letter *y* is used by itself at the end of multisyllabic words to represent a vowel phoneme, it represents _____.
4. Explain when the letter *r* is part of a vowel grapheme.

See the Answers section for the answers to Review 10.

Vowel Phonemes

voiced vowel	**1.** There are no voiceless vowel phonemes. All vowel phonemes are _____; we vibrate our vocal cords when producing all (voiceless, voiced) _____ phonemes. (vowel, consonant)
a *a* *ai* *ay*	**2.** The 20 vowel phonemes, the graphemes representing them, and the key words used to refer to them are begun in this frame and continued in the next eight frames. They are marked with asterisks. *The vowel grapheme _____ represents /a/ as in *at*. *The vowel grapheme _____ also represents /ā/ as in *ate* or *bacon*. (The pattern of the syllable in which *a* occurs will help the reader know which phoneme it represents. More will be said about this shortly.) The phoneme /ā/ is also predictably represented by the vowel team patterns _____ (*raid*) and _____ (*say*).
e *ea* *e* *ee* *ea*	**3.** *The vowel grapheme _____ represents /e/ as in *edge*. The phoneme /e/ is also represented by the vowel team _____ (*bread*). *The vowel grapheme _____ also represents /ē/ as in *eve* or *me*. (The pattern of the syllable in which *e* occurs will help the reader know which phoneme it represents.) The phoneme /ē/ is also predictably represented by the vowel team patterns _____ (*feet*) and _____ (*eat*).
i *i* *y* *igh* pattern	**4.** *The vowel grapheme _____ represents /i/ as in *it*. *The vowel grapheme _____ also represents /ī/ as in *ice* and *ci.der*. The phoneme /ī/ is also predictably represented by _____ (*my* or *rhyme*) and the vowel team pattern _____ (*night*). (Again, the _____ of the syllable or the vowel team will help the (pattern, size) reader know which phoneme is represented.)

o *a* *aw* *au*	**5.** *The vowel grapheme _____ represents /o/ as in *ox*. The phoneme /o/ is also predictably represented by _____ when it is preceded by a *w* (*water*) or followed by an *l* (*ball*). It is also predictably represented by the vowel teams _____ (*saw*) and _____ (*fraud*).
o *oa* *ow*	*The vowel grapheme _____ also represents /ō/ as in *ode* and *so*. The phoneme /ō/ is also predictably represented by the vowel teams _____ (*soap*) and _____ (*show*). (The syllable and letter patterns will help the reader determine which phoneme is being represented.)
u *u* syllable *ew* *ue*	**6.** *The vowel grapheme _____ represents /u/ as in *up*. *The vowel grapheme _____ also represents /ū/ as in *use* or *u.nite*. (The pattern of the _____ in which *u* occurs will help the (syllable, letters) reader know which phoneme it represents.) The phoneme /ū/ is also represented by the vowel teams _____ (*few*) and _____ (*cue*).
oo *u* *ew* *ue* *oo*	**7.** *The vowel grapheme _____ represents /o͞o/ as in *moon*. The letter _____ in such words as *rude,* and the vowel teams _____ (*blew*) and _____ (*blue*) also represent /oo/. *The vowel grapheme _____ also represents /oo/ as in *book*.
ow *ou* *oy* *oi*	**8.** *The vowel graphemes _____ and _____ represent /ou/ as in *cow* and *found*. *The vowel graphemes _____ and _____ represent /oi/ as in *boy* and *coin*.
ur *ir* *er* *ar* *or*	**9.** *The vowel graphemes _____, _____, and _____ represent /ûr/ as in *hurt, first, fern*. *The vowel grapheme _____ represents /ar/ as in *car*. *The vowel grapheme _____ represents /or/ as in *for*.

air, are, ere *ear* *eer, ear* *ire*	**10.** *The vowel graphemes _____, _____, _____, and _____ represent /âr/ as in *hair, care, there,* and *bear.* *The vowel graphemes _____ and _____ represent /ir/ as in *deer* and *year.* *The vowel grapheme _____ represents /īr/ as in *fire.*
	11. The symbols encased within the sound markers / / in frames 2 through 10 above identify the 20 vowel phonemes. An asterisk (*) was used whenever a new phoneme was introduced. The following words are written phonemically (according to their sounds). Spell each word correctly:
geese *reading* *badge* *fusion* *stretch*	gēs _____ rē.ding _____ baj _____ fū.zhun _____ strech _____
	12. Using the symbols for consonant and vowel phonemes encased within the sound markers / /, write the following words phonemically:
kum.plēt *dogz* *es.tab.lish* *rē.sunt.lē* *stâr*	*complete* _____ *dogs* _____ *establish* _____ *recently* _____ *stare* _____
/ûr/	**13.** Write the symbol that represents the vowel sound in the word *thirst.* _____
/o͞o/	**14.** Write the symbol that represents the vowel sound in the word *crude.* _____
/oo/	**15.** Write the symbol that represents the vowel sound in the word *put.* _____

/ā/	**16.** Write the symbol that represents the vowel sound in the word *break.* _____
/ar/	**17.** Write the symbol that represents the vowel sound in the word *start.* _____
/âr/	**18.** Write the symbol that represents the vowel sound in the word *stare.* _____
/ou/	**19.** Write the symbol that represents the vowel sound in the word *how.* _____
/oi/	**20.** Write the symbol that represents the vowel sound in the word *joint.* _____
/ū/	**21.** Write the symbol that represents the vowel sound in the word *fuse.* _____
/o/	**22.** Write the symbol that represents the vowel sound in the word *hop.* _____
/a/ /e/ /ē/ /ī/	**23.** Write the symbols for the vowel sounds in the following words: strap _____ next _____ street _____ my _____
/i/ /ō/ /u/ /or/ /ir/	**24.** Write the symbols for the vowel sounds in the following words: hymn _____ soap _____ much _____ stork _____ cheer _____

Review 11   **1.** There are voiceless and voiced consonant phonemes; however, there
are no _____ vowel phonemes.
2. There are 20 vowel phonemes. Write the symbols for each vowel
phoneme and give a word example for each.

See the Answers section for the answers to Review 11.

Long Vowel Phonemes and Graphemes

eve *ice* *open* *use*	**1.** Long vowel phonemes are the sounds of the vowels' names. The long sound of the letter *a* is /ā/ as in *ate*. The long sound of the grapheme *e* is /ē/ as in _____. The long sound of the grapheme *i* (*edge, eve*) is /ī/ as in _____. The long sound of the grapheme *o* is /ō/ as in (*ice, it*) _____, and the long sound of the grapheme *u* is /ū/ as in (*open, odd*) _____. (*use, up*)
name	**2.** We write a *macron* (—) over the vowel letter to indicate the long sound of the vowel. The macron is used to indicate that the sound of the vowel is the same as the _____ of the vowel. (name, pattern)
mane	**3.** The word element *macro* in the word *macron* means "long" or "great." If we were writing words phonemically, a macron would be placed over the *a* in the word _____. (*man, mane*)
stāk *men.chun* *sēk* *fūz* *bōn*	**4.** Write the following words phonemically: steak _____ men.tion _____ seek _____ fuse _____ bone _____

long *e* doesn't represent consonant	**5.** It was mentioned earlier that the pattern of the syllable indicates to the reader which phoneme a vowel grapheme is representing. Read the following words: *came, time, tone, use, eve.* The vowel phoneme in each word is _____. Each word ends with the letter _____, (long, short) which _____ a sound. The pattern of these single-syllable words (represents, doesn't represent) is a VCe pattern. That is, the written syllable contains *one* vowel (V) grapheme, followed by *one* _____ (C) unit, followed by the letter (consonant, vowel) *e,* which is silent.
long	**6.** Vowel graphemes in the VCe pattern generally represent _____ vowel phonemes. (long, short)
cape, wine, cope, *use, bathe, lathe*	**7.** Write the words containing long vowel sounds from the following list: *cap, cape, wine, win, cope, cop, us, use, bathe, bath, lathe.* _____ _____
yes one digraph	**8.** Do the words *bathe, blithe,* and *lathe* fit the VCe pattern? _____ (yes, no) The grapheme *th* in these words represents _____ consonant (How many?) unit/s. Therefore, the (C) consonant in the VCe pattern can be either a single consonant or a consonant _____. (digraph, blend)
no *come, some, love*	**9.** Are all vowel phonemes in VCe patterned words long? _____ (yes, no) Although the pattern is quite consistent, there are vowels in VCe patterned words that are not long. From the list of words that follows, write those that do not contain a long vowel phoneme: *stone, come, these, some, fate, love.* _____.

e	**10.** Since the letter *v* never ends a word without the letter _____ after it, you cannot use the VCe pattern with words ending in *ve*. Sometimes it works (*drive*), and sometimes it doesn't (*prove*), and sometimes it works in one context but not in another (*live*).
short	**11.** Words with consonant blends between the vowel and the silent *e* (*pulse, rinse, fence*) are a VCCe pattern, and the vowel phonemes in these words are usually _____. (long, short)
one long	**12.** We have discovered that when we see one vowel in a written syllable followed by _____ consonant unit and a final *e*, the (one, two) vowel grapheme is likely to represent its _____ sound.
long after	**13.** There is another syllable pattern that suggests to the reader that the vowel grapheme represents its long sound. Read the following words: *so, go, me, he, ti.ger, pi.lot, ba.con, la.bor, mu.sic,* and *hu.mor.* The vowel grapheme in the first four words and the first syllable of the last six words represent a _____ vowel phoneme. Each syllable with (short, long) the long vowel phoneme ends _____ the vowel grapheme. (after, before)
long	**14.** Written syllables ending in a single-letter vowel grapheme are called *open syllables*. The vowel sound represented by these graphemes is generally _____. (short, long)
she, fro.zen, cra.zy, mo.tel, spi.der	**15.** Write the words that contain open syllables: *com.plete, she, suf.fer, fro.zen, cra.zy, mo.tel, spi.der, cam.el.* _____ _____

the VCe pattern (*rope*) and the open syllable pattern (*so*)	**16.** The syllable patterns suggesting that vowel graphemes represent long vowel phonemes are _____ _____ _____
sûr.kus jip.sē Frīdāy plāt nō.shun	**17.** Write the following words phonemically: cir.cus _____ gyp.sy _____ Fri.day _____ plate _____ no.tion _____
long the syllable pattern of *snake* is VCe	**18.** The vowel grapheme *a* in the word *snake* represents the _____ (long, short) vowel phoneme because _____ _____
long the syllable *fa* in the word *favor* is an open syllable	**19.** The vowel grapheme *a* in the word *fa.vor* represents the _____ (long, short) vowel phoneme because _____ _____ _____ _____
vowel	**20.** Open syllables (*ti.ger, ba.con, me, she, so*) end in single _____ (consonant, vowel) graphemes.
gone, the, to, do	**21.** Although the VCe syllable pattern and open syllable pattern are quite consistent in predicting long vowel phonemes, there are, of course, unusual situations in which the vowels in these syllable patterns represent something other than the long sound. From the list of words that follows, write those words that contain vowels that represent something other than the predictable long sound: *gone, smile, the, to, strike, do, wide, shame, la.dy.* _____

i	**22.** When *y* functions as a vowel in single-syllable words, it represents phonemes in the same way the letter _____ represents them. (*e, i*)
i *i*	When the letter *y* is in an open syllable (*cry my, fly*), it represents the same sound the letter _____ represents in the open syllable (*mi.ser, di.ver, fi.nal*). When the letter *y* is the vowel in the VCe pattern (*rhyme*), it represents the same sound the letter _____ represents in the VCe syllable (*time, bike, dice*).

Review 12

1. We write a _____ over vowel letters to indicate that they represent the long sound of the vowel.

2. The two syllable patterns that predict when single-letter vowel graphemes represent their long vowel sounds are _____.

3. Single-letter vowel graphemes in VCCe syllable patterns represent their _____.

4. Since the letter *v* never ends a word without an _____ after it, you cannot use the VCe pattern with words ending in _____.

See the Answers section for the answers to Review 12.

Short Vowel Phonemes and Graphemes

	1. In this section we introduce the short vowel sounds and the syllable pattern that indicates when the single vowel grapheme represents the short vowel phoneme.
short	As you read the italicized words that follow, listen carefully to the vowel sound in each word and determine whether the vowel sound is long or short. In the word *at*, the vowel grapheme *a* represents the _____ vowel phoneme. (long, short)
short long	**2.** In the word *edge*, the vowel grapheme *e* represents the _____ (long, short) vowel phoneme. In the word *be* the vowel grapheme *e* represents the _____ vowel phoneme. (long, short)

long short	**3.** In the word *ice* the vowel grapheme *i* represents the _____ <div align="right">(long, short)</div>vowel phoneme. In the word *it* the vowel grapheme *i* represents the _____ vowel phoneme. (long, short)
short long	**4.** In the word *ox* the grapheme *o* represents the _____ vowel <div align="right">(long, short)</div>phoneme. In the word *so* the vowel grapheme *o* represents the _____ vowel phoneme. (long, short)
long short	**5.** In the word *use,* the vowel grapheme *u* represents the _____ <div align="right">(long, short)</div>vowel phoneme. In the word *up* the vowel grapheme *u* represents the _____ vowel phoneme. (long, short)
macron	**6.** In order to distinguish long vowel phonemes from short vowel phonemes, we place a _____ over the vowel graphemes <div align="center">(macron, curve)</div>representing the long vowel phonemes.
short long short	**7.** Some dictionaries place a diacritical mark called a breve, ˘, over vowel graphemes to indicate when they are representing short vowel phonemes.* In these situations, the short sound of *a* would be represented as /ă/. However, because English words contain more _____ vowel <div align="right">(long, short)</div>sounds than _____ vowel sounds, most individuals now leave the (long, short) graphemes representing _____ vowel phonemes unmarked to (long, short) save the cost and effort involved in marking them. *The linguistic relationship of "breve" to "short" can be observed in such words as *abbreviate* and *brevity*.

/a/	**8.** In this text all vowel graphemes representing short vowel phonemes will not have a breve over them. Therefore, the short sound of *a* will be represented as _____
catch, desk, hunch, bath, sack, dog, up, add, pest consonant consonant	**9.** Read the following words. Circle those with vowel graphemes representing short vowel phonemes: catch desk lame hunch wine bath sack fake dog up rope so me add pest All of the written words with vowel graphemes representing short vowel sounds end with _____ letters that represent _____ (consonant, vowel) (consonant, vowel) phonemes.
open	**10.** We call syllables ending in single-letter vowel graphemes (*so*) _____ syllables. (open, VCe) We call syllables ending in consonant graphemes (*sob*) closed syllables. *Note:* Both open and closed syllables contain only one vowel letter.
short long	**11.** The vowel phonemes represented by vowel graphemes in closed syllables are generally _____. The vowel phonemes represented (long, short) by vowel graphemes in open and VCe syllables are generally _____. (long, short)
gum, camp, tent, kiss, yes, rock, bump	**12.** Read the following words. Circle those words that are closed syllables: *gum camp zone tent kiss lo yes vice rock hope name bump say me*

consonant	**13.** Read the following closed syllable words: *up, bet, best, wish, lunch.* Closed syllables do not need to begin with _____ graphemes
	(vowel, consonant)
single	(*up*). Closed syllables may end with a _____ consonant letter
blend	(*bet*); they may end with a consonant _____ (*best*); they may end
	(blend, digraph)
digraph	with a consonant _____ (*wish*); or they may end with a
	(blend, digraph)
single	consonant digraph blended with a_____ consonant (*lunch*).
consonant	**14.** The phoneme heard at the end of closed syllables is a _____
	(vowel, consonant)
	phoneme, and the phoneme represented by the single vowel is
short	_____.
	(long, short)
	Consider the following words: *fir, her, hair, fur, for, far.* You learned
	earlier that vowels plus *r* represent _____ phonemes called
vowel	(consonant, vowel)
murmur diphthongs	_____ _____. Therefore, since these words end in vowel
are not	phonemes rather than consonant phonemes, they _____ closed
	(are, are not)
	syllable words.
closed	**15.** Syllables that end in consonant phonemes are called _____
	(open, closed)
	syllables.
are not	**16.** Syllables that end in murmur diphthongs _____ closed
	(are, are not)
	syllables because murmur diphthongs represent vowel phonemes. Syllables with murmur diphthongs belong to the group of syllables called vowel team syllables. Vowel team syllables will be discussed later.

vowel team	**17.** The words *hurt, first, germ,* and *fork* are examples of ____________ (open, closed, vowel team) syllables.
open	**18.** The first syllable in the words ***pa***.*per,* ***ca***.*ble,* ***do***.*nate,* and ***ra***.*cer* are examples of _________ syllables. (open, closed, vowel team)
closed	**19.** The first syllable in the words ***win***.*ter,* ***sev***.*en,* ***mag***.*ic,* and ***nap***.*kin* are examples of _________ syllables. (open, closed, vowel team)
pitch, gust, *lid, tend, stump,* *slept, blond, stomp, brush*	**20.** Read the following words and circle all closed syllable words: *pitch porch gust sharp page* *she lid tend squirt stump three* *slept blond starch slope stomp brush*
       ost *old* *oll* *olt* *ind* *ild*	**21.** A *rime* in single-syllable words consists of the vowel and everything that follows it (*ot,* for example in the words *c**ot**, d**ot**, g**ot**, h**ot**, j**ot**, l**ot**, n**ot**, p**ot**, r**ot**, t**ot**, bl**ot**, kn**ot**, pl**ot**, sh**ot**, tr**ot**.* There are six rimes that we call "foolers" because the vowel phoneme represented by the vowel letter is long rather than short. See if you can find the "foolers" and circle them. *ab* *cab, crab, dab, jab, scab, stab* *ost* *post, most, ghost, host* *an* *can, fan, man, pan, ran, tan* *old* *bold, cold, told, sold, gold, hold* *oll* *toll, roll, poll, stroll, troll* *olt* *bolt, colt, jolt* *ame* *came, game, lame, name, same, tame* *ind* *bind, mind, hind, kind, find, grind* *ild* *wild, mild, child*

/j/	**22.** You learned earlier that whenever *ge* occurs at the end of a word (*page, huge*), the letters *ge* predictably represent the phoneme _____. The *e* at the end of the syllable also helps the reader (/j/, /g/) predict the vowel phoneme in the word. In such words as *rage, stage,* and *cage,* we have the VCe pattern, suggesting that the vowel phoneme
long	is_____. However, in such words as *bridge, dodge,* and *edge,* we
	(long, short)
short	have the VCCe pattern, suggesting that the vowel phoneme is _____.
	(long, short)
is	**23.** The letter *d* in the *dge* grapheme _____ silent.
	(is, is not)
	Read the following words and listen carefully to the ending sound of each: *wage, fudge, sage, badge, age, smudge, huge, lodge, rage.* The ending
is the same	consonant phoneme in all of these words _____, even though the
	(is different, is the same)
different	spellings of these consonant phoneme are sometimes _____. The
	(the same, different)
	consonant phoneme heard at the end of *smudge* and *huge* is
/j/ short	_____. The vowel phoneme in the word *smudge* is _____,
	(long, short)
long	and the vowel phoneme in the word *huge* is _____.
	(long, short)
	24. In words such as *badge* and *cage,* the *e* after the *g* is needed to indicate that the consonant phoneme at the end of the words is /j/. With the word *cage,* there is no problem in predicting the vowel
VCe	phoneme because the syllable pattern is _____. However, with words like *badge,* there had to be some way to show that the vowel grapheme in the word represented the short vowel phoneme instead of the long one. Therefore, a *d* was placed before the *ge,* making the
VCCe	syllable pattern _____. However, the *d* wasn't needed to represent a phoneme, so it isn't heard in the spoken word. Therefore,
/j/	*dge* at the end of words represents the phoneme _____, as does the grapheme *ge.*

VCCe short /n/ /j/	**25.** Words such as *hinge, lunge, cringe,* and *plunge* reveal how words ending in *ge* are written to predict both the ending consonant phoneme and the vowel phoneme. Each of these words has a _____ syllable pattern, the vowel graphemes represent _____ vowel phonemes, the consonant *n* before the *ge* in each (short, long) word represents the phoneme _____, and the grapheme *ge* represents the phoneme _____.
ge /j/ murmur diphthongs /ur/ /or/ /ar/	**26.** Read the following words: *verge, forge, large, merge, purge, surge, gorge.* These words all end with the same two letters, _____. The ending consonant phoneme in all of these words is _____. The vowels in all of these words are called _____ _____. Therefore, these words belong to the vowel team syllable group. Write the symbol representing the vowel phoneme in the words *verge, merge, purge,* and *surge.* _____. Write the symbol representing the vowel phoneme in the words *forge* and *gorge.* _____. Write the symbol representing the vowel phoneme in the word *large.* _____.
      dge	**27.** The *dge* and *ge* word endings not only provide helpful clues for phoneme identification, but a knowledge of these endings can also help a person's spelling. When you hear the long vowel phoneme or a murmur diphthong phoneme in a word that ends in /j/, the spelling of /j/ is *ge*. When you hear the short vowel phoneme in a word ending in /j/, the spelling of /j/ is _____.
i *i sit*	**28.** When *y* functions as a vowel in closed syllable words, it represents phonemes in the same way the letter _____ represents them. Consider the following words: *myth, hymn,* and *gym.* The phoneme represented by *y* in these closed syllables is the same phoneme represented by the letter _____ in the closed syllable _____. (*sit, edge*)

syllable	**29.** You have learned that vowel phonemes can be predicted by the _____ pattern in which the vowel grapheme occurs. Vowel (syllable, sentence) phonemes can also be predicted by certain letter patterns.
/o/ /o/	**30.** The consonant letters *w* and *l* seem to have a controlling effect on the vowel letter *a*. Read the following words: *water, want, watch, wash, wander, swallow, also, small, call, talk, salt, ball, false.* The *wa* letter pattern in the first six words predicts that the vowel phoneme *a* will represent the phoneme _____. The *al* letter pattern in words six through thirteen predicts that the vowel phoneme *a* will represent the phoneme _____.

A B C Review 13

1. Some dictionaries place a diacritical mark called a _____ over vowel letters to indicate they are representing short vowel phonemes.

2. American English words contain more _____ vowel phonemes
                                                                        (long, short)
than _____ vowel phonemes.
        (long, short)

3. Which syllable pattern indicates that the single vowel in a word or syllable represents the short vowel phoneme?

4. Words ending in murmur diphthongs (are, are not) closed syllables.

5. Write the six "fooler" phonograms.

6. When *y* represents vowels in single-syllable words, it represents _____.

See the Answers section for the answers to Review 13.

Vowel Teams

closed	**1.** We ended our study of the vowel phonemes that are predicted by vowels in open, VCe, _____, and VCCe syllable patterns by introducing the concept that vowel phonemes can also be predicted by certain letter patterns.

vowel team /ā/	**2.** Some of the letter patterns that predictably represent vowel phonemes are called vowel teams. A vowel team is a vowel combined with some other letter to represent a vowel phoneme. The letters *ai* in the word *paint* are an example of a _____ _____. The *ai* vowel team in the word *paint* represents the vowel phoneme _____.
murmur diphthongs *or ir* teams	**3.** Vowel team syllables are different from open, closed, and VCe syllables. You learned earlier that _____ _____ such as (murmur diphthongs, vowel blends) those in the words *porch* and *bird* belong to the group of syllables called vowel team syllables. Therefore, the murmur diphthongs _____ and _____ in the words *porch* and *bird* are vowel _____.
diphthong	***Murmur Diphthongs*** **4.** When vowel letters are followed by the letter _____ in a syllable, the vowel and the *r* represent a murmur _____ (diphthong, digraph) phoneme.
phoneme	**5.** A murmur diphthong grapheme is one grapheme representing one *r*-controlled vowel _____ and should not be confused with the single-letter grapheme *r*.
herd, card, first, repair, burn, chair, fork, hear	**6.** From the list of words that follows, write those that contain murmur diphthongs: *rustle, herd, card, rang, rainbow, first, repair, roast, burn, chair, fork, race, hear.* _____ _____
murmur diphthongs	**7.** The letter combinations *ir, er, ur, or, ar, air, eer, ear, ire,* and *are* represent vowel phonemes and are called _____.

the same /ûr/ /ûr/ /ûr/	**8.** Read the following words aloud and listen carefully to the vowel sound in each word: *dirt, swirl, shirt, thirst, verb, herd, term, clerk, nurse, turn, curse, curl.* The vowel sound in each word is _____. · (different, the same) The vowel team *ir* represents the murmur diphthong phoneme _____; the vowel team *er* represents the phoneme _____; and the vowel team *ur* represents the phoneme _____.
the same murmur diphthong phoneme	**9.** The vowel teams *ir, er,* and *ur* are called the /ur/ triplets because they represent _____ _____.

/or/
 	
the same
 	
the same
	10. The vowel team *or* represents the phoneme _____. Read the following words: *fork, storm, shore, tore, sport, horn, sore, store.* The *or* vowel team in all of these words represents _____ phoneme/s.
	                                                                    (different, the same)
	Some of the words end in the letter *e,* but the vowel phoneme represented by the *or* vowel team is _____ in all words.
	                                                                    (different, the same)

/ûr/ *w* /ûr/	**11.** Read the following words aloud and listen carefully to the vowel sound in each word: *word, work, world, worth, worry, worst, worms.* The vowel phoneme in each word is _____. The letter before each *or* vowel team is _____. We can say that this letter controls the *or* vowel team so that when it appears before the vowel team, the vowel phoneme the vowel team represents is _____, rather than /or/.

12. Read the following words aloud and listen carefully to the vowel phoneme in each word: *worked, short, worse, morn, worried, torn, workmen, cord.* Write the words in the proper columns below.

/or/	/ur/
_____	_____
_____	_____
_____	_____
_____	_____

short   worked

morn   worse

torn   worried

cord   workmen

/or/

w

/ûr/

The *or* vowel team represents the phoneme _____, unless the letter _____ precedes it. When a *w* precedes the vowel team *or, or* represents the phoneme _____.

/ar/

different

/ar/

/âr/

13. The vowel team *ar* represents the phoneme _____ (*snarl*). Read the following words: *starch, shark, park, yarn, sharp, care, share, bare, spare, dare.* The *ar* and *are* vowel teams in all of these words represent _____ phoneme/s. The *ar* vowel team represents the
(different, the same)
phoneme _____, and the *are* vowel team represents the phoneme _____.

/âr/

14. In the 5,000 most frequently used words, the *are* vowel team represents the phoneme _____ in every word in which it occurs, except the word *are.*

air

/âr/

15. Read the following words: *hair, pair, chair, fair, pairs, fairly, repair.* The vowel team in these words is _____. The *air* vowel team consistently represents the phoneme _____.

are   air

16. The two vowel teams consistently representing the murmur diphthong phoneme /ar/ are _____ and _____.

/ûr/ /âr/ /ar/	**17.** The *eer* vowel team consistently represents the gliding murmur diphthong phoneme /ir/ (*steer*). The *ear* vowel team represents that same murmur diphthong phoneme about 58% of the time, but it also represents the phoneme _____ (*earth*) 28% of the time, the phoneme _____ (*bear*) 12% of the time, and the phoneme _____ (*heart*) 2% of the time.

vowel team
 	
vowel
 	
/ou/ /oi/
	Vowel Diphthongs
	18. You learned earlier in this text that vowel diphthongs are also found in syllables called _____ _____ syllables.
	       (open, closed, VCe, vowel team)
	A diphthong is a special gliding _____ sound. Only two
	       (vowel, consonant)
	of our 18 vowel phonemes are classified as diphthongs. They are both heard in the word *cowboy*. These phonemes are _____ and _____.

/ou/ *ou* *ow*	**19.** Read and study the following words: *trout, couch, cloud, found, house, scout, brown, cow, growl, down, clown, frown.* The vowel diphthong phoneme in all of these words is _____. The vowel teams that represent the phoneme /ou/ are _____ and _____.
/oi/ *oy oi*	**20.** Read and study the following words: *toy, boy, joy, coy, coin, voice, oil, noise.* The vowel diphthong phoneme in all of these words is _____. The vowel teams that represent the phoneme /oi/ are _____ and _____.
enjoy, moist, destroy, joint, annoy, void, employ, groin, decoy, broil, loyal, spoil, voyage	**21.** Read the following words and circle all those that contain the vowel diphthong /oi/: *enjoy loose moist moon destroy book joint annoy cool void employ loaves groin load decoy broil famous loyal brook spoil voyage.*

crouch, frown, mound, howl, drown, mouse, count, scowl	**22.** Read the following words and circle all those that contain the vowel diphthong /ou/: *crouch crook frown shrewd mound blew threw howl drown shoot mouse look count scowl*
ou ow *oi oy*	**23.** There are two vowel teams that represent the diphthong phoneme /ou/. They are _____ and _____. There are two vowel teams that represent the diphthong phoneme /oi/. They are _____ and _____.
/oi/ /ou/	**24.** The vowel teams *oi* and *oy* consistently predict the vowel diphthong phoneme _____. However, the vowel teams *ou* and *ow* are not as consistent in predicting the vowel diphthong phoneme _____.

town snow
gown blow
frown known
drown grown
howl flown
crown blown
slow
show
	25. Read and study the following words: *snow, blow, town, gown, known, grown, frown, flown, drown, blown, howl, crown, slow, show.* Write all of the words that have the same vowel sound as *cow* underneath it. Write all of the words that have the same vowel sound as *glow* underneath it:
	
	      cow *glow*
	      _____ _____
	      _____ _____
	      _____ _____
	      _____ _____
	      _____ _____
	      _____ _____
	      _____ _____
	                   _____

/ou/ /ō/	**26.** The vowel team *ow* represents both the vowel diphthong phoneme _____ as in *fowl* and the long vowel phoneme _____ as in *so.* It represents the diphthong phoneme about 45% of the time and the long vowel phoneme about 55% of the time.

/u/ /ō/ /o͞o/ /o/ /oo/ /or/ /ûr/	**27.** The vowel team *ou* represents the vowel diphthong phoneme /ou/ about 60% of the time. However, it represents the phoneme _____ as in the word *country* about 18% of the time. It represents the phoneme _____ as in the word *soul* about 10% of the time, and about 12% of the time it represents other phonemes. It represents the phoneme _____ as in *group*, the phoneme _____ as in *sought*, and the phoneme _____ as in *should*. The grapheme *our* represents the murmur diphthong phoneme _____ as in *court* or _____ as in *courage*.

two
 	
one
	Vowel Digraphs
	
	28. A vowel digraph (*soap*) is a _____ letter grapheme
	                       (How many?)
	representing _____ phoneme. Vowel diphthong phonemes are
	        (How many?)
	gliding vowel sounds, and murmur diphthong phonemes are *r*-controlled vowel sounds. The phonemes represented by vowel digraphs, however, are neither gliding nor *r*-controlled.

teams trigraph	**29.** The following vowel _____ are called vowel digraphs: *ai, ay, ee, oa, ea, aw, au, ew, ue, oo, ie, ui, ey,* and *ei*. The vowel team *igh* is called a vowel _____ because three letters represent one phoneme. (digraph, trigraph)
a /ā/	**30.** The digraphs *ai, ay, ee,* and *oa* are the most reliable of all the vowel digraphs. They consistently represent predictable phonemes. The digraphs *ai* (*rain, saint*) and *ay* (*day play*) represent the same vowel phoneme represented by the letter _____ when it is in open and (a, i, y) VCe syllables. Ninety-nine percent of the time, the digraph *ay* represents the phoneme _____, and 96% of the time, the digraph *ai* represents that sound.

e	**31.** The digraph *ee* (*see, feet*) consistently represents (99% of the time) the same vowel phoneme represented by the letter _____ when it is in open and VCe syllables.
o	**32.** The digraph *oa* (*boat, soap*) represents (95% of the time) the same vowel phoneme represented by the letter _____ when it is in open and VCe syllables.
sed, plad, sez, kē, ben, brod	**33.** Although the *ai, ay, ee,* and *oa* digraphs are very reliable, on rare occasions these digraphs represent phonemes other than those that would be predicted. Read the following words aloud and listen to the vowel phonemes in each word: *said, plaid, says, quay, been, broad.* Using the phoneme symbols presented in this text, write each of these words phonemically. _____
weak sweat *tease dead* *clean bread* *bead head*	**34.** The digraph *ea* consistently represents one of two sounds, and there is no reliable way to determine which sound it will represent. Read the following words aloud: *weak, tease, sweat, dead, clean, bead, bread, head.* Write the words that have the same vowel sound as *speak* underneath it, and write the words that have the same vowel sound as *thread* underneath it. *speak* *thread* _____ _____ _____ _____ _____ _____ _____ _____ _____ _____
/ē/ /e/ /ā/	**35.** The *ea* digraph represents the phoneme heard in the word *tea* most of the time. It represents the phoneme _____ about 74% of the time and the phoneme _____ about 25% of the time. In the words *great, steak, break,* and *yea,* the *ea* digraph represents the phoneme _____.

/o/ /a/	**36.** The digraphs *aw* (*saw*) and *au* (*sauce*) consistently represent the phoneme _____. On rare occasions, the *au* digraph represents the phoneme _____ as in *laugh*.
two *pool, moon, shoot* *good, wood, took*	**37.** Read the following words aloud and listen carefully to the vowel sound in each: *pool, moon, shoot, good, wood, took*. The *oo* digraph represents _____ phonemes. (How many?) Write the words in which the digraph *oo* represents the /o͞o/ phoneme: _____ Write the words in which the digraph *oo* represents the /oo/ phoneme: _____
/oo/ /u/ /or/	**38.** The digraph *oo* represents the phoneme /o͞o/ about 70% of the time it occurs in words. About 28% of the time, it represents the phoneme _____, and in words such as *blood* and *flood*, it represents the phoneme _____. The *oor* vowel team in the words *door* and *floor* represents the murmur diphthong phoneme _____.
/o͞o/ *fuel, few, cue, pew*	**39.** The digraphs *ew* (*new*) and *ue* (*due*) consistently represent the phoneme _____. Sometimes these digraphs represent the consonant phoneme /y/ blended with the vowel phoneme /oo/. From the words that follow write those in which the digraphs *ew* and *ue* represent the phonemes /yoo/: *threw, due, fuel, few, cue, pew*. _____
/yo͞o/ /ō/	**40.** The digraph *ew* represents the phoneme /o͞o/ about 95% of the time it occurs in words. About 4.5% of the time, it represents the phoneme _____ as in *hew, mew,* and *fewer*. In the word *sew*, however, the digraph *ew* represents the phoneme _____.

/o͞o/ /yo͞o/	**41.** The digraph *ue* represents the phoneme _____ about 94% of the time (*glue*). About 5% of the time, it represents the phonemes _____ as in *hue, fuel, value,* and *continue*.
u /k/ /w/ /k/	**42.** Readers need to be careful not to confuse the vowel digraph *ue* with the letters *que* in such words as *question, sequence, frequent,* and *unique*. The letter *q* does not appear in written words without the letter _____ after it. When *qu* begins words, the phonemes represented by that digraph are usually _____ and _____ blended together. When *que* is found at the end of words (*technique*) it usually represents the phoneme _____.
/ē/ /ī/ /e/	**43.** The remaining digraphs (*ie, ui, ey,* and *ei*) are fairly unreliable. The digraph *ie* (*piece*) represents the phoneme _____ about 65% of the time, it (*pie*) represents the phoneme _____ about 26% of the time, and it (*friend*) represents the phoneme _____ about 9% of the time.
/o͞o/ /i/	**44.** The digraph *ui* (*fruit*) represents the phoneme _____ about 67% of the time, and it (*build*) represents the phoneme _____ about 33% of the time. Readers need to be careful, however, not to confuse the vowel digraph *ui* with the letters *qui* in such words as *quick, liquid,* and *equipment*.
/ē/ /ā/	**45.** The digraph *ey* (*key*) represents the phoneme _____ about 70% of the time, and it (*they*) represents the phoneme _____ about 30% of the time.
/ē/ /ā/	**46.** The digraph *ei* (*seize*) represents the phoneme _____ about 39% of the time. It (*vein*) represents the phoneme _____ about 52% of the time (this percentage includes the *eigh* grapheme in such words as *weigh*), and it represents other phonemes (*heifer*) about 9% of the time.

 **Review 14**

1. A vowel team is _____.

2. When there is a vowel team in a syllable, that syllable is called

_____.

3. When vowel letters are followed by the letter *r* in a syllable, the team of letters (the vowel/s and the *r*) is called a

_____.

4. When the letter *w* precedes an *or,* the *or* represents the phoneme

_____.

5. A vowel diphthong is a gliding vowel sound. Write the four vowel diphthong graphemes and provide a sample word for each.

6. The vowel diphthong graphemes _____ and _____ reliably predict the vowel diphthong phonemes they represent, but the diphthong graphemes _____ and _____ are not so reliable.

7. The vowel team *ow* represents the _____ phoneme about 55% of the time and the _____ phoneme about 45% of the time.

8. How would you describe the reliability of the grapheme *ou* in predicting vowel phonemes?

9. A vowel digraph is _____.

10. The four most reliable digraphs (95–99%) are _____.

11. The digraph *ea* represents the phoneme _____ about 74% of the time and the phoneme _____ about 25% of the time.

12. The digraphs *aw* and *au* reliably represent the phoneme

_____.

13. The digraph *oo* represents the phoneme _____ about 70% of the time and the phoneme _____ about 28% of the time.

14. The *ew* and *ue* digraphs represent the phoneme _____ about 94–95% of the time and the phonemes _____ about 4.5–5% of the time.

15. How would you describe the reliability of the graphemes *ie, ue, ey,* and *ei?*

See the Answers section for the answers to Review 14.

A REVIEW OF PHONEMES AND THE GRAPHEMES MOST FREQUENTLY REPRESENTING THEM

There are 20 vowel phonemes represented by vowel graphemes. They are:

/a/	*at*	/ē/	*eve, feet, eat, me*
/ā/	*ate, raid, say, ba.con*	/ir/	*deer, year*
/i/	*it*	/o/	*off, saw, fraud, ball*
/ī/	*ice, ci.der, high*	/ō/	*so, oak, ode, show*
/u/	*up*	/oo/	*book, put*
/ū/	*use, few, cue, u.nite*	/o͞o/	*moon, rude, blue, grew*
/ûr/	*bird, fur, fern*	/ar/	*car*
/or/	*for*	/oi/	*boy, oil*
/ou/	*cow, found*	/âr/	*hair, care, there, bear*
/e/	*edge, bread*	/ īr/	*fire*

There are 25 consonant phonemes represented by the following graphemes:

/b/	*bat*	/d/	*dog*
/f/	*fish*	/g/	*go*
/h/	*had*	/j/	*jump, gem, rage, fudge*
/k/	*kiss, cat, kick*	/l/	*lamp*
/m/	*man*	/n/	*no*
/p/	*pan*	/r/	*run*
/s/	*sun, cent, geese*	/t/	*teeth*
/v/	*voice*	/w/	*watch*
/y/	*yes*	/z/	*zoo, dogs, rose*
/sh/	*shoe*	/ch/	*church*
/th/	*the*	/th/	*thing*
/ng/	*sing*	/zh/	*measure*
/hw/	*white*		

Chapter 4

Onsets and Rimes

Phonics is the study of phoneme/grapheme relationships within syllables. There are different ways to analyze syllables. One way is to analyze them according to their onsets and rimes. When viewed in this fashion, the syllable is an acoustically unanalyzable spoken unit. However, the approach is popular among many educators, and this approach has some definite advantages when teaching very young children phonics. This chapter will help you understand what onsets and rimes are and how viewing syllables from the "onset and rime" perspective can help young children develop phonemic awareness and beginning phonics knowledge. The next chapter will provide more information about syllables, help you analyze the syllable as an acoustically analyzable spoken unit, and help you understand the role of syllabication and phonics in learning to read multisyllabic words.

rime onset	**1.** Many reading educators analyze syllables psychologically in terms of onsets and rimes. The syllable's _____ is the rhyming (onset, rime) component in the syllable (*map*, *trap*), and the syllables's _____ is the component before the rhyming component (*map*, (onset, rime) *trap*).
onset rime, single-consonant grapheme	**2.** In the single-syllable word *jump*, the grapheme *j* is the syllable's _____, and the graphemes *ump* comprise the syllable's (onset, rime) _____. The onset in the word *jump* is a _____. (onset, rime) (single-consonant grapheme, consonant digraph)
onset, rime consonant blend	**3.** In the word *stop*, the graphemes *st* comprise the syllable's _____ and the graphemes *op* are the syllable's _____. In (onset, rime), (onset, rime) the word *stop*, the onset is a _____. (consonant blend, consonant digraph)

onset, rime consonant digraph	**4.** In the word *ship,* the graphemes *sh* comprise the syllable's _____, and the graphemes *ip* are the syllable's _____. (onset, rime) (onset, rime) In the word *ship,* the onset is a _____. (consonant blend, consonant digraph)
single consonant blend, digraph	**5.** Syllable onsets may be a _____ (*line*), a (single consonant, blend, digraph) _____ (*spine*), or a _____ (*shine*). (single consonant, blend, digraph) (single consonant, blend, digraph)
single consonant	**6.** Syllable onsets may also be a blend of a consonant digraph and a _____ (*shrink*). (single consonant, blend, digraph)
3 1 1 3 2 2 3 3	**7.** Using the following symbols (1 = single consonant; 2 = consonant digraph; 3 = consonant blend), write the number that most appropriately describes the onset in each word: _____*strap* _____*nice* _____*land* _____*cross* _____*shoot* _____*thorn* _____*slide* _____*black*

no
 	
yes
	8. Consider the following single-syllable words: *job, am, end, frost, odd, slouch, up, to.* Do all syllables contain an onset? _____ Do all
	                                                              (yes, no)
	syllables contain a rime? _____
	                                  (yes, no)

a. All syllables contain one vowel sound.	**9.** What is the distinguishing characteristic of all syllables? Underline one of the following statements: a. All syllables contain one vowel sound. b. All syllables contain onsets and rimes.

top, band, lost, jump	**10.** Consider the following single-syllable words: *start, top, cross, band, lost, shirt, jump.* Write the words containing the onsets easiest for children to hear: _____
easier digraph blend	**11.** Onsets representing one consonant phoneme are _____ for (easier, more difficult) children to hear than consonant blend onsets. Consonant _____ onsets are easier for children to hear than consonant (blend, digraph) _____ onsets. (blend, digraph)
one	**12.** All rimes contain _____ vowel phoneme(s). (How many?)
a vowel	**13.** Consider the following words that are separated according to their onsets and rimes: b ake p orch j ail r ain t est n o s ay f ast b ird d og s oap c ar All rimes begin with _____.
o og, est, ast ake ain, ay, orch, oap, ail, ird, ar	**14.** In your study of vowels, you learned about open, closed, vowel team, and VCe syllables. Write the rime in the preceding frame in which the vowel is open. _____ Write the rimes in the preceding frame in which the vowels are closed. _____ Write the rime that is a VCe. _____ Write the rimes with vowel teams. _____ _____

open, VCe, vowel team	**15.** Rimes are the part of the syllable containing the vowel grapheme. The vowels in rimes may be classified as closed, _____, _____, or _____.
ew no do not	**16.** Consider the following words: *few, sew, dew.* The rime in each of these words is _____. Do these words rhyme? _____. It (yes, no) is appropriate to say that words having the same rime _____ (do, do not) always rhyme.
phonemes	**17.** Many teachers begin their phonemic awareness training for young children using rhyming words. Once children are able to perceive rhymes in rhyming words, teachers then help them isolate the beginning phoneme in each word. They engage in this practice because children's phonological awareness of rhymes precedes an awareness of _____. (syllables, phonemes)
rhyming alliteration	**18.** Incidentally, since children are able to perceive rhyming components of words before they are able to hear the consonant sounds preceding them, _____ books are often more relevant (rhyming, alliteration) for preschool children than books stressing _____ (rhyming, alliteration*) *Alliteration is the emphasis on the initial sounds in words spoken or written closely together: *Tom told Tamara to take a towel.*
rime onset	**19.** Since young children find it easier to perceive the _____ in (onset, rime) a syllable before perceiving its _____, many first grade (onset, rime) teachers also begin their phonics instruction using rimes. Rhyming words are written in a column on the chalkboard, and children learn to associate beginning consonant sounds with the onsets representing them as they are isolated from the rimes.

ock	**20.** For example, the rime _____ is found in all of the following words: *sock, rock, dock, lock,* and *mock.* Children are shown these words, helped to isolate the phoneme represented by each onset in each word, and helped to associate each isolated phoneme with the onset representing it.
phonemes	**21.** Young children are able to isolate phonemes represented by onsets before they are able to isolate all of the individual _____ (phonemes, graphemes) in a word. Therefore, initial phonemic awareness training and phonics instruction using onsets and rimes become an important first step in the development of higher levels of phonemic awareness and phonics knowledge.
cop, hop, mop, pop, top	**22.** As teachers help children become aware of initial consonant phonemes by studying rimes and onsets, they also help them learn to write the graphemes representing the onsets. For example, write five words by combining each of the five onsets *c, h, m, p,* and *t* to the rime *op:* _____
phonemes	**23.** As children grow in phonemic awareness and phonics knowledge, however, they need to move beyond onsets and rimes so they can learn how all speech sounds, or _____, are represented by graphemes in words.

 **Review 15**

1. Syllables (are, are not) acoustically analyzable spoken units when they are analyzed according to onsets and rimes.

2. In the word *shine,* the onset is _____, and the rime is_____.

3. The part of the word before the vowel is called _____.

4. Onsets can be either single consonants, consonant _____, or consonant _____.

5. Do all syllables contain an onset?

6. All rimes begin with a _____.

7. Do all syllables contain a rime?

8. The distinguishing characteristic of all syllables is that

_____.

9. The vowels in rimes can be classifies as open, _____,

_____, or _____.

See the Answers section for the answers to Review 15.

Chapter 5

Syllabication and Accent

Remember to place the mask over the left-hand column. Write your responses in the right-hand column before you pull the mask down.

The Syllable

vowel sound	**1.** A syllable is the smallest part of a word containing one _____ . It is also the smallest pronunciation unit in the (vowel, vowel sound) language because it is the smallest part of the word that can be pronounced without distortion problems.
vowel syllables	**2.** Since each syllable contains only one _____ phoneme, (consonant, vowel) the number of vowel phonemes you hear in a word equals the number of _____ in that word. (syllables, vowels)
voiced	**3.** All vowel phonemes are _____ phonemes. Therefore, if (voiceless, voiced) you touch the part of your throat containing the vocal cords, you can feel the vibration of the vocal cords as you say the syllables of a word. *Note:* Consonant phonemes, voiced or voiceless, are coarticulated with vowel phonemes, so we can't detect them as easily as we can vowel phonemes.

	4. Place your hand against your larynx (the larynx is the structure at the upper end of the trachea containing the vocal cords). Read the following words aloud and write the number of vibrations you feel as you say the words:
3 2 1 3 1 2	_____ *yesterday* _____ *complete* _____ *seed* _____ *obsolete* _____ *fair* _____ *sofa*
feel	**5.** If you can hear the vowel sounds in words, you can determine the number of syllables they contain. However, if you can't hear vowel sounds, you can _____ them by saying the words aloud while your hand is against your larynx.
phoneme 1 2	**6.** A syllable may have more than one vowel letter but only one vowel _____ . How many syllables are in the word *kissed*? (grapheme, phoneme) _____. How many vowel letters are in the word *kissed*? _____.
1 2 one	**7.** How many syllables are in the word *seat*? _____. How many vowel letters are in the word *seat*? _____. All syllables contain _____ vowel phoneme. (How many?)
graphemes phonemes	### Why Study Syllables? **8.** Before we discuss syllables in more detail, let's talk about why reading teachers are concerned about syllablication. Phonics is a study of the relationship that exists between the _____ in (graphemes, phonemes) written words and the _____ in spoken words. (graphemes, phonemes)

syllables	**9.** A study of phonics involves a study of _____ (syllables, onsets and rimes) because the pattern of the written syllable suggests to the reader which phoneme the vowel grapheme is representing.
closed syllable open syllable	**10.** Grapheme/phoneme relationships are influenced by whether the vowel grapheme in the word is in the open, closed, or VCe syllable. In the word *map*, the letter *a* represents its short sound because the word *map* is a(n) _____ . In the (closed syllable, open syllable) word *so*, the letter *o* represents its long sound because the word *so* is a(n) _____ . (closed syllable, open syllable)
long short	**11.** Vowel graphemes in open syllables (*so, me, spi.der, pa.per, bu.gle*) predictably represent _____ vowel phonemes. Vowel (short, long) graphemes in closed syllables (*got, met, spin, past, bug*) predictably represent _____ vowel phonemes. (short, long)
does not	**12.** In the word *map*, the letter *a* represents its short sound, and in the word *maple*, the letter *a* _____ represent its short sound. To a (does, does not) child who doesn't understand the relationship between syllabication and phonics, this may be confusing.
short no	**13.** Let's look at the problem once more. In the word *hot*, the letter *o* represents its _____ sound because the word is a closed (short, long) syllable. However, does the letter *o* in the word *hotel* represent its short sound? _____ (yes, no)

open	**14.** The confusion children may have with words like *map* and *maple* is eliminated when they understand that the first syllable in the word *maple* is not *map*, but *ma* (*ma.ple*). The letter *a* in the word *map* is short because it is a closed syllable, but the letter *a* in the syllable *ma* is long because it is an _____ syllable.
a closed an open	**15.** The syllables in the word *hotel* are *ho.tel*. Therefore, the *o* in the word *hot* is short because *hot* is _____ syllable, and the *o* in the <center>(an open, a closed)</center> syllable *ho* is long because *ho* is _____ syllable. <center>(an open, a closed)</center>
fi	**16.** In the words *fatal* and *fiber,* young children often focus their attention on what they think are familiar rimes within the words, like *fat* and *fib,* rather than on the appropriate first syllable in each word, which in this case would be *fa* and _____, respectively.
multisyllabic	**17.** Onsets and rimes instruction is a good way to introduce young children to initial consonant sounds and phonograms. It also provides them with a good introduction to phonemic awareness. However, focusing on rimes at the expense of syllable patterns may confuse children who may think they see the rime *map* in *maple*, or *hot* in *hotel*, or *not* in *notice*, etc. Children need to be able to see appropriate "word chunks" in _____ words, and understanding (multisyllabic, single-syllable) where the syllables are in these words will help them reach that goal.
phonics	**18.** Therefore, you will study syllabication so you can help young readers find the appropriate syllable patterns in unfamiliar multisyllabic words, so they can use their _____ knowledge to (phonics, syllabication) identify them. As we continue our discussion of syllabication, keep this goal in mind.

Accented and Unaccented Syllables and the Schwa Phoneme

syllable	**1.** When we pronounce words of more than one syllable, we accent (emphasize) one of the syllables more than the others. We show this emphasis or stress by placing an accent mark (') at the end of the accented _____ . The vowels in syllables that are not (phoneme, syllable) accented often represent a phoneme that we call the schwa.

two
 	
 accented /ō/
 	
 unaccented
 	
 /u/
 up
	2. In the word *sofa* there are _____ syllables because the word
	         (How many?)
	 contains two vowel phonemes. The vowel phoneme in the first syllable
	 (*so'*) is _____ , and the phoneme is _____. The
	    (accented, unaccented)
	 vowel phoneme in the second syllable (*fa*) is _____ ,
	                 (accented, unaccented)
	 and the phoneme is _____. It is the same phoneme we hear at
	 the beginning of the word _____ . It is called the *schwa phoneme*.
	         (up, use)

unaccented	**3.** The schwa phoneme is the phoneme that is generally used in _____ syllables. When we accent or emphasize (accented, unaccented) syllables, the schwa phoneme is not used.

first
 	
 second   first
 	
 second
	4. In the word *pi'.lot*, the _____ syllable is accented, and the
	         (first, second)
	 _____ syllable is unaccented. The vowel in the _____
	 (first, second) (first, second)
	 syllable represents its long sound, and the vowel in the _____
	                 (first, second)
	 syllable represents the schwa sound.

second	**5.** In the word *a.lone'* the _____ syllable is accented, and the (first, second)
first first	_____ syllable is unaccented. The vowel in the _____ (first, second) (first, second) syllable represents the schwa sound, and the vowel in the
second	_____ syllable represents its long sound. (first, second)
	6. In words of more than one syllable, more than one syllable may be stressed. Read the following words aloud. Listen carefully for the schwa phoneme in each word. Write the syllables in each word phonemically, using the phonemic symbols presented in the text, and indicate which syllable (first, second, third) contains the schwa phoneme:
	Word Syllable Containing Schwa
kum plān' 1	*complain* _____ _____
bar' bu kyoō' 2	*barbecue* _____ _____
nav' u gāt' 2	*navigate* _____ _____
mel' un 2	*melon* _____ _____
plaz' mu 2	*plasma* _____ _____
kum plēt' 1	*complete* _____ _____
	7. The schwa phoneme is not found in all multisyllabic words. Circle the multisyllabic words below that do not contain the schwa.
panic intrust never	*panic button intrust animal never*
	8. <u>Open Syllable</u> <u>Closed Syllable</u> <u>Vowel Team Syllable</u>
	fe' ver *rob' in* *dai' ly*
	go' pher *pen' cil* *loy' al*
	a go' *con struct'* *com plain'*
	Vowel graphemes in accented syllables represent the vowel phonemes
syllable	suggested by the _____ pattern in which they occur, or they (letter, syllable)
	represent the phonemes suggested by the vowel team pattern in the vowel team syllable.

schwa murmur diphthong, *y*	**9.** Vowel graphemes in unaccented syllables often represent the _____ phoneme. Vowel graphemes in unaccented syllables do not represent the schwa if the unaccented syllable (*tim' ber*) ends in a _____ , or (*hap' py*) the letter _____ . (murmur diphthong, consonant)
/ī/ /ē/	**10.** Read the following words and listen carefully to the vowel phoneme the grapheme *y* represents in accented and unaccented syllables: *de ny', ap ply', ba' by, par' ty.* The grapheme *y* represents the phoneme _____ in accented syllables, and the phoneme _____ in unaccented syllables.
accent schwa	**11.** When attempting to decode multisyllabic words not recognized by sight, it is often helpful to have some idea where to place the _____ on a syllable and when to try the _____ (accent, mark) (schwa, long *e*) phoneme. There are some clues regarding where the accent may be found in words.

Accent Placement Clues

accented	**1.** All single-syllable words are considered to be _____ (accented, unaccented) even though dictionaries do not place accent marks on them.
root word affixes	**2.** Prefixes (*alive*) and suffixes (*hateful*) are often separate syllables. When a word contains affixes, the _____ are/is more (affixes, root word) likely to receive the accent than the _____ . (affixes, root word)
first	**3.** In compound words (*homework, fireman*), the accent usually falls on or within the _____ word. (first, second)

first
 	
second
	4. In words that are used as both nouns and verbs (*object, conduct*) the accent is placed on the _____ syllable when used as nouns
	                    (first, second)
	and on the _____ syllable when used as verbs.
	                    (first, second)

first unaccented	**5.** In two-syllable words the accent is usually placed on the _____ syllable (*cli' mate*), unless the word begins with a prefix (*a* (first, second) *rise'*). Prefixes such as the one in the word *arise* are _____. (accented, unaccented)

<u>a</u>noint, <u>con</u>spire,
<u>un</u>real <u>ig</u>nore, <u>pro</u>claim
unaccented
 	
accented
 	
ignore, proclaim
	6. All of the following words contain prefixes. Read them aloud and underline the prefixes that are unaccented:
	a.noint con.spire un.real ig.nore pro.claim
	
	In words containing prefixes, the prefix is generally _____ ,
	                                    (accented, unaccented)
	and the root word is generally _____ .
	                                    (accented, unaccented)
	The vowel graphemes in prefixes do not always represent the schwa phoneme. Which of the words above do not contain the schwa sound?
	_____

farm'er, short'est,
laugh'ing, joy'ful,
glad'ness, fool'ish,
point'less, wait'er
 	
unaccented
 	
accented
	7. All of the following words contain suffixes or inflectional endings. Read them aloud and write the accent mark over the accented syllable in each word:
	farm.er short.est laugh.ing joy.ful glad.ness
	fool.ish point.less wait.er
	
	In words containing suffixes, the suffix is generally _____
	                                    (accented, unaccented)
	and the root word is generally _____ .
	                                    (accented, unaccented)

robbed *bagged* *wished* *kissed* *seated* *loaded* *root word*	**8.** The inflectional ending *ed* is not always a syllable. Read the following words aloud: *wished, kissed, robbed, bagged, seated, loaded*. The ending *ed* represents the phoneme /d/ in the words _____ and _____ because it follows voiced consonants. The *ed* ending represents the phoneme /t/ in the words _____ and _____ because it follows voiceless consonants. The *ed* ending represents the syllable /ud/ in the words _____ and _____ because the *ed* follows either a *t* or a *d*. When the *ed* ending represents a syllable, the accent is placed on the _____ . (ending, root word)
na *des*	**9.** Words consisting of three or more syllables are likely to have both a primary accent and a secondary accent. In the word *des.ti.na.tion*, the primary accent is on the syllable _____, and the secondary accent is on the syllable _____ .
me o *pli tion* schwa	**10.** In words of more than two syllables, accented and unaccented syllables usually alternate with each other. In the word *me.tab.o.lism*, the two unaccented syllables are _____ and _____. In the word *com.pli.ca.tion*, the two unaccented syllables are _____ and _____. The vowels in all of the unaccented syllables in these words represent the _____ phoneme.
grav i ta' tion, ex ten' sion, *sym pa thet' ic,* *ex pen' sive, fric'tion,* *con vul' sion*	**11.** In most multisyllabic words ending in *tion, sion, ic,* and *sive*, the primary accent falls on the syllable preceding these endings. Place the primary accent on the following words (notice the stress and schwa pattern of alternation): *grav i ta tion* *ex ten sion* *sym pa thet ic* *ex pen sive* *fric tion* *con vul sion*

vol'un tar y, col'um nist, *har'mo nize, op'ti mism,* *cru'ci fy, grat'i tude,* *ge og'ra phy, cel'e brate,* *lav'a tor y*	**12.** In most multisyllabic words ending in *ary, ist, ize, ism, fy, tude, y, ate,* and *tory,* the primary accent falls on the syllable before the syllable preceding these endings. Place the primary accent on the following words:

vol un tar y   *col um nist*   *har mo nize*
op ti mism   *cru ci fy*   *grat i tude*
ge og ra phy   *cel e brate*   *lav a tor y*

im pec' ca ble, *e mer' gen cy,* *an' i mal, A mer' i can,* *var' i ous, dif' fer ent,* *sim' i lar, av' er age,* *ad jec' tive, dis' tance,* *sen' tence, pos'si ble*	**13.** In most multisyllabic words ending in *al, an, ent/ant, ous, ar, ence/ance, able/ible, age, tive,* and *ency/ancy,* the primary accent falls on the syllable before the syllable preceding the ending *if* there is only one consonant before the suffix. If there are two consonants before the suffix, the primary accent falls on the syllable preceding the ending. Place the primary accent on the following words:

im pec ca ble   *e mer gen cy*   *an i mal*
A mer i can   *var i ous*   *dif fer ent*
sim i lar   *av er age*   *ad jec tive*
dis tance   *sen tence*   *pos si ble*

 **Review 16**

1. What is a syllable?
2. The number of vowel sounds you hear in a word equals

   _____ .

3. We can "feel" syllables because _____ .
4. Why study syllabication?
5. Explain the concept of accented and unaccented syllables.
6. When *y* occurs in the accented syllable it represents the

   _____ phoneme, and when it occurs in the unaccented syllable

   it represents the _____ phoneme.
7. Where is the accent generally placed in compound words?
8. Where is the accent generally placed in words containing prefixes, suffixes, and inflectional endings?
9. Where is the accent generally placed in two-syllable words?
10. When is the *ed* inflectional ending a syllable?

11. State the accent generalization for words ending in the suffixes *tion, sion, ic,* and *sive.*

12. State the accent generalization for words ending in the suffixes *ary, ist, ize, ism, fy, tude, y, ate,* and *tory.*

13. State the accent generalization for words ending in the suffixes *al, an, ent/ant, ous, ar, ence/ance, able/ible, age, tive,* and *ency/ancy.*

See the Answers section for the answers to Review 16.

Syllable Division Clues

patterns	**1.** The most important issue in syllabication for the reading teacher is where the syllabic divisions occur. This information is important to beginning readers because phonics knowledge loses its effectiveness when applied to words of more than one syllable if the syllable _____ in multisyllabic words are not perceived. (accents, patterns)
vowel one VCe vowel team	**2.** The approach to the division of syllables taken in this text is different from traditional approaches. The approach is simple, but linguistically sound. The key to syllabication is the _____ . <div style="text-align:right">(vowel, beginning consonants)</div> Each syllable contains _____ vowel phoneme, even though it <div style="text-align:center">(How many?)</div> may contain more than one vowel letter. The two syllable patterns containing more than one vowel letter are the _____ pattern <div style="text-align:right">(closed, VCe)</div> and the _____ pattern. <div style="text-align:center">(open, vowel team)</div>

represent phonemes	**3.** Since each syllable contains only one vowel sound, we can identiy the number of syllables in a word if we can identify the number of vowels in the word that _____ . In order to do, this we must (represent phonemes, are silent)
one	know that vowel teams represent _____ phoneme(s), that the *e* (How many?)
is silent	vowel in VCe syllables _____, that the *e* in *dge* (represents one sound, is silent)
a silent	and *ge* graphemes at the end of words _____ , (represents one sound, is silent)
phoneme	that the letter *y* represents a vowel _____ when it isn't used to begin words or syllables, and that the letters *le* at the end of multisyllabic words represent the syllable /ul/.
consonant	**4.** We must also know that when the letters *ci* and *ti* are followed by vowels (*facial, direction*), they represent _____ phonemes, (vowel, consonant)
/j/	and that when the letters *gi* and *ge* are followed by vowels (*legion, pigeon*) those letters represent the phoneme _____ . When we know the vowel graphemes that represent vowel phonemes, we can identify the number of syllables in a word by just looking at it.
distance, finally, thousand, explain, firsthand, discharge, complete	**5.** Underline all of the vowels or vowel teams that represent one phoneme in the following words: *distance* *finally* *thousand* *explain* *firsthand* *discharge* *complete*
syllables	The number of vowels or vowel teams that you have underlined in each word equals the number of _____ in that word.

phonemes	**6.** A beginning point for the identification of syllable boundaries, then, is to locate the vowels in a word that represent _____ .

7. Once you are able to identify the vowel letters representing phonemes in words, you are ready to discover some basis linguistic patterns related to syllabication. Study the words in each column below:

Column 1	**Column 2**
admit	*fever*
butter	*label*
complete	*pilot*
athlete	*ether*
unchain	*wagon*
discharge	*seven*
harmful	*level*
	whether

two

All of the words in both columns contain _____ vowel
(How many?)

two

phonemes. All of the words have _____ syllables.
(How many?)

two or more

8. Look again at the words in frame 7. The words in column 1 have _____ consonant letter(s) between the vowels representing
(How many?)

one

vowel phonemes. The words in column 2 have _____
(How many?)

consonant letter(s) between the vowels representing vowel phonemes.

Key: Multisyllabic words have either one consonant unit between vowels representing phonemes or they have two or more. (Consonant units are consonants or consonant digraphs.)

	9. Continue to study the words in frame 7. Focus on the words in column 1. Notice that when two or more consonant units separate vowels representing phonemes (*admit*), the first syllable ends after the first consonant unit (*ad*) , and the second syllable begins with whatever consonant units are left (*mit*). Write the syllable divisions for the rest of the words in column 1 of frame 7: _____
but.ter, com.plete, *ath.lete, un.chain* *dis.charge, harm.ful*	_____ _____
consonant	**10.** Our first syllabication generalization is: When there are two or more consonant units between vowels representing phonemes, the first syllable ends after the first _____ unit.
one open short	**11.** Look at the words in column 2 in frame 7. All of these words have _____ consonant unit/s between vowels representing (How many?) phonemes. However, the first syllable ends after the first vowel in the first four words (*fe.ver, la.bel, pi.lot, e.ther*), while the first syllable ends after the consonant unit in the last four words (*wheth.er, wag.on, sev.en, lev.el*). When the first syllable ends after the vowel, that syllable is _____ , and the vowel in the syllable represents its long (open, closed) sound. When the first syllable ends after the consonant unit, that syllable is closed, and the vowel in the syllable represents its _____ sound.
consonant unit	**12.** Fifty-five percent of the time that one consonant unit separates vowels representing phonemes, the first syllable ends after the vowel, and 45% of the time the first syllable ends after the _____ .

shi.ny, mer.chant, *pu.pil, spi.der, frol.ic,* *gav.el, bish.op, chap.el*	**13.** Our second syllabication generalization is: When there is one consonant unit between vowels representing phonemes, separate the syllable after the first vowel and pronounce the word. If it doesn't make sense, separate the syllable after the consonant unit. Write the syllable divisions for the following words using this generalization: *shiny, merchant, pupil, spider, frolic, gavel, bishop, chapel* _____ _____ _____

/ul/
 	
one
 	
there are two
consonant units
between the *le* and
the vowel preceding it.
	14. A special linguistic pattern involves the use of *le* at the end of multisyllabic words (*maple, babble, candle, able, bugle.*) In these situations, the *le* represents a syllable, and the *le* syllable represents the phonemes _____ . Once you realize that the *le* grapheme
	             (/ul/, /lu/)
	represents a syllable, you simply look at the *le,* the vowel before it, and the number of consonant units between the two, and you can apply either of our generalizations to find the syllable division. For example, in the word *maple* there is/are _____ consonant unit(s)
	             (one, two)
	between the *le* and the vowel *a,* so you can use the second generalization to find the syllable boundaries. You would use the first generalization to find the syllable boundaries in the word *babble* because
	_____
	_____

tick.le, no.ble, fid.dle, *ca.ble, tat.tle*	**15.** Use the appropriate generalization to help you find the syllable divisions for the following words: *tickle, noble, fiddle, cable, tattle.* _____ _____
syllables	**16.** Combine your knowledge of prefixes and suffixes with your knowledge of the two syllabication generalizations, and the ease with which you find the syllable divisions in multisyllabic words increases. Prefixes (*alone*) and suffixes (*vengeful*) are often separate _____ , but not always (*agreeable*).

ary, ism, tory, able/ible, ency/ancy	**17.** Examine the following suffixes that are most often used in words of more than two syllables and write those that are not separate syllables: *ion, sion, ic, sive, ary, ist, ize, ism, fy, tude, y, ate, tory, al, an, ent/ant, ous, ar, ence/ance, able/ible, age, tive,* and *ency/ancy.* _____ _____ _____
ble schwa	*impossible* *terrible* *responsible* *vegetable* *available* **18.** The suffixes *able* and *ible* are separated between the vowel and the letters _____, and the vowels *a* and *i* usually represent the _____ phoneme.
/âr/ /ē/	*necessary* *dictionary* *ordinary* *library* *military* **19.** The suffix *ary* is separated between the *ar* and the *y,* and the *ar* grapheme represents the phoneme _____ while the *y* grapheme represents the phoneme _____.
or y /ur/	*history* *factory* *victory* *laboratory* *territory* *dormitory* **20.** The suffix *ory* is separated between the _____ and the _____, and the *or* grapheme represents /ur/ or /or/ depending on the accent. When the *or* and *ar* graphemes are in the unaccented syllable (*color, buzzard*), they represent the phoneme _____.
n c s m	*frequency* *occupancy* *optimism* *hypnotism* **21.** The suffixes *ency/ancy* are separated between the letters _____ and _____ while the suffix *ism* is separated between the letters _____ and _____. A schwa phoneme is inserted between the graphemes *is* (/iz/) and *m* (/um/).

	painted *wanted* *landed* *handed*
t *d*	**22.** Remember that the *ed* inflectional ending is only a syllable when it is preceded by the letters _____ or _____.
/us/ /shun/ /shun/	*famous* *tremendous* *information* *direction* *television* *division* **23.** The suffixes *ous, tion,* and *sion* are used so frequently in multisyllabic words that it is helpful to look for these syllable units and to learn the phonemes that each represents. The *ous* grapheme represents the phonemes _____; the *tion* grapheme usually represents the phonemes _____; and the *sion* grapheme represents the phonemes _____.
	24. Finally, if you want to become very skilled in syllable division, add to everything you have learned the accent and schwa pattern of alternation discussed in the Accent Placement Clues section of this text.

Answer the questions in Review 17. Then you will be ready for the posttest. Good luck!

Review 17

1. Where do we begin the task of identifying syllable boundaries?
2. What must we know in order to determine visually which vowel letters in words represent vowel sounds?
3. After we have identified the vowel graphemes representing phonemes in a word, how do we determine the syllable boundaries?

See the Answers section for the answers to Review 17.

Self-Evaluation: A Posttest ━━━━━━

This test will help you evaluate your growth in phonics knowledge and issues related to phonics. Read each item carefully, including all of the choices. Circle the letter (a, b, c, d, or e) to indicate your best answer. Be sure to respond to all test items.

I. Multiple Choice. Select the best answer.

1. Which of the following most adequately completes the sentence?
   Language can be

   a. either associative or communicative.
   b. either expressive or receptive.
   c. either oral or written.
   d. All of the above.
   e. Both b and c.

2. Which of the following most adequately completes the sentence?
   The major reason we study phonics is to

   a. learn about consonant and vowel sounds.
   b. learn how to "sound out" words.
   c. learn how the spoken language relates to the written language.
   d. become phonemically aware.
   e. Both b and c.

3. How many phonemes are in the word *lunch?*

   a. one   b. two   c. four   d. six   e. seven

4. How many graphemes are in the word *lunch?*

   a. one   b. two   c. four   d. six   e. seven

5. Which of the following most adequately completes the sentence?
   The meanings young readers acquire from reading are largely based on

   a. written context.
   b. prosody.
   c. decoding.
   d. their knowledge of spoken words.
   e. phonics.

6. Which of the following most adequately completes the sentence?
   The written language is

   a. difficult to understand.
   b. as easy to acquire as the oral language.
   c. used more often in schools than the oral language.
   d. a representation of the oral language.
   e. a primary language form.

7. Which of the following statements are correct?
   a. A phoneme is the written representation of a grapheme.
   b. A grapheme is the written representation of a phoneme.
   c. A phoneme is the smallest unit of sound in a word.
   d. Graphemes and letters are synonomous terms.
   e. Statements b and c are correct.

8. Which of the following statements are correct?
   a. The letter x has no sound of its own.
   b. The letter c has no sound of its own.
   c. The letters y and w are used to represent both consonant and vowel phonemes.
   d. The letter q has no sound of its own.
   e. All of the statements above are correct.

9. Which of the following most adequately completes the sentence?
   The differences in the meaning that we associate with spoken words are affected mostly by
   a. graphemes.
   b. phonemes.
   c. syllables.
   d. phonological awareness.
   e. syntax.

10. Which of the following most adequately completes the sentence?
    If we didn't have a written language, there would be little reason to
    a. learn about syntax.
    b. study phonics.
    c. develop phonemic awareness.
    d. learn about text structure.
    e. Both b and c.

11. The letter y is most likely to be a consonant when
    a. it is the first letter in a word or syllable.
    b. it is the final letter in a word or syllable.
    c. it occurs in the middle of syllable.
    d. it follows the letter a in a word or syllable.
    e. None of the above

12. Which of the following most adequately completes the sentence?
    Most of the consonant speech sounds are predictably represented by
    a. 18 consonant letters and 5 consonant digraphs.
    b. 21 consonant letters.
    c. single-letter consonants and consonant blends.
    d. 21 consonant phonemes.
    e. The written form of the American English language is too irregular for any safe predictions.

13. The consonant digraph is illustrated by
    a. the *oa* in *soap.*
    b. the *th* in *with.*
    c. the *st* in *stop.*
    d. the *nt* in *bent.*
    e. the *gh* in *though.*

14. The voiced equivalent for the consonant sound represented by the *t* in *tie* is
    a. the consonant sound represented by the *d* in *dog.*
    b. the consonant sound represent by the *b* in *bug.*
    c. the consonant sound represented by the *g* in *go.*
    d. the consonant sound represented by the *v* in *van.*
    e. the consonant sound represented by the *z* in *zoo.*

15. The voiceless equivalent for the consonant sound represented by the *g* in *go* is
    a. the consonant sound represented by the *f* in *fun.*
    b. the consonant sound represented by the *s* in *sit.*
    c. the consonant sound represented by the *ch* in *chin.*
    d. the consonant sound represented by the *t* in *top.*
    e. the consonant sound represented by the *c* in *can.*

16. Which of the following most adequately completes the sentence?
    Consonant phonemes and graphemes are
    a. used in the middle of syllables.
    b. used at the beginning and ending of syllables.
    c. more important than vowel phonemes and graphemes.
    d. Both a and b.
    e. None of the above.

17. Which of the following most adequately completes the sentence?
    The consonant letter *q* is not really needed to represent consonant phonemes because
    a. it never occurs in words without the letter *u* after it.
    b. other letters represent the sound/s it represents.
    c. it looks too much like the letter *g.*
    d. Both a and b.
    e. All of the above.

18. The consonant letter *s* most frequently represents the sound/s heard in
    a. *ship.*　　b. *zone.*　　c. *sugar.*　　d. *so.*　　e. Both b and d.

19. The word *laugh* ends with the same sound as the sound represented by
    a. the *f* in *of.*
    b. the *ph* in *graph.*
    c. the *gh* in *caught.*
    d. the *gh* in *ghost.*
    e. Both a and b.

20. The consonant letter *c* followed by an *e* is most likely to represent the same sound represented by
    a. the letter *c* in *ocean.*
    b. the letter *s* in *some.*
    c. the letter *c* when followed by *o.*
    d. the letter *c* when followed by *i.*
    e. Both b and d.

21. The consonant letter *g* followed by a *u* is most likely to represent the same sound represented by
    a. the *j* in *jump.*
    b. the *gh* in *ghastly.*
    c. the *g* in *sing.*
    d. the letter *g* followed by *i.*
    e. Both a and d.

22. The open syllable in the nonsense word *tamel* would most likely rhyme with
    a. *ham.*   **b.** *pay.*   **c.** *fell.*   **d.** *game.*   **e.** *come.*

23. A vowel diphthong is best illustrated by the vowels representing the sound of
    a. *oo* as in *took.*
    b. *ou* as in *trout.*
    c. *ai* as in *said.*
    d. *oy* as in *joy.*
    e. Both b and d.

24. The schwa sound is represented by
    a. the *ai* in *certain.*
    b. the *ay* as in *day.*
    c. the *ou* as in *famous.*
    d. the *e* as in *wished.*
    e. Both a and c.

25. An example of a closed syllable is found in which of the following words?
    a. *mine*   **b.** *me*   **c.** *stretch*   **d.** *high*   **e.** *tea*

26. Which of the following has an incorrect diacritical mark?
    a. *tăll*   **b.** *băck*   **c.** *ŭp*   **d.** *dĭtch*   **e.** *pĭg*

27. Which of the following has an incorrect diacritical mark?
    a. *fūse*   **b.** *ēve*   **c.** *tīme*   **d.** *lōve*   **e.** *stāge*

28. When the single vowel *a* is followed by a single consonant and a final *e*, the *a* would most likely have the sound of
    a. the *ai* in *aim.*
    b. the *a* in *have.*
    c. the *a* in *ball.*
    d. the *ay* in *day.*
    e. Both a and d.

29. If the vowel *o* was the only and final vowel in a syllable, the *o* would most likely represent the same sound as

    a. the *o* in *mother.*
    b. the *a* in *was.*
    c. the *o* in *do.*
    d. the *ew* in *sew.*
    e. None of the above.

30. If the single vowel *a* was in a syllable ending with one or more consonants, the *a* would most likely represent the same sound as

    a. the *ea* in *great.*
    b. the *ai* in *plaid.*
    c. the *a* in *fall.*
    d. the *au* in *gauge.*
    e. None of the above.

31. The word containing a murmur diphthong is

    a. *coat.*   b. *bead.*   c. *hurt.*   d. *town.*   e. *rail.*

32. When the letters *ai* appear together in a syllable, they usually represent the same sound as

    a. the *a* as in *rag.*
    b. the *i* as in *risk.*
    c. the *aw* as in *lawn.*
    d. the *ey* as in *they.*
    e. the *a* as in *want.*

33. An example of a vowel team syllable is

    a. *game.*   b. *so.*   c. *stamp.*   d. *create.*   e. *coach.*

II. Multiple Choice. Select the word in each row in which the primary accent is correctly placed.

34. *permissible*	a. *per'missible*	b. *permis'sible*	c. *permissi' ble*	d. *permissible'*
35. *metropolitan*	a. *met'ropolitan*	b. *metro'politan*	c. *metropol'itan*	d. *metropoli'tan*
36. *appropriate*	a. *ap'propriate*	b. *appro'priate*	c. *appropri'ate*	d. *appropriate'*
37. *interruption*	a. *in'terruption*	b. *inter'ruption*	c. *interrup'tion*	d. *interruption'*

III. Multiple Choice. Select the word in each row that is incorrectly syllabicated.

38. a. *la bor*	b. *so da*	c. *gra vy*	d. *ca mel*	e. *de mon*
39. a. *em blem*	b. *com plete*	c. *bur den*	d. *ex cept*	e. *mons ter*
40. a. *merch an dise*	b. *ath lete*	c. *e ther*	d. *watch ful*	e. *dis charge*
41. a. *re gion*	b. *pi geon*	c. *gi ant*	d. *page ant*	e. *treach er ous*
42. a. *sym pa thet ic*	b. *con vul sion*	c. *ge og ra phy*	d. *im pec ca ble*	e. *tre mend ous*

IV. Multiple Choice. Select the words in each item (a, b, c) that contain a sound that the letter or group of letters at the left might represent. If none of the words contain a sound represented by the letter or group of letters, mark e. If all of the words contain a sound represented by the letter or group of letters, mark d.

43. *ti*   **a.** *choose*   **b.** *wish*   **c.** *machine*   **d.** All   **e.** None

44. *ci*   **a.** *sharp*   **b.** *sip*   **c.** *session*   **d.** All   **e.** None

45. *ge*   **a.** *gue*ss   **b.** *jello*   **c.** *jump*   **d.** All   **e.** None

46. *ce*   **a.** *single*   **b.** *car*   **c.** *keep*   **d.** All   **e.** None

V. Multiple Choice. Select the word in each item (a, b, c) that contains the same sound as that represented by the underlined part of the word at the left. If none of the words contain that sound, mark e. If all of the words contain that sound, mark d.

47. <u>h</u>orse   **a.** *honor*   **b.** *whom*   **c.** *right*   **d.** All   **e.** None

48. m<u>oo</u>n   **a.** *few*   **b.** *cue*   **c.** *to*   **d.** All   **e.** None

49. <u>w</u>atch   **a.** *plow*   **b.** *who*   **c.** *once*   **d.** All   **e.** None

50. si<u>ng</u>   **a.** *ranger*   **b.** *tank*   **c.** *gem*   **d.** All   **e.** None

See page 221 for answers to Self-Evaluation: A Posttest.

Self-Evaluation: A Posttest   Number correct _____

Self-Evaluation: A Pretest   Number correct _____

Part Two

Classroom Phonics Activities

Chapter 6

Teaching Phonics to Children

PHONICS KNOWLEDGE

The major purpose of this book is to enhance your knowledge of phonics; that is, to help you consciously understand the relationships existing between spoken and written language. If you have carefully studied the material presented so far, you have learned how American English speech sounds are represented by an alphabetic code in written words. This knowledge should help you become a better teacher.

Knowledgeable teachers, in any area of study, tend to make wiser instructional decisions than less knowledgeable teachers, simply because they have a better understanding of what they are teaching. You have probably sensed by now that not all phonics knowledge is of equal importance. If you have, you will probably make good decisions about what phonics patterns and principles should be taught to children. If you haven't, then you will want to read this, and the remaining part of the book, very carefully. There are some phonics principles and patterns outlined for you in the first section of the text that you will not want to teach to all children. There are even some that you may not want to teach to any child. You might ask then, "Why did you go into so much detail?" My answers to that question are, "The more you know about phonics, the clearer your perceptions will be about what is and what is not critical to teach children," *and* "Since you must be able to respond intelligently to the many questions children ask as they are learning about phonics, it is important for you to understand more about phonics than you intend to teach."

The decisions classroom teachers make about phonics instruction have far-reaching effects on children's literacy development. Some teachers spend so much time teaching children phonics that the children have little time left for reading and writing. Children in these classrooms are often deprived of opportunities to enjoy good literature and to "use" the written language as it was meant to be used. Their literacy development is often slow, and their motivation for learning how to read and write is often poor. Other teachers totally ignore the teaching of phonics, or give it little conscious attention in their instructional programs. Children in these classrooms are often left to discover the alphabetic principle on their own—an extremely difficult task for many children. Because children in these classrooms are deprived of meaningful opportunities to develop phonemic awareness and phonics knowledge, their literacy development is often hindered, their self-images are generally low, and their attitudes toward reading and writing are often poor.

Effective literacy teachers never teach children everything they know about phonics. They teach them only what they need to know in order to develop a good understanding of the alphabetic principle—the basic principle on which reading and writing is based. However, they also recognize that phonics knowledge facilitates word recognition growth, word recognition growth affects reading fluency, and reading fluency affects reading comprehension. Therefore, effective literacy teachers do not avoid the teaching of phonics either!

Finally, effective teachers strive for an effective literacy program. They seek a balance in learning to read and write, learning to enjoy reading and writing, and learning to use reading and writing in functional ways. In the "learning to read and write" area they also seek a balance of focus on "lower-order" and "higher-order" processes; that is, they try to balance their instruction so that children learn both the lower-order processes of decoding and encoding written language and the higher-order processes of constructing and reconstructing written discourse. They recognize that the mastery of encoding and decoding enables individuals to engage independently in the higher-level processes. Therefore, they give proper attention to children's development in this area. They also recognize, however, that the enhancement of basic-, connecting-, and controlling-thinking processes and language/schemata should not be delayed until the lower-order processes are mastered. Therefore, they begin the development of these higher-order processes while assisting children to read material they can't read by themselves.

In short, effective literacy teachers know that skilled readers (1) are automatic decoders; (2) employ both bottom-up and top-down strategies to make sense of print; (3) understand language (schemata/vocabulary, figurative language, parsing, prosodic features of print); (4) read between and beyond lines of print; (5) have multiple reading rates; (6) are able to focus on the "big" ideas presented in written text and perceive how those ideas relate to each other; and (7) control their own comprehension of written text. Since effective teachers have a clear vision of the end product of literacy instruction, they provide an effective literacy program that focuses on all seven areas of development. While phonics knowledge is important in this whole process, it should never overshadow other important areas of literacy knowledge.

PHONICS INSTRUCTION

A secondary purpose of this book is to introduce you to various phonics activities designed to help children develop their own strategies for identifying written words while also enhancing their word recognition abilities. These activities are presented in the next section of the book.

The teaching of phonics has been, and will probably always be, a topic surrounded with controversy. Suggestions for teaching phonics are many and varied. Some are effective in terms of their impact on children's reading growth, and some are not. Some are efficient in terms of the classroom time taken for this purpose, and some are not. The teaching of phonics is a subject I have treated extensively in other books, and a full treatment of the topic is beyond the scope of this book. However, some simple, basic teaching activities, which are very effective in helping children learn how to use phonics in reading and writing, are not beyond the scope of this book. These activities are outlined for you in the next section. They are easy to teach, children enjoy them, and they work!

The position taken in this book is that phonics teaching can be effective within the reading and writing context, or it can be effective outside of that context; it depends on the teacher. Some teachers are effective using either approach, while others seem to be effective with only out-of-context "mini-lessons" or within-context phonics instruction.

Instruction in phonics helps children become better readers and writers. However, phonics instruction is *not* reading or writing. Phonics is a study of the *form* of written text, not its *function*. Phonics instruction should not interfere with children's functional reading and writing experiences in the classroom, but sometimes teachers who try to teach it within the reading and writing context do that very thing.

Furthermore, although sentiment at times is against teaching phonics "out of context," there are some legitimate reasons for ignoring that sentiment. First, research supports the effectiveness of the practice. Second, research reveals that children do not find phonics instruction meaningless as some individuals claim. Third, research reveals that children enjoy it instead of dislike it as some suggest. In sum, research findings reveal that brief "out of context" phonics instruction in an otherwise predominantly holistic environment improves children's reading and writing achievement, helps them understand how print and speech are related, and is associated with positive attitudes toward reading (see Eldredge, 1995).

The decision to teach phonics in or out of context is a choice you must make for yourself. You may elect to do some of both. Both approaches can be effective when provided by knowledgeable teachers who are sensitive to students' needs.

Explicit phonics instruction need not take much classroom time. Daily 10-minute periods of systematic phonics instruction are adequate, if teachers focus on the right things.

Effective phonics instruction (1) will not absorb much classroom time; (2) will not communicate to children that phonics is reading; (3) will avoid phoneme distortion; (4) will be taught as a strategy to be used, not just skills to be learned; (5) will help children determine vowel sounds in words by syllable patterns; (6) will help children sound out words; (7) will be accomplished without the use of workbooks or handouts; (8) will be based on sound linguistic principles; and (9) will support teachers who wish to emphasize relevant reading and writing activities in the classroom.

Phonics should be taught as a strategy for children to use rather than just skills for them to learn. Children should be taught how to use phonics knowledge along with their syntax and vocabulary knowledge to strategically decode unfamiliar words through the process of contextual analysis. This is an important decoding strategy for children to develop. However, phonics knowledge can also be used by children to strategically sound out words. I teach children to use the following strategy when identifying a word by sounds: First, determine the vowel sound in the unknown word (the syllable pattern or the vowel team pattern helps here). Second, blend the consonant sound before the vowel sound with the vowel sound (this eliminates any phoneme distortion). Third, isolate the consonant sound after the vowel sound. Fourth, blend everything together. For example: If using the strategy with the word *jump*, you would first determine the vowel sound. The vowel sound is /u/. The word is a closed syllable word, so the vowel sound is short. Second, blend the consonant sound before the vowel sound with the vowel sound: /ju/. Third, isolate the consonant sound/s after the vowel sound: /m-p/. Fourth, blend everything together: /ju//m-p/ = /jump/.

I teach children to use this phonics strategy when other methods fail. If they are able to recognize a word by sight, there is no reason to sound it out. Furthermore, words do not need to be sounded out if children are able to identify them by analogy or by the contextual information provided in the sentence, since these identification strategies are much more efficient than phonics. However, if children do not recognize a written word, and if they cannot identify it by analogy or context, then they should use this strategy.

When teaching phonics to very young children who have not yet developed the ability to hear all of the phonemes in spoken words, I use rhyming books and games to help them develop rhyming awareness and onset awareness. Children learn to associate the single consonant letters in rhyming words with the consonant sounds representing them while at the same time developing the phonemic awareness abilities needed for successful reading and writing. Only after children experience initial success with onsets and rimes do I introduce the phonics strategy to them.

I use the principles of social mediation, zone of proximal development, and scaffolding as I teach children to use the phonics strategy. That is, I do with them what they are incapable of doing for themselves until they are able to use the strategy without help (Eldredge, 1995).

While I am teaching children how to develop the strategy for sounding out words, I am also introducing them to the phonics elements and patterns in the following simple sequence:

1. Five short vowel sounds
2. Initial consonant sounds (the most predictable sound associated with each consonant)
3. Final consonant sounds (the most predictable sound associated with each consonant)
4. Vowel principles (determining long and short vowel sounds by syllable pattern)
5. Vowel teams (determining vowel sounds by letter clusters—most predictable sounds)
6. Consonant digraph sounds (digraphs in both the initial and final position of words)
7. Consonant blends (blends in both the initial and final position)
8. The letter *y* as a vowel

The 10-minute phonics instruction briefly described here is succinct, systematic, and intensive. It complements holistic, informal decoding strategies such as the "Shared Book Experience," "Shared Music Experience," "Shared Rhythm Experience," "Group Assisted Reading," "Dyad Reading," "Tape Assisted Reading," and the Language Experience Approach (LEA). It also complements holistic writing experiences in which children use invented spelling while moving toward the orthographic stage of reading acquisition.

Chapter 7

Developmental Stages of Decoding

Decoding refers to the process of translating written text into language. There are many ways to decode written words. Proficient readers do it by a process called word recognition; they quickly recognize written words by their spellings. When good readers do not recognize written words, they generally identify them by analogy or by context. However, beginning or poor readers cannot use these word identification strategies because their word recognition vocabularies are too small.

Unless a sufficient number of written words are stored in the memory of a reader, the identification of unfamiliar words by analogy or context becomes impossible. When readers identify words by analogy, they search in their lexical memory for a word containing the same rime (*can, man, tan, ran,* etc.) or beginning (*back, bat, band, bad,* etc.) so they can identify unfamiliar words (*ban,* for example). If the number of sight words in memory is insufficient, the identification of unfamiliar words by analogy becomes difficult, if not impossible.

When readers identify words by contextual analysis, they use various language cues to make logical guesses. They use syntax cues, which suggest the function of the unfamiliar word (Is it naming something? Is it describing something? Is it describing some action?); graphophonic cues, which indicate the beginning sound of the unfamiliar word; and semantic cues, which indicate whether certain words would make sense in a particular sentence. For example, in the sentence "The dog b _____ at the cat," the reader might identify the unknown word *barked* by thinking "What action word beginning with the letter *b* would make sense in this sentence?" However, if the reader could not read all of the words around the word *barked,* then the use of context for the identification of that word would be impossible. Therefore, the use of analogy and context for word identification is dependent on the size of the reader's word recognition vocabulary.

When we teach phonics to children, we equip them with a necessary tool for identifying words by context. Once their sight vocabularies are sufficient, they can use this process independently for word identification. More important, however, phonics knowledge also equips them with the tools needed to identify unfamiliar words by their letter-sound sequences (i.e., to "sound out" unfamiliar words). This is an important practical skill for young readers to acquire. However, it is not the primary reason for teaching phonics to young children.

Phonics knowledge equips children with the tools they need to remember a word's spelling. A word's spelling sets it apart from all other words, and it is the word's spelling that is stored in lexical memory so it can be recognized. Therefore, the primary purpose for teaching phonics to children is to help them develop their word recognition abilities.

Recent research suggests that children go through predictable developmental stages in "sounding out" written words. These stages are closely related to their developmental spelling stages and to their levels of phonemic awareness. The findings of this research help teachers understand how children learn to sound out unfamiliar words, and they also provide teachers with important information regarding appropriate phonics activities for children at various stages of development.

Since children have not developed strategies for sounding out words when they first begin to read, they try to remember written words by some visual features. When they begin to develop sounding out strategies, however, the first words they are able to decode are simple, single-syllable words—words beginning with a single consonant, containing only one vowel, and ending with a single consonant (e.g., *man, big, sit,* etc.). Research findings indicate that children learn to decode these consonant-vowel-consonant (CVC) words before they are able to sound out words containing consonant digraphs (*sh, th,* etc.), consonant blends (*bl, st,* etc.), vowel teams (*oa* as in *soap, ai* as in *rain,* etc.), and words organized in a VCe pattern (*bone, came,* etc.).

The first CVC words children are able to decode contain predictable consonant letters in the initial and final positions. They are unable to sound out words beginning with a *q* or with a *c* representing /s/ until much later. You have already learned that the letter *q* is paired with a *u* in words (*quit, quiet*), and the letter *c* represents /s/ when it is followed by an *e, i,* or *y* (*cent, rice, city, cycle*). Therefore, when these letters occur in words, they are not simple CVC words. The easiest consonants for children to decode in CVC words are listed in the following order: *n, b, t, z, l, p, m, f, k, x* representing /ks/, *c* representing /k/, *d, r, s, h, j, g* representing either /g/ or /j/, *y,* and *w.* The most difficult consonants for children to decode in CVC words are *v, qu,* and *c* representing /s/.

The ability to sound out words containing consonant digraphs (*ch, sh,* etc.) and blends (*st, fl,* etc.) occurs *after* children develop the ability to decode CVC words. Words containing the *sh* digraph seem to be the easiest for young children to decode, followed by words containing *ch* and *ng.* The easiest consonant blends for children to decode in the initial position of words seem to be *sl* and *fl,* and the easiest consonant blends for children to decode in the final position of words seem to be *ft* and *st.*

Children develop the ability to sound out words containing simple vowel teams (*keep*) before they are able to consistently decode words in the VCe pattern (*hope*). However, children have more difficulty with some vowel teams than others, so there isn't a clear trend suggesting that vowel team words are easier for children to decode than VCe words. Children find it difficult to decode words containing *y* as a vowel, but the most difficult words for children to decode are those containing complex consonant clusters (**ranch, scratch, graph, stretch,** etc.) and silent letters (*know, write, gnat*).

The most important findings of the developmental decoding stages data are as follows:

1. Children go through predictable developmental decoding stages, and children's decoding growth follows a consistent pattern from grade one through grade three.

2. Children's ability to sound out words closely parallels their developmental spelling stages, and is dependent on their levels of phonemic awareness.

3. Children are able to sound out simple CVC words before they are able to sound out words containing consonant clusters (blends and digraphs),

and before they are able to decode VCe words and words containing vowel teams.

4. The most difficult words for children to sound out are those containing difficult vowel teams (*oi, ou*), complex consonant clusters (*squ, scr, str, nge, ph*), and silent letters (*gn, wr, kn*).

5. Children's ability to sound out words is significantly related to their over-all word recognition abilities, their reading fluency, and their reading comprehension.

We now realize that phonics knowledge is needed for optimal sight word recognition growth. Sight word learning is not a paired-associate memory process, as originally believed, but a process involving the establishment of systematic connections between the spellings and pronunciations of words. Phonics knowledge facilitates these connections.

Reading is a complex process involving the use of many knowledge sources. Phonics knowledge is just one of those sources. Phonics knowledge, however, contributes significantly to a person's overall decoding ability. Without the ability to translate the written text into language, readers could not access their vocabulary, syntax, schemata, or discourse knowledge to construct meaning.

The teaching activities that follow are based on "phonemic awareness" research (research suggesting how children develop the ability to hear phonemes in spoken words), phonics knowledge research, and research on children's developmental stages of decoding.

Chapter 8

Early Experiences with Written Text

READING BOOKS WITH CHILDREN

It is a well-established fact that reading books to and with children positively impacts their reading growth. The early, enjoyable experiences children have with books provide them with the motive to learn to read. If children are able to see the text while it is being read, and if parents and teachers track the print with a finger as they read the story with emotion and expression, the reading experience is even more valuable. From these early reading experiences with written text young children learn the important concepts they need to read independently. Some of these important concepts are that (1) written words represent spoken words; (2) alphabetic letters are used to make written words; (3) written words are read from the left to the right, and from the top to the bottom; (4) the spaces that separate written words are larger than the spaces that separate letters within written words; and (5) punctuation marks help us know when to raise the pitch of our voice, stress words, and pause while reading.

One of the most important concepts for young children to learn is word awareness. Word awareness refers to the ability to perceive individual words within sentences. The syllable is the smallest pronunciation unit in the language; that is, syllables are the sound units we hear as we speak. Some words are made of only one syllable, but other words are comprised of two, three, or more syllables. These multisyllabic words confuse us as we seek to understand a spoken language. As we listen to the pronunciation units (syllables) in speech, we might say to ourselves, "Does the sound I just heard end the word, or is it the beginning of another word?" Young children reveal this confusion when they ask teachers to help them spell such words as *gimme* (rather than *give me*) or *wanna* (rather than *want a*).

Children must be able to develop word awareness with the spoken language before, or at the same time as, they develop word awareness with the written language. In the written language, the spaces between written words separate them. Children must be able to match spoken words with the written ones representing them in order to read. One of the most effective ways to help children develop word awareness is to read stories to, or with, them. Let them see the pages of print as you read the story, and touch the words as you read them. I will demonstrate other word awareness activities shortly.

Another important concept related to the development of phonics knowledge and reading is rhyme awareness. Children develop an awareness of rhyming words before they develop an awareness of a word's beginning phonemes. After children have developed rhyme awareness, it is relatively easy to introduce them to initial phoneme sounds. Rhyming words beginning with different consonant sounds can be used to teach children the relationships between the initial letter of a word and the phoneme it represents. Thus, children begin their first phonics lessons.

To illustrate a variety of activities you can use with a story to develop children's awareness of both words and rhymes, I have written an alphabet book (Figure 1) that can be made into a "big" book. Books with large print are useful for teaching begin-

---

Alphabet Sounds
by J. Lloyd Eldredge

A is for **at,** imagine that!
B is for **bug,** but not for cat.

C is for **cake,** something good to eat.
D is for **duck,** but not for meat.

E is for **edge,** but don't fall off!
F is for **fish,** but not for cough.

G is for **girl,** and not for squirrel.
H is for **hair,** but not for curl.

I is for **itch,** that's not fun!
J is for **jump,** but not for run.

K is for **kid,** a baby goat.
L is for **lamp,** but not for coat.

M is for **milk,** cows make that!
N is for **nut,** but not for hat.

O is for **ox,** who pulls anything.
P is for **pup,** but not for ring.

Q is for **quit,** I won't do that!
R is for **rake,** but not for bat.

S is for **sit,** I love my chair!
T is for **top,** but not for bear.

U is for **us,** we love each other!
V is for **van,** but not for brother.

W is for **wake,** and not for bake.
X is for **"ks,"** a sound fun to make.

Y is for **you,** and not for me.
Z is for **zoo,** but not for tree.

Figure 1

ning reading concepts because all of the children in the classroom can see the words and punctuation marks in books as they are read. As the teacher tracks the print, children can also develop the concepts of left-to-right and top-to-bottom directionality.

Not only is an alphabet book useful for teaching word and rhyme awareness, but it can also be used to help children learn the names of the alphabet letters and the sounds that are represented by them.

USING BOOKS TO DEVELOP WORD AWARENESS

On large cards, draw pictures of the key words used in *Alphabet Sounds*. (If you prefer, you can cut out the pictures from magazines or old workbooks.) Underneath each picture, write the key word. The noun pictures you should have are *bug, cat, cake, duck, meat, fish, girl, squirrel, hair, kid* (baby goat), *lamp, coat, milk, nut, hat, ox, pup, ring, rake, bat, chair, top, bear, van, zoo,* and *tree.* You will need to be a little creative to draw pictures of someone sitting in a chair (*sit*); someone jumping (*jump*); someone running (*run*); someone baking (*bake*); someone waking up (*wake*); the edge of a trampoline, mountain, or bed (*edge*); and a curl of smoke or hair (*curl*). Some words are difficult to illustrate, so pictures will not be used. However, a card should be made for each of those words: *at, itch, quit, us, other, brother,* "ks," *you,* and *me.* (Although some of the words are hard to illustrate, the words chosen for the alphabet rhyming book, particularly the vowel words, were carefully selected for purposes that will be explained later.)

Show each picture card to the children and tell them the word that goes with each one. Distribute the cards to various children and ask them to hold up their card when the appropriate word is read.

General instructions for reading *Alphabet Sounds*. Read *Alphabet Sounds* with the children, two lines at a time. Before reading each pair of lines, ask the children with the appropriate word cards to come to the front of the class and stand next to the big book. Line them up in the order their words will appear. Each child should hold up his/her word card as it is read. As you read *Alphabet Sounds* with the children, teach them to add voice and facial expressions, plus hand and arm movements, to make the experience enjoyable and meaningful.

Word cards for the first two lines: **at, bug, cat**

Suggested action: Throw hands up in the air for "imagine that!"

> **A** is for **at,** imagine that!
>
> **B** is for **bug,** but not for cat.

Word cards for the next two lines: **cake, duck, meat**

Suggested actions: Rub stomachs and smack lips for "something good to eat."

> **C** is for **cake,** something good to eat.
>
> **D** is for **duck,** but not for meat.

Word cards for the next two lines: **edge, fish**

Suggested actions: One jump backward after "but don't fall off!" Cough after "but not for cough."

E is for **edge,** but don't fall off!

F is for **fish,** but not for cough.

Word cards for the next two lines: **girl, squirrel, hair, curl**

G is for **girl,** and not for squirrel.

H is for **hair,** but not for curl.

Word cards for the next two lines: **itch, jump, run**

Suggested actions: Scratching self for "itch, that's not fun!" Jump in air once, then run in place for "jump, but not for run."

I is for **itch,** that's not fun!

J is for **jump,** but not for run.

Word cards for the next two lines: **kid, lamp, coat**

K is for **kid,** a baby goat.

L is for **lamp,** but not for coat.

Word cards for the next two lines: **milk, nut, hat**

M is for **milk,** cows make that!

N is for **nut,** but not for hat.

Word cards for the next two lines: **ox, pup, ring**

Suggested action: Pretend to pull an imaginary rope for "who pulls anything."

O is for **ox,** who pulls anything.

P is for **pup,** but not for ring.

Word cards for the next two lines: **quit, rake, bat**

Suggested action: Shake head for "I won't do that!"

Q is for **quit,** I won't do that!

R is for **rake,** but not for bat.

Word cards for the next two lines: **sit, chair, top, bear**

Suggested actions: Sit down for "sit." Hands over heart; move bodies to the right and to the left for "I love my chair!"

S is for **sit,** I love my chair!

T is for **top,** but not for bear.

Word cards for the next two lines: **us, other, van, brother**

Suggested action: Move hands in sweeping motion to indicate all class members for "us."

> **U** is for **us,** we love each other!
>
> **V** is for **van,** but not for brother.

Word cards for the next two lines: **wake, bake,** "ks"

Suggested action: Children all say "ks."

> **W** is for **wake,** and not for bake.
>
> **X** is for "**ks,**" a sound fun to make.

Word cards for the next two lines: **you, me, zoo, tree**

Suggested actions: Point to others for "you," and point to self for "me."

> **Y** is for **you,** and not for me.
>
> **Z** is for **zoo,** but not for tree.

Matching Words (Word Awareness)

Make separate word cards for all of the letters, words, and punctuation marks used in *Alphabet Sounds.* None of the word cards should have pictures on them since we want the children to rely on each word's letter sequences. Some of the words, such as *is* and *for,* are used in every line at least once. Other words, such as *but* and *not,* are also used frequently. Since this matching activity is done with only two lines of the book at a time, you may want to make only five or six copies of these frequently used words. You will probably want to laminate all of the cards you make, however, so they can be used many times.

Begin the matching activity by distributing to selected children all of the cards containing the letters, words, and punctuation marks used in the first two lines of *Alphabet Sounds.* Ask the children receiving the cards to look at their words, letters, or punctuation marks carefully. Tell them they are going to make the first two lines of the big book by organizing themselves, and the cards they have been given, in front of the class, so that the letters, words, and punctuation marks are in the same order as they are in the first two sentences of *Alphabet Sounds.* Display the first two lines of *Alphabet Sounds* and ask the children to read the sentences with you:

> **A** is for **at,** imagine that!
>
> **B** is for **bug,** but not for cat.

Point to each word as you lead the unison reading of each sentence. Instruct the children with the cards to look at them to see if their word matches any of those in the sentences. Read the two lines again and ask the children with the cards to come to the front of the class and get in the right order to make the two sentences.

Help them to get in the right order if they need your help. Three children will have a *for* word card, and two of them will have an *is* card. You may want to tell the children with the *is* and *for* cards which sentences they are to be in, and you may want to tell the children with the two *for* cards in the second sentence which one will appear first and which one will appear second. Help those with the punctuation marks to get in the right order and explain to the children the purpose of these marks. When all of the children are in the right order, the children in their seats should read the sentence as you touch the head of each child representing a letter or word.

Ask the children with the word cards to return them to you and return to their seats. Display the next two lines of *Alphabet Sounds* and help the children read them as before:

> **C** is for **cake,** something good to eat.
>
> **D** is for **duck,** but not for meat.

Again, distribute letter, punctuation, and word cards to selected students, have them reconstruct the sentences, and have the children in their seats read them as you touch the head of each child holding a letter or word card. Continue this activity with the other pairs of lines in *Alphabet Sounds.*

Children enjoy this matching activity, and by participating in the activity, they learn that written words represent spoken words, that letters are used to make words, that spaces in sentences separate individual words, that we read from the left to the right and go from the top of the page to the bottom, and that punctuation marks help us read with expression. Furthermore, some children will also begin to recognize individual words by their letter sequences.

Find the Missing Word

In this activity you will use the word cards you made for the matching activity, and you will use only two lines of the book at a time just as you did in the matching activity.

Begin the missing words activity by distributing to selected children all of the cards containing the letters, words, and punctuation marks used in two of the lines of *Alphabet Sounds.* Display the two lines of *Alphabet Sounds,* and ask the children to read the sentences with you:

> **M** is for **milk,** cows make that!
>
> **N** is for **nut,** but not for hat.

Point to each word as you lead the unison reading of each sentence. Instruct the children with the cards to look at them to see if their word matches any of those in the sentences. Read the two lines again, and ask the children with the cards to come to the front of the class and get in the right order to make the two sentences. When all of the children are in the right order, have the children in their seats read the sentences as you touch the head of each child representing a letter or word.

Close the *Alphabet Sounds* big book so the children cannot see the two lines of print from the book, but leave the children in front of the class holding their cards.

Ask the children at their seats to close their eyes while you have one of the children in the second line turn his/her card over. The children's sentences are now constructed as follows:

M is for **milk,** cows make that!

N is for _____, but not for hat.

Point to each word as you lead the unison reading of each sentence. When you come to the missing word, skip over it and continue reading the rest of the words. Ask the children to guess the word that is missing. Once the missing word is identified, it is turned over and read. Continue the activity by hiding various words:

1. **M** is for **milk,** cows make that!

   N is for **nut,** but not for _____ .

2. **M** is for _____, cows make that!

   N is for **nut,** but not for hat.

3. **M** is for **milk,** _____ make that!

   N is for **nut,** but not for hat.

Once the children have success with the activity, have them guess the missing word without the unison reading of the sentence:

M is for **milk,** cows _____ that!

N is for **nut,** but not for hat.

Eventually, have the children in front of the classroom hide more than one word:

M is for **milk,** cows make _____!

N is for **nut,** but _____ for hat.

You will probably want to continue this activity with other couplets in *Alphabet Sounds.* Children find the missing words activity enjoyable, and the activity helps them develop word awareness, reading for meaning, making predictions, reading with expression, and print directionality. Furthermore, more children will also begin to recognize individual words by their letter sequences.

Sorting Words According to the Number of Letters

You will use the same word cards in the sorting words activity that you used in the word matching and missing words activities. However, you will need only one copy of each unique word used in *Alphabet Sounds: at, and, a, anything, bug, but, baby, bat, bear, brother, bake, cat, cake, cough, curl, coat, cows, chair, duck, don't, do, eat, edge, each, for, fall, fish, fun, good, girl, goat, hair, hat, is, imagine, itch, I, jump, kid, lamp, love, meat, milk, make, my, me, not, nut, off, ox, other, pulls, pup, quit, run, ring, rake, something, squirrel, sit, sound, that, to, that's, top, tree, us, van, who, won't, we, wake, you, zoo.*

Begin this activity by distributing all of the word cards to the children in your classroom. Explain to them that they are going to help you organize all of the words in *Alphabet Sounds* according to how many letters each word has. Write "1" on the chalkboard and have all of the children who have a word made up of only one letter bring it up to the chalkboard. Children should bring up the words *a* and *I*. Put a piece of masking tape on the back of each word and read each one as you stick it onto the chalkboard under the numeral 1. Next write "2" on the chalkboard and ask the children to find the words that have just two letters in them. Have them brought up to the chalkboard, read them, and stick them onto the chalkboard under the numeral 2. Those words would be *at, do, is, my, me, ox, to, us,* and *we.*

Continue to sort the words in this fashion until all 74 words are sorted and displayed on the chalkboard:

1	2	3	4	5	7
I	at	and	baby	cough	brother
a	do	bug	bear	chair	imagine
	is	but	bake	other	
	my	bat	cake	pulls	
	me	cat	curl	sound	
	ox	eat	coat	that's	
	to	for	cows		
	us	fun	duck		
	we	hat	don't	8	9
		kid	edge		
		not	each	anything	something
		nut	fall	squirrel	
		off	fish		
		pup	good		
		run	girl		
		sit	goat		
		top	hair		
		van	itch		
		who	jump		
		you	lamp		
		zoo	love		
			meat		
			milk		
			make		
			quit		
			ring		
			rake		
			that		
			tree		
			won't		
			wake		

Children find the sorting activity interesting, and the activity helps them understand that words can be made of just one letter or, in this example, as many as nine. Research studies reveal that many first grade children believe that all words are made up of the same number of letters—about five or six.

Sorting Words by Initial Letters

The same word cards you used in the previous activity are used in this activity. Begin the activity by distributing all of the word cards to the children in your classroom. Explain to them that they are going to help you organize all of the words in *Alphabet Sounds* according to the first letter in each word. Write "a" on the chalkboard and have all of the children who have a word beginning with the letter *a* bring it up to the chalkboard. Children should bring up the words *at, and, a,* and *anything.* Put a piece of masking tape on the back of these words and stick them onto the chalkboard under the letter *a.*

Next write "b" on the chalkboard and ask the children to find the words that begin with the letter *b.* Have them brought up to the chalkboard and stick them onto the chalkboard under the letter *b.* Those words would be *bug, but, baby, bat, bear, brother,* and *bake.*

Continue to sort the words in this fashion until all 74 words are sorted and displayed on the chalkboard:

a	b	c	d	e	f
at	bug	cat	duck	eat	for
and	but	cake	don't	edge	fall
a	baby	cough	do	each	fish
anything	bat	curl			fun
	bear	coat			
	brother	cows			
	bake	chair*			

g	h	i	j	k	l
good	hair	is	jump	kid	lamp
girl	hat	imagine			love
goat		itch			
		I			

m	n	o	p	q	r
meat	not	off	pull	quit	run
milk	nut	ox	pup		ring
make		other			rake
my					
me					

s	t	u	v	w	y	z
something	that*	us	van	who	you	zoo
squirrel	to			won't		
sit	that's*			we		
sound	top			wake		
	tree					

Note: These words begin with digraphs (*ch, th*), so technically speaking they do not begin with *c* and *t*, but with *ch* and *th*. However, children at this stage of development would not understand this concept so, at this time, when they sort these words according to the first letter of each word, we do not tell them that they are wrong.

This sorting activity focuses children's attention on letters. It develops, or in some cases reinforces, the understanding that words are made of letters. It also helps them recognize that different words can begin with the same letter.

USING BOOKS TO DEVELOP AWARENESS OF RHYME

Explain to children that rhyming words have the same ending sound. Tell them that *tail* and *nail* are rhyming words because they sound alike at the end. Repeat the words *tail* and *nail,* and ask the children to say them while they listen carefully to the ending sounds of the words. Tell them that *tail* and *cake* are not rhyming words because they do not sound alike at the end.

As you read *Alphabet Sounds* with the children, ask them to raise their hands when they hear words that rhyme. They will enjoy the activity, and it will help them develop an awareness of rhyme.

Help Children Discriminate Between Rhyming and Nonrhyming Words

Read the first two lines of the big book with the children:

A is for **at,** imagine that!

B is for **bug,** but not for cat.

Ask the children if they can find the rhyming words in the first two lines of *Alphabet Sounds.* If they have difficulty with this task, read the lines again, say the words *at, that,* and *cat,* and help the children see that the ending sounds of the three words are alike.

Place some masking tape on the back of the word card *dog* and stick it to the book over the word *cat.* The first two lines of the book now look like this:

A is for **at,** imagine that!

B is for **bug,** but not for dog.

Read these lines with the children and ask them if the words *that* and *dog* have the same ending sounds. Remind them that if words do not have the same ending sound, they are not rhyming words. Help the children conclude that the words *that* and *dog* do not rhyme.

Write the following words on the chalkboard:

th<u>at</u>   th<u>at</u>

d<u>og</u>   c<u>at</u>

The rhymes in many of the rhyming words will be spelled alike. This relationship between "same sounds" and "same spellings" in rhyming words is important for young children to perceive. Help them see that the ending letters of the nonrhyming words are different, while the ending letters of the rhyming words are often the same.

Read the second two lines of the big book with the children, and ask the children to find the rhyming words:

> C is for **cake,** something good to eat.
>
> D is for **duck,** but not for meat.

If the children have difficulty perceiving *eat* and *meat* as rhyming words, read the lines again, repeat the words *eat* and *meat,* and help them hear the rhymes.

Place some masking tape on the back of the word card *fish* and stick it to the book over the word *meat.* The second two lines of the book now look like this:

> C is for **cake,** something good to eat.
>
> D is for **duck,** but not for fish.

Read these lines with the children and ask them if the words *eat* and *fish* have the same ending sounds. Help them conclude that the words *eat* and *fish* do not rhyme.

Write the following words on the chalkboard:

<u>eat</u>   <u>eat</u>

<u>fish</u>   m<u>eat</u>

Again, help the children see that the ending letters of the nonrhyming words are different, while the ending letters of the rhyming words are often the same.

Continue this activity with lines 9 and 10, lines 11 and 12, lines 13 and 14, lines 15 and 16, lines 17 and 18, lines 21 and 22, and lines 23 and 24 of the big book. The rhyming words *off* and *cough* in lines 5 and 6, the rhyming words *squirrel* and *curl* in lines 7 and 8, the rhyming words *chair* and *bear* in lines 19 and 20, and the rhyming words *me* and *tree* in lines 25 and 26 are not spelled alike. Therefore, after you have worked with the "same sounds/same spellings" rhymes, introduce children to the "same sounds/different spellings" rhymes, and help them understand that some rhyming sounds are spelled differently.

Creating Rhymes

Word walls can be constructed by the teacher or the children to enhance children's awareness of rhyming words (see Figure 2).

Begin the creating rhymes activity by reading the first two lines of the big book with the children:

> **A** is for **at,** imagine that!
>
> **B** is for **bug,** but not for cat.

Now that the children can differentiate between rhyming and nonrhyming words, they are ready to create some rhymes of their own. Use the chalkboard to record the children's work. First, on the chalkboard, copy all of the words of the first two lines of *Alphabet Sounds,* except the last word:

> **A** is for **at,** imagine that!
>
> **B** is for **bug,** but not for _____.

Tell the children that you want them to complete the last line by finding another word to rhyme with the word *that.* Record each child's responses on the chalkboard, one at a time, by writing the rhyming word and the name of the child identifying it. For example:

> **A** is for **at,** imagine that!
>
> **B** is for **bug,** but not for hat. (Teresa)

Figure 2 Rhyming Words Word Wall

Read the revised couplet with the children. Ask them to verify whether Teresa's word does or does not rhyme with the word *that* by helping them decide if the words *that* and *hat* sound alike at the end. Also help them decide if the rhyming parts of *that* and *hat* are spelled alike.

Erase Teresa's rhyme from the chalkboard. Ask for other contributions and repeat the process. Other possible contributions:

> **A** is for **at,** imagine that!
>
> **B** is for **bug,** but not for rat. (Carlos)
>
> **A** is for **at,** imagine that!
>
> **B** is for **bug,** but not for fat. (Tony)
>
> **A** is for **at,** imagine that!
>
> **B** is for **bug,** but not for pat. (Michelle)
>
> **A** is for **at,** imagine that!
>
> **B** is for **bug,** but not for flat. (Dale)
>
> **A** is for **at,** imagine that!
>
> **B** is for **bug,** but not for sat. (Nicole)
>
> **A** is for **at,** imagine that!
>
> **B** is for **bug,** but not for mat. (Troy)

If some of the children offer nonrhyming words, accept their contributions just as you would rhyming words (see Phillip's contribution below). Write the child's word at the end of the line, and write the child's name next to the word. Read the revised product and make a positive comment about the contribution. For example, Phillip's word begins like *cat* (the word used in *Alphabet Sounds*), and the last letter of his word is the same as the last letter in the word *that.* Help the children decide, however, if the words *that* and *cut* rhyme by using the same evaluative criteria used with Teresa's contribution.

> **A** is for **at,** imagine that!
>
> **B** is for **bug,** but not for cut. (Phillip)

DEVELOPING PHONEMIC AWARENESS AND SIMPLE PHONICS KNOWLEDGE

Phonemic awareness is being aware that spoken words are made of phonemes—the basic sound units used to create spoken words. Research studies on phonemic awareness reveal that children develop an awareness of words before they develop an awareness of words that rhyme. Studies also reveal that children develop an awareness of rhyming words before they begin to develop an awareness of phonemes. Once they begin to be aware of phonemes, however, their awareness generally grows in predictable stages.

The levels of phonemic awareness, in the order children generally develop them, are as follows:

1. Identifying simple single-syllable words when they are spoken in phonemes. (For example, when hearing /m/ /a/ /s/ /k/, the child can identify the word *mask.*)

2. Associating isolated phonemes with the initial sounds of familiar words. (For example, when hearing /p/, the child can say a word beginning with that phoneme, such as *push, people,* or *pan.*)

3. Isolating the beginning phonemes of familiar words. (For example, when given a word such as *man,* the child will be able to say /m/.)

4. Associating isolated phonemes with the final sounds of familiar words. (For example, when hearing /t/, the child can say a word ending with that phoneme, such as *cat, sit, cut,* or *pet.*)

5. Isolating the ending phonemes of familiar words. (For example, when given a word such as *hat,* the child will be able to say /t/.)

6. Associating isolated phonemes with vowel sounds of familiar words. (For example, when hearing /a/, the child can say a word with that vowel sound, such as *man, bag, lamp,* or *can.*)

7. Isolating the vowel phonemes in familiar words. (For example, when given a word such as *man,* the child will be able to say /a/.)

8. Isolating all the phonemes in simple single-syllable words. (For example, when given a word such as *sit,* the child will be able to say /s/ /i/ /t/.)

9. Counting phonemes in words. (For example, when given a word such as *jump,* the child will be able to say that the word contains four phonemes.)

10. Saying words without the initial phoneme. (For example, when asked to say the word *mask* without /m/, the child will be able to say *ask.*)

11. Saying words without the final phoneme. (For example, when asked to say the word *paint* without /t/, the child will be able to say *pain.*)

12. Saying words by substituting new phonemes for the original ones. (For example, when asked to substitute /a/ in the word *quack* with /i/, the child will be able to say *quick.*)

Without phonemic awareness, phonics instruction would be meaningless. Phonics knowledge is a knowledge of the letters in written words that represent the phonemes in spoken words. Unless children can hear the phonemes in spoken words, they cannot learn to associate letters, or anything else, with them.

Teachers can provide instruction that will help children develop an awareness of phonemes in the initial position of words while also learning the letters that represent these phonemes. In other words, children can learn some phonics knowledge at the same time they are developing phonemic awareness. You learned in Part One of this book that this instruction generally begins after children have developed an awareness of words that rhyme. You also learned that this instruction helps children focus on the onsets and rimes of single-syllable words. Remember, a single-syllable word can be analyzed by its **rime** (the ending part of the word beginning with its vowel) and the letter, or letters, that come before the rime, called the **onset.** By helping children learn to hear the various consonant phonemes in rhyming words, and then helping them learn which consonant letters represent those phonemes (onsets), children begin to develop both phonemic awareness and phonics knowledge.

Key Words and Pictures for Rimes

The 36 key words shown in Figure 3 contain the following rimes: *ack, ag, ail, ain, ake, ale, ame, amp, an, ank, ap, ash, at, ate, ay, eat, ell, en, est, ick, ide, ill, in, ine, ing, ink, ip, it, ock, oke, op, ot, uck, ug, ump, and unk.* These key words also contain 18 different onsets: *b, c, d, g, h, j, l, m, n, p, r, s, t, v, w, ch, sh,* and *wh.* The 18 onsets and 36 rimes organized in various ways would produce hundreds of words.

Each child should have a copy of the key words and pictures to use for reference purposes. They may want to refer to the pictures from time to time to help them remember the sounds of the rimes and the onsets that precede them.

Using Rhyming Words to Teach Initial Consonant Phonemes and Graphemes

As children participate in the activities and games that follow, they should develop the ability to isolate onset sounds from the rimes (a phonemic awareness task) and associate the onset sounds with the letter/s representing them (a phonics task). They will also learn to associate the sound of rimes with the letters representing them, make words using the onsets and rimes, and create "hink pinks" (example: *fat cat*).

Making Words with Onsets and Rimes. Begin this activity by making word cards for the following words: *van, can, fan, man, pan, ran, tan.* Draw a line to separate

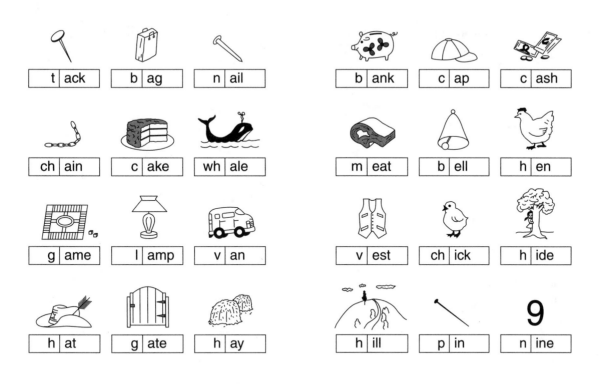

Figure 3

the onset from the rime in each of these words, put some masking tape on the back of each word card, and place them on the chalkboard. For example:

v	an

c	an

f	an

m	an

p	an

r	an

t	an

Read the words with the children, and ask them to verify whether these words do or do not rhyme. Help them decide if the words sound alike at the end. Help them decide if the rhyming parts of the words are spelled alike.

With a pair or scissors cut the word card *van* into two parts, the onset and the rime. Put masking tape on both parts and place them back on the chalkboard next to each other.

Say the word *van* and ask the children if they can say the sound that begins the word. Some of the children will be able to say /v/. Point to the letter *v* and tell them that this is the letter that is used to write that sound. Say the sounds represented by the onset and the rime as you point to each (/v/ . . . /an/). Ask the children to isolate the onset and rime as you point to each word part, and then repeat the word.

Next, cut the onsets off the remaining words, put masking tape on each on-set and rime, and place all of the word parts back on the chalkboard:

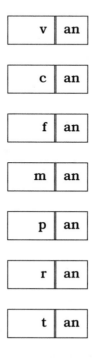

Say each word as you point to it, ask the children to say its beginning sound, and then show them the letter representing that sound. Then, isolate the sound of each word's onset and rime, and ask the children to do the same. (You may want to move the onset and rime away from each other as you say each word part.) Place the onset and rime back together while you and the children say the sounds represented by each, and then say the word.

Next, place only one *an* rime on the chalkboard, with all of the onsets in a column next to the rime:

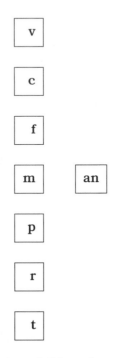

This part of the activity gives children the opportunity to isolate the beginning phonemes of dictated words, select the appropriate letter for each phoneme isolated, and move the letter to the rime to make words. For example, you say the word *pan*, the children would say (/p/), and a selected child would move the letter representing /p/ next to the rime /an/ to make the word *pan*. This process would be repeated with all of the onsets.

Next, distribute seven word cards (*van, can, fan, man, pan, ran, tan*) to each dyad group in the classroom. (A dyad is a group of two.) Ask the children in each dyad to cut the onset off each word with a pair of scissors. First, ask them to put six of the *an* rimes aside and work with only one rime. As you dictate words, each student team will make those words by moving the appropriate onsets to the *an* rime. Reinforce correct responses using the chalkboard, or by using large word cards prepared for the activity. Second, give the student teams an opportunity to reconstruct all seven words using all of the rimes and onsets available to them. The steps in this reconstruction process would be: (1) move an onset to a rime; (2) isolate the sounds of the onset and rime, in that order; and (3) identify the word.

This activity may be repeated as often as desired using various rimes and onsets (see the list of common rimes in the appendix).

Option: You may wish to use a flannelboard rather than a chalkboard for this activity or any of the other activities in the book requiring the use of manipulatives.

If so, the manipulatives would need to be prepared to stick on the flannelboard. Magnets and metal boards are also effective if you want to make your manipulatives from magnet sheets.

Making Words Game

This game can be played with two players, two small groups of players, or the entire classroom divided into two groups. The materials needed are two copies of one rime card (*ack*, for example) and cards for all of the single-letter consonants in the alphabet.

Procedures: Each player or team of players is given one of the rime cards. The rime cards are placed face up on the desk or posted on the chalkboard with masking tape. All of the consonant cards are turned face down so they cannot be identified. Each player or team of players randomly picks eight consonant cards, turns them over so they can be identified, and places them in a column on the desk or chalkboard:

Team (or Player) One

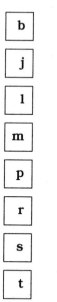

b	ack
j	
l	
m	
p	
r	
s	
t	

Team (or Player) Two

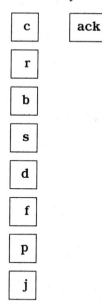

c	ack
r	
b	
s	
d	
f	
p	
j	

Each player should have a copy of the key words and pictures for rimes to help them associate the onsets and rimes with the sounds they represent. The players, or teams, take turns. A child on the first team moves the *b* onset next to the *ack* rime and says the sound represented by the onset followed by the sound represented by the rime (example: "b" . . . "ack"). If the two sounds make a word, the team gets two points. If the two sounds do not make a word, as would be the case with the child on the second team (example: "k" . . . "ack"), but the child says the sounds correctly and correctly acknowledges that a real word has not been made, the team gets one point. Play continues in this fashion until the children have tested all of their onsets and have made as many words as possible.

The players may continue to play the game with the same rime by randomly drawing single-letter onsets again, until they become familiar with the rime. The game may also be continued with other rimes so children can become familiar with them as well. However, this activity is meant to be enjoyed by children rather than forced on them, so let their interests dictate how often and how extensively this activity is pursued.

Later on, after the children have had success with the single-letter onsets, the game may be played with consonant digraph onsets and *qu*. You probably remember that the consonant digraphs *th, sh, ch,* and *wh* each represent one sound. Depending on the word, the *th* digraph represents either a voiced or voicelss sound: *that* or *thing*. You may also remember that the letter *q* doesn't occur without a *u* after it; so when *qu* begins words, it represents the "kw" sound heard in the word *quit*.

As the players gain more phonics knowledge, they will also be able to make words with consonant blends. For example, after the word *t ack* has been made by a player, the onset *s* could be placed next to the onset *t* to make another word: *st ack*. **However, at this point in the child's development you should limit the game to the use of single-letter onsets only.**

Creating Hink Pinks. Begin this activity by making two *at* rime cards and cards for the following onsets: *b, c, f, h, m, r, s,* and *v*. Put masking tape on the back of each card and place them on the chalkboard in the following manner:

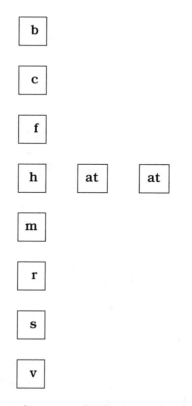

Explain to the children that some rhyming words when they are said together can be used to make words for funny pictures. Move the *f* onset card next to the first *at* rime, and move the *c* onset card next to the second *at* rime as shown:

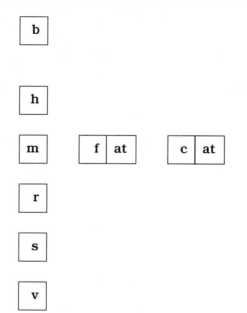

Ask the children to identify the two words you have made. If the children have difficulty identifying the words, help them use the strategy they developed while playing the Making Words Game. Point to the onset and rime while saying, "/f/ . . . /at/ makes the word _____." Repeat this process with the next word, if necessary. After the words have been identified, tell them that you have made a "hink pink." A hink pink is two rhyming words that can be used for drawing funny pictures. Give them the opportunity to write these words on a piece of art paper and draw a picture of a fat cat above the words.

Invite the children to try to create another hink pink using the *at* rime cards and the eight onsets posted on the chalkboard. They might create:

1. | f | at | | r | at |

2. | f | at | | h | at |

3. | f | at | | b | at |

This hink pink activity may be repeated using various rimes and onsets.

Hink Pink Game

This game can be played with two players, two small groups of players, or the entire classroom divided into two groups. The materials needed are two sets of cards for all of the single-letter consonant onsets and two sets of cards for all of the rimes.

Procedures: Each player or team of players is given all of the onset cards. The onset cards are placed in a column in alphabetical order face up on the desk, or posted on the chalkboard with masking tape. One set of rime cards is stacked in a pile face up, and the other set is stacked in a pile face down so they can't be identified. Each player or team of players randomly picks a rime card from the set placed face down and places it face up on the desk, or posts it on the chalkboard. The match for the rime picked is found from the other rime card stack and placed beside it.

Team (or Player) One

Team (or Player) Two

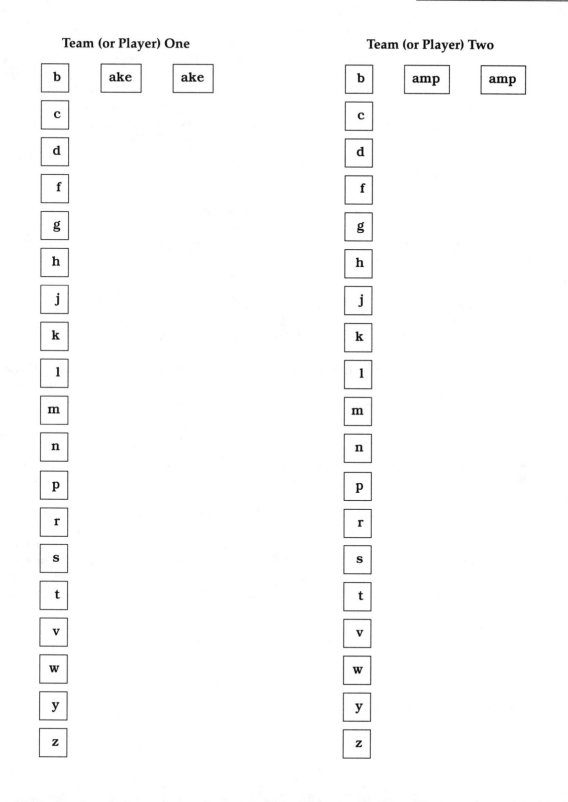

Each player should have a copy of the key words and pictures for rimes to help them associate the onsets and rimes with the sounds they represent. Both players or teams are given a reasonable amount of time to make a "hink pink" using the rhymes chosen and any of the onsets on the desk or chalkboard. For example, the first player or team might make the hink pink *fake cake,* and the second player or team might make *damp lamp.* Each time a player makes a hink pink within the time allotted, the player gets two points. The game continues by each player or team randomly selecting a new rime. Players may wish to write down the hink pinks they create and illustrate them later.

Matching Consonant Letters and Word Cards

Helping young children learn the sounds associated with single consonant letters is best facilitated by pictures and key words. Copies of the pictures and key words representing common rimes and onsets will be an important reference resource for these children for some time to come. They will help children remember not only consonant letter/sound relationships, but also common rimes. Later, these pictures and key words will help children learn about consonant digraphs and the syllable patterns predicting for the reader the vowel sounds in written words.

The rhyming activities and games presented thus far should help children learn the letters representing consonant phonemes. We are now ready to go back to *Alphabet Sounds* and help children learn to associate each consonant sound with one simple key word.

Alphabet Sounds provides a key word for the 21 consonant letters so that children will have a handy reference to associate the sounds represented by each consonant letter. All of the key words are presented in alphabetical order in the big book, which makes it easy for the children to locate a specific consonant quickly.

This matching activity helps children master the common sounds represented by consonant letters and helps those who do not master them learn to use *Alphabet Sounds* as a tool to assist them in that task. Begin this activity by making 20 lowercase letter cards for all of the consonant letters, except *x*. After these cards have been made, have the children sit in a large circle. Distribute the lowercase letter cards to the children. Then give them the 20 uppercase consonant letter cards and the reference word cards for those letters that were made for the matching words activity (some of the children will have more than one card):

B	b	bug		K	k	kid		S	s	sit				
C	c	cake		L	l	lamp		T	t	top				
D	d	duck		M	m	milk		V	v	van				
F	f	fish		N	n	nut		W	w	wake				
G	g	girl		P	p	pup		Y	y	you				
H	h	hair		Q	q	quit		Z	z	zoo				
J	j	jump		R	r	rake								

Say the consonant letters used for beginning word sounds, in alphabet order. Ask the children holding the appropriate word card, and the appropriate lower- and uppercase letter cards, to hold them up when the letter is said. When all three cards are held up, help the children say, in unison, the letter name, the letter sound, and the key word. For example, "B . . . /b/ . . . bug."

Using Key Words to Build Word Walls for Beginning Consonant Sounds

This activity is designed to help children associate consonant letters with the sounds they represent in the initial position of words. Display on the wall the following 18 picture/word cards made for *Alphabet Sounds: bug, cake, duck, fish, girl, hair, jump, kid, lamp, milk, nut, pup, rake, sit, top, van, wake,* and *zoo.* Also display the *quit* and *you* cards, with the letters *q* and *y* above the appropriate words, instead of pictures. The wall may be covered with white paper so children can write their words on it, or the children may tape or "tack" their words to the wall, if more appropriate.

The word wall is made by the children. When they find a word beginning with one of the 20 consonant sounds posted on the wall, they add it to the wall. A portion of the chart might look like Figure 4.

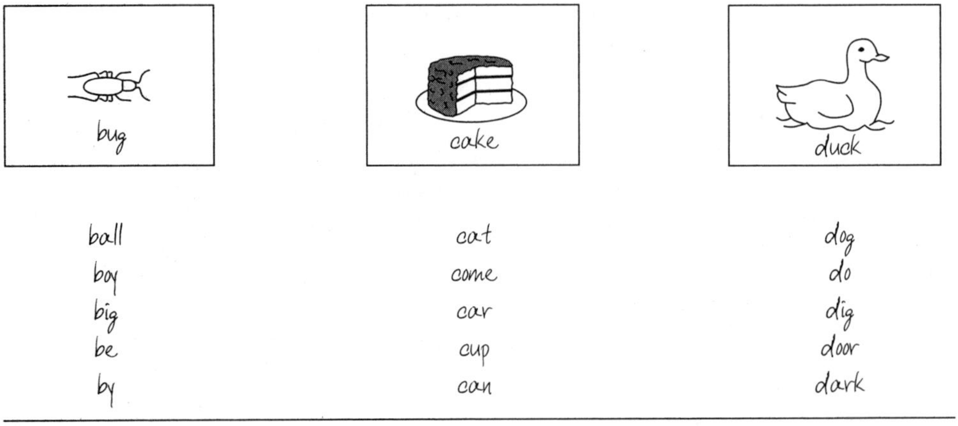

| bug | cake | duck |

ball | cat | dog
boy | come | do
big | car | dig
be | cup | door
by | can | dark

Figure 4   Partial Word Wall for Beginning Consonant Sounds

More Onset and Rime Games

As children participate in the games that follow, they will begin to develop their phonics knowledge by associating written rimes with sounds, making words using the onsets and rimes, and sorting words according to beginning consonant sounds. In addition, they will be working with words containing the VCe syllable pattern (*hate*) and the VC syllable pattern (*hat*), exposing them to two syllable patterns predicting vowel sounds.

Creating Words with Common Rimes. This game can be played with two players, two small groups of players, or the entire classroom divided into two groups. The materials needed are two *t* onset cards and cards for all of the common rimes: *ack, ag, ail, ain, ake, ale, ame, amp, an, ank, ap, ash, at, ate, ay, eat, ell, en, est, ick, ide, ill, in, ine, ing, ink, ip, it, ock, oke, op, ot, uck, ug, ump,* and *unk*.

Procedures: Each player or team of players is given one of the *t* onset cards. The onset cards are placed on the desk or posted on the chalkboard with masking tape. All of the rhyme cards are turned face down so they cannot be identified. Each player or team of players randomly picks eight rimes, turns them over so they can be identified, and places them on the desk or chalkboard in a column:

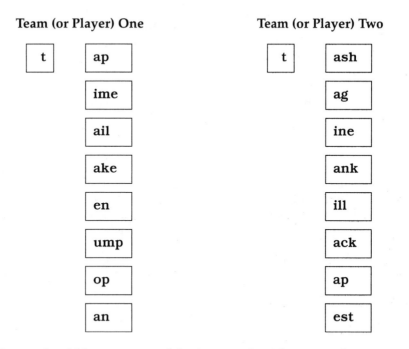

Team (or Player) One   Team (or Player) Two

t	ap		t	ash
	ime			ag
	ail			ine
	ake			ank
	en			ill
	ump			ack
	op			ap
	an			est

Players should have a copy of the key words and pictures for rimes to help them associate the onsets and rimes with the sounds they represent. The players or team members take turns. A child on the first team moves the *t* onset next to the *ap* rime and says the sound represented by the onset followed by the sound represented by the rime (example: "t" . . . "ap"). If the two sounds make a word, the team gets two points. If the two sounds do not make a word, as would be the case with the child on the second team (example: "t" . . . "ash"), but the child says the sounds correctly and correctly acknowledges that a real word has not been made, the team gets one point. Play continues in this fashion until the children have tested all of their rimes and have made as many words as possible.

The players may continue to play the game with the same onset by randomly drawing rimes again, or they can use a different onset. Players should be able to play this game with all of the single-letter onsets.

Creating Words with Two Onsets and Common Rimes. This game can be played with two players, two small groups of players, or the entire classroom divided into two groups. The materials needed are two *d* onset cards, two *b* onset cards, and all of the rime cards.

Procedures: Each player or team of players is given a *d* and a *b* onset card. The onset cards are placed on the desk or posted on the chalkboard. Each player or team is given a copy of all of the rime cards.

Team (or Player) One   **Team (or Player) Two**

Both players or teams are given a reasonable amount of time to (1) place all of the rimes between the two onsets that could be used to make real words with both the onset *d* **and** the onset *b* (for example, the *ump* rime would make the word *dump* with the *d* onset and the word *bump* with the *b* onset); (2) place all of the rimes next to the *d* onset that would make real words with the onset *d*, but not with the onset *b* (for example, *damp*); and (3) place all of the rimes next to the *b* onset that would make real words with the onset *b*, but not with the onset *d* (for example, *bake*).

Example: **Team (or Player) One**

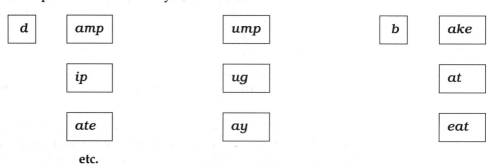

etc.

At the end of the allotted time, the players or teams check each other's work and a point is given for each correct word identified.

The children may want to write down each word correctly identified on a separate piece of paper so they can be mixed up, read, and sorted into columns later according to beginning consonant sounds. For example:

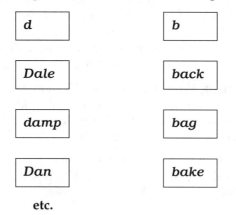

etc.

The game continues by using other single-letter onset pairs. A variation of this game is to allow the players or teams to randomly pick the onset pairs.

Creating Words with Closed and VCe Rimes. This game can be played with two players, two small groups of players, or the entire classroom divided into two groups. The materials needed are two *in* rime cards, two *ine* rime cards, and all of the onset cards except *c, h, j, y,* and *z.*

Procedures: Each player or team of players is given an *in* rime card and an *ine* rime card. The rime cards are placed on the desk or posted on the chalkboard. Each player or team is given all of the onset cards except the ones excluded.

Team (or Player) One   **Team (or Player) Two**

Both players or teams are given a reasonable amount of time to (1) place all of the onsets between the two rimes that could be used to make real words with both the rime *in* **and** the rime *ine* (for example, the *f* onset would make the word *fin* with the *in* rime and the word *fine* with the *ine* rime); (2) place all of the onsets next to the *in* rime that would make real words with the rime *in,* but not with the rime *ine* (for example, *bin*); and (3) place all of the onsets next to the *ine* rime that would make real words with the *ine* rime, but not with the *in* rime (for example, *line*).

Example: **Team (or Player) One**

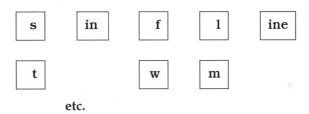

etc.

At the end of the allotted time, the players or teams check each other's work and a point is given for each correct word identified. Children may want to write down each word correctly identified on a separate piece of paper so they can be mixed up, read, and sorted into columns later according to rimes. For example:

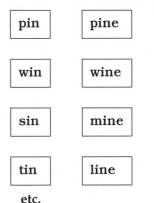

etc.

When children see the words in separate rime lists, some of them may discover that the vowel sounds in the words ending with a consonant (*in*) represent the short vowel sound, and the vowel sounds in the words ending with a consonant and an *e* (*ine*) represent the long sound of the vowel. This is an important phonics pattern for children to discover. However, if they do not make the discovery, do not force the issue at this stage of development.

Later, children may discover that they can combine single-letter onsets to make words beginning with consonant blends (examples: *grin, brine, spin, spine, swine, twin, twine, shrine*). However, at this stage of development, that probably won't happen.

You may continue this game by using the rimes *at* and *ate* and the rimes *ack* and *ake*. With the first pair of rimes, use all of the onsets except *j, k, n, w, y,* and *z*. With the second pair of rimes, use all of the onsets except *d, g, k, n, v, y,* and *z*.

Again, the children may want to write down all of the words correctly identified on a separate piece of paper so they can be mixed up, read, and sorted into columns according to the rhyme pattern. For example:

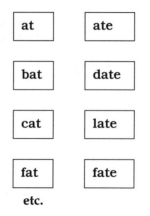

etc.

Making Words with Ending Consonant Graphemes

You have probably noticed that the activities and games presented thus far have been organized around children's developmental stages of phonemic awareness. Phonics instruction for children is meaningless without phonemic awareness. Therefore, beginning phonics instruction should follow children's phonemic awareness development.

Developmentally speaking, children are able to hear rhyming words before they are able to hear beginning consonant phonemes in words. They are also able to hear single-consonant phonemes at the beginning of words before they are able to hear single-consonant phonemes at the end of words. Furthermore, they are able to hear single final consonant phonemes at the end of words before they are able to hear vowel phonemes in the medial position of words.

Activities focused on words' final phonemes, although challenging to some, are appropriate for children who can hear words' initial consonant phonemes and identify the letters representing them. Therefore, final consonant phoneme segmentation, and letter association with the phonemes isolated, are the next area of focus. Begin your final consonant instruction by making word cards for the following words: *bug, bus, but, bud, bun, buzz, buck.* Draw a line to separate the final consonant grapheme from the rest of the word, put some masking tape on the back of each word card, and place them on the chalkboard. For example:

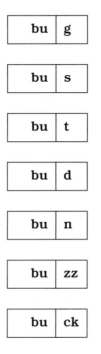

Read the words for the children. Then say each word in two parts. The first part is the beginning consonant phoneme coarticulated with the vowel sound, and the second part is the ending consonant phoneme. For example, /bu/ ... /g/; /bu/ ... /s/; /bu/ ... /t/; etc. Ask the children to verify whether these words do or do not sound alike at the beginning. Help the children decide if the beginning parts of the words are spelled alike.

With a pair of scissors cut the word card *bug* into two parts: the consonant-vowel and the ending consonant. Put masking tape on both parts and place them on the chalkboard next to each other.

Say the word *bug* and ask the children to tell you the sound they hear at the end of the word *bug.* Repeat the sound (/g/). Point to the letter *g* and tell them that *g* is the letter used to write that sound. Say the sounds represented by the letters in the first part of the word followed by the ending consonant, and point to each part as you say it (for example, /bu/ . . . /g/). Ask the children to say the word in two parts as you point to each part.

Next, cut the ending consonants off the remaining words, put masking tape on each word part, and place all of the word parts back on the chalkboard:

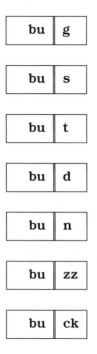

Say each word as you point to it (for example, *bug*), and ask the children if they can hear the ending sound of the word (/g/). Help them if they need help. After the ending sound has been identified, point to the letter, or letters, in the word representing the sound and tell them the name of the letter/s. Then say the word in two parts and ask the children to repeat each word part as you point to it. You may want to move the two parts of the word to different places on the chalkboard as you say them.

Next, place only one *bu* card on the chalkboard, with all of the final consonant graphemes in a column next to the *bu* card:

g

s

t

bu   d

n

zz

ck

This activity gives children the opportunity to isolate the ending phoneme of a word; select the letter, or letters, representing the phoneme; and move the letter/s to the beginning consonant-vowel to make the word. First, say a word (*bus,* for example). Ask the children to tell you the sound they hear at the ending of the word (/s/). Help them if they need help. Ask one of the children to come to the chalkboard and move the letter representing /s/ next to /bu/ to make the word *bus.* Repeat this process with all of the other words.

Distribute seven word cards (*bug, bus, but, bud, bun, buzz, back*) to each dyad group in the classroom. Ask the children in each dyad to cut the *bu* beginning off each word with a pair of scissors. First, ask them to put six of the *bu* beginnings aside and work with only one of them. As you dictate words, each student team will make those words by moving the appropriate ending to the *bu* beginning. Reinforce correct responses using the chalkboard, or by using large word cards prepared for the activity. Second, give the student teams an opportunity to reconstruct all seven words using all of the beginnings and endings available to them. The steps in this reconstruction process would be: (1) move an ending to a *bu* beginning; (2) isolate the sounds of the beginning and ending, in that order (/bu/ . . . /g/); and (3) identify the word.

You may repeat this activity as often as you like, using common word beginnings and various final consonant graphemes.

Using Key Words to Build Walls for Ending Consonant Sounds

Key word pictures are helpful in building word walls for ending consonant sounds, just as they were in building word walls for initial consonant phonemes. Display the following 15 picture/word cards: *tub, kid, roof, bug, cage, duck, girl, gum, van, pup, us, hat, five, ox,* and *fuzz* on the wall. You have already made many of these word cards for previous activities. The new picture/word cards to make are *tub, roof, cage, gum, five,* and *fuzz.* You may elect to cut pictures from books or magazines, rather than draw them. However, the pictures with the word cards help young children remember the sounds that are represented by the ending consonant letters.

Incidentally, the grapheme representing /j/ at the end of words is spelled *ge,* so the word *cage* is the key word representing that ending consonant phoneme. When the letter *v* occurs at the end of words, it always has an *e* after it, so the word *five* is the key word for the ending phoneme /v/.

Display the 15 key picture/word cards on the wall so children can write, tape, or "tack" other words under the appropriate card. Because an *e* is written after consonant letters in VCe patterned syllables to indicate that the vowels in those syllables are long, some of the ending consonant sounds will be spelled with an *e* after the consonant (*tube, hate, ride*), and some will be spelled without the *e* (*tub, hat, rid*). However, the consonant phonemes are the same, and the experience may help children discover this important "concept of print." A portion of the chart might look like Figure 5.

bug	van	hat
bag	ten	cat
dog	ran	pet
log	sun	boat
pig	can	gate
leg	win	hot
big	fun	hit

Figure 5   Partial Word Wall for Ending Consonant Sounds

Using Key Words to Teach Short Vowel Sounds

Becoming aware of vowel phonemes in the medial position of words is very difficult for young children. Therefore, helping them hear vowel sounds is best accomplished by using simple single-syllable words with the vowels at the beginning of the words. The key vowel words in *Alphabet Sounds* were chosen with this in mind.

    Alphabet Sounds provides a key word for each of the five short vowel sounds. Incidentally, short vowel sounds are used more frequently in words than any other sounds. These five key words give children something they can use to associate the short vowel sounds with the letters representing them.

    Begin this activity by making five word cards for the five short vowel key words presented in *Alphabet Sounds.* Cut the words apart after the vowel, put masking tape on each word part, and place the word parts on the chalkboard:

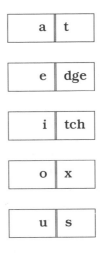

    Say each word as you point to it (example: *at*). Say each word part as you point to it (example: /a/ . . . /t/). Ask the children if they can identify the beginning sound of the word (example: /a/). Help them if they need help. After the beginning sound has been identified, point to the letter in the word representing that sound and tell them the name of the letter (*a*). Then say the word in two parts and ask the children to repeat each word part as you point to it. You may want to move the two parts of the word to different places on the chalkboard as you say the parts.

Matching Vowel Letters and Word Cards

Make five lowercase letter cards for all of the five vowels. Next, have the children sit in a large circle, and distribute the lowercase letter cards to them. Then distribute five uppercase vowel letter cards, and the reference word cards for those letters, that you made for the Matching Words Game. The cards involved in this activity are:

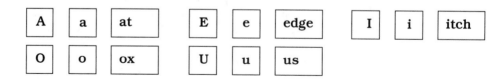

Begin the activity with the *Alphabet Sounds* big book. Read with the children the lines that present the vowel letters. Leave the big book open so the children can refer to it, if needed. Tell the children that you are going to say the vowel letters that represent the vowel sounds in words, in alphabetical order. Tell them that the children having the lower- and uppercase vowel letter cards should hold them up when the appropriate letter is said, and the child having the word card beginning with the vowel sound represented by that letter should also hold up that card. When all three cards are held up, the children should be instructed to say in unison the letter name, the letter sound, and the key word (for example, "A . . . /a/ . . . at").

Using Key Words to Build Walls for Vowel Sounds

Make five letter cards for all of the five vowel letters. Display them on a wall. Also display the five key word cards for short vowel sounds. Explain to the children that each vowel letter represents two sounds. Tell them that the sounds most frequently represented by the vowel letters are the sounds represented by the key words. Point to the key words on the bulletin board. Tell them that the other sounds represented by each vowel letter are the sounds we hear when we say the names of the vowels. Point to the letter cards on the bulletin board.

Explain to the children that they will use this wall to write (or paste or "tack") words containing long and short vowel sounds. When they find a word they want to add to the chart, they simply write it under the proper key word or letter. A portion of the chart might look like Figure 6.

Building a word wall for vowel sounds helps children discover that there are different ways to spell vowel sounds. The activity will also prepare them to understand more advanced phonics concepts introduced later on, such as vowel team patterns and syllable patterns. These concepts need to be understood in order for them to predict when vowel letters represent long and short vowel sounds.

at
an add
ask ant
mad and

edge
end bed
desk mess
red

itch
if in big
is sit

ox
on off
box dog
rock

us
up bus but
duck pup

a
ate age rain
day play

e
eat see
me he
each

i
ice my
night by
try

o
soap coat
road

u
use

Figure 6 Partial Word Wall for Vowel Sounds

Using Word Walls for Phonics Games

Word walls can be used for playing simple informal phonics games with children. For example, you might pick a word from the beginning consonant sounds word wall and ask the children to guess the word you have picked from clues you provide for them. For example, you might say, "I'm thinking of a word that begins with the letter *t*. It has a long vowel sound." The children might guess the words *time, take,* or *teacher.* You would then offer another clue, such as, "The word ends with the /m/ sound."

Similar games to enhance children's phonics awareness and development can be played using any of the word walls the children have constructed in the classroom.

EARLY WRITING ACTIVITIES

Children should be given opportunities to write as soon as they become aware of writing. Encouraging children to write is perhaps one of the best ways to help them develop both phonemic awareness and phonics knowledge, especially when they are encouraged to write with invented spellings.

The earliest writing experiences provided for children, however, will probably be those using the Language Experience Approach (LEA) to reading. This approach has been used effectively in classrooms for years. The LEA begins with shared experiences. When teachers and children share experiences in the classroom or on field trips, they first discuss them and then write about them. The children themselves provide the content for the written work. Teachers write down what children say, and the children watch them do it. Teachers repeat each word a child says while writing it down. Afterward, the teacher and the children read what was said. Sometimes children copy down the written product so they can read it to others (see Figures 7 and 8).

Many benefits are associated with using the LEA to introduce children to reading and writing. First, the written products resulting from this approach contain children's sentence patterns and words. Children often find it difficult to understand writing containing the syntax patterns and vocabulary of adults. By controlling the syntax and vocabulary variables in children's reading material, reading comprehension is easy, and children are able to focus their undivided at-

> Last Thursday our class went to Pumpkin Land. We got lost in the corn maze. After we got out of the corn maze we saw a train and took our pictures. We played on the playground and saw some animals. We went through the spook alley and picked out our pumpkins. Pumpkin Land was cool!

Figure 7 Language Experience Chart

Figure 8   Language Experience Chart

tention on how speech is mapped onto print. Second, children begin to realize that what is said can be written and read. They begin to see how speaking, listening, reading, and writing are all related. Third, through the LEA, the writing process can be introduced to children. In this way, they become aware of the process writers use as they write—a process that begins with getting ideas for writing, followed by writing those ideas, followed by revising and reorganizing those ideas, followed by editing the written work, and ending with sharing or publishing the written work. Finally, the LEA provides a natural bridge to independent writing. That is, children develop an increased interest in producing their own written work using whatever skills and tools they have acquired.

I recommend that you introduce children to writing early; that you use the LEA frequently, helping children record experiences important to them; and that you encourage children to do independent writing early, regardless of their level of literacy development.

Writing Alphabet Books

In addition to other writing, you and the children might want to rewrite *Alphabet Sounds*. This activity should extend children's phonics growth, involve them in writing, and give them an opportunity to be creative. Use the LEA as the writing vehicle for the activity. Begin by writing the first two lines of *Alphabet Sounds* on the chalkboard:

> **A** is for **at,** imagine that!
>
> **B** is for **bug,** but not for cat.

Read the lines with the children. Invite them to come up with a different word for the word *at.* Explain to them that the word chosen must begin with the /a/ sound. Various children might suggest words such as *apple, am, add,* etc. Obtain group consensus on the word to use. After they have decided on the word, erase the word *at* and write the word selected by the children in its place:

> **A** is for **apple,** imagine that!
>
> **B** is for **bug,** but not for cat.

Read the revised version with the children. Next ask them to identify a different word for the word *bug* in the second line. Explain that the word chosen must begin with the same beginning sound as the word *bug.* Repeat the process used previously to help them select their replacement word. The revised version might be:

> **A** is for **apple,** imagine that!
>
> **B** is for **boy,** but not for cat.

Continue this process with all of the other lines in *Alphabet Sounds.* After the revised version of *Alphabet Sounds* has been written, the children should have the opportunity to copy the new version, in their best handwriting, so they can read it to their parents or some other person.

Early Spelling Experiences

As children continue to develop phonemic awareness and early phonics knowledge, give them opportunities to engage in simple spelling activities. Spelling instruction should also be organized around children's phonemic awareness development. First, give children the opportunity to spell initial consonant sounds.

For example, you might give the children a copy of the following and ask them to spell the words you dictate by writing in the missing letters:

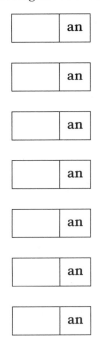

Say, "Spell the word *van*." "Spell the word *fan*." "Spell the word *can*." "Spell the word *man*." "Spell the word *pan*." "Spell the word *ran*." "Spell the word *tan*."

Second, give children an opportunity to spell ending consonant sounds. For example, you might give children a copy of the following and ask them to spell the words you say by writing in the missing letters:

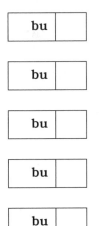

Say, "Spell the word *bug*." "Spell the word *but*." "Spell the word *bun*." "Spell the word *bus*." "Spell the word *bud*."

Finally, give children an opportunity to spell medial vowel sounds. For example, you might give children a copy of the following and ask them to spell the words you say by writing in the missing letters:

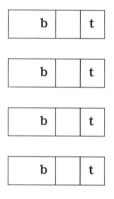

Say, "Spell the word *bat*." "Spell the word *but*." "Spell the word *bet*." "Spell the word *bit*."

Writing with Sentence Starters

This writing activity helps children learn to write and read common nouns. A simple sentence starter, such as "I see a . . . ," is written on a chart or chalkboard. The children supply words they see in the classroom, and the teacher writes those words:

> *I see a book.*
>
> *I see a chair.*
>
> *I see a desk.*
>
> *I see a picture.*
>
> etc.

Later, children might add other nouns not found in the classroom to the sentence starter such as animals (*rabbit, deer, lion, pig,* etc.), fruits/vegetables (*pear, apple, peach, carrot, tomato,* etc.), people (*mailman, policeman, artist,* etc.), and so on. An example of a sentence starter is found in Figure 9.

Figure 9 Sentence Starter

Writing with Invented Spellings Using Key Words

This activity helps children use invented spellings to write. Begin the activity by displaying the following *Alphabet Sounds* key word cards (along with their pictures): *bug, cake, dog, fish, girl, hair, jump, kid, lamp, milk, nut, pup, quit, rake, sit, top, van, wake, you,* and *zoo.* The focus of those cards is on initial consonant sounds. Also display the following picture/word cards used for referencing the ending consonant sounds: *tub, kid, roof, bug, cage, duck, girl, gum, van, us, hat, five, ox,* and *fuzz* on the wall. **The pictures that accompany the word cards provide the children with letter-sound references when memory fails them.** Arrange the cards so the initial consonant sounds are in alphabetical order, and, if appropriate, group ending consonant cards with the card containing the same consonant sound in the initial position. For example:

b	c	d	f	g	h
bug	cake	**d**og	fish	girl	hair
tu**b**		kid	roof	bug	

j	k	l	m	n	p
jump	kid	lamp	milk	nut	**p**up
ca**g**e	duck	girl	gum	van	

q	r	s	t	v	w
quit	**r**ake	**s**it	**t**op	**v**an	**w**ake
		u**s**	ha**t**	fi**v**e	

x	y	z
o**x**	**y**ou	**z**oo
		fu**zz**

In addition display the five short vowel reference cards used in *Alphabet Sounds: at, edge, itch, ox,* and *us,* and create and display a second card for each vowel letter with a macron over the vowel to indicate its long sound. For example:

a	e	i	o	u
at	**e**dge	**i**t	**o**x	**u**s
$\bar{a}$	$\bar{e}$	$\bar{\imath}$	$\bar{o}$	$\bar{u}$

Explain to the children that you want them to begin to do some of their own writing. Suggest that they may want to (1) write notes to classmates or parents, (2) write about some of their experiences at home or school, (3) keep journals, or (4) write short stories. Tell them that when they do their independent writing, they are to try to write words by sounds. They should say the sounds of the words they want to write and use the cards displayed in the classroom to help them remember how to write those sounds.

Remind the children that the long sounds of vowels are the same sounds as the sounds of their names. Explain to them that there are many different ways to write long vowel sounds, and they will learn how to write them while they are learning how to write. However, in the meantime when they want to write words with long vowel sounds, encourage them to write the appropriate vowel letter and put a line over it so everyone will know the word they are trying to write. (*Note:* As you involve children in the writing process, they will learn that there is a scheduled time during this process when writers correct their spelling errors. It will be during this time that correct spellings for words with long vowel sounds are provided. When children are ready to share their written work with others, their final products will reflect those spelling corrections.)

Explain to the children that you will provide them with brief daily lessons designed to help them better learn how to write words by sounds. Demononstrate the first mini-lesson by using the following cards:

a	t

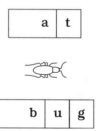

b	u	g

Figure 10 Children Learn to Write by Writing
David, Age 6

Review the five sounds in the words *at* and *bug* with the children by isolating the sounds in each word as the appropriate letters are touched. For example, say *at* followed by /a/ . . . /t/ while pointing to the proper letters in the word. Then say *bug* followed by /b/ . . . /u/ . . . /g/. Randomly, touch letters in both words, and elicit the correct sounds from the children.

Ask the children to write the word *but*. Isolate all of the sounds in the word for them: /b/ . . . /u/ . . . /t/. Help them concentrate on the first sound, and help them find the appropriate letter from the cards to represent /b/. Repeat this process with the phonemes /u/ and /t/. Explain that when they write a word by sounds, they need to say all of the sounds in the word and write something for each sound. Have them write other words (*tag, bat, tug, gag,* etc.) using the five sounds in these two words.

Continue this activity on a daily basis with other word cards until the children can write something for all of the phonemes they hear in words. However, do not spend an excessive amount of time on the activity at any one time (no more than 10 minutes in one sitting). Short daily mini-lessons on writing words by sounds are better than longer, sporadic lessons.

This word writing activity will help children develop confidence in their ability to use invented spelling and increase their involvement in independent writing. Too much cannot be said about the importance of independent writing for young children. Young children who are encouraged to write on a regular basis, and who are taught to write words by sounds, tend to be better writers and spellers than children not provided with this help (Eldredge & Baird, 1996).

Explain to the children that they can write almost any word they can say, if they can do two things. First, they need to be able to hear the individual sounds (phonemes) in the word they want to write. Second, they need to be able to write letters (graphemes) representing all of those sounds. Although many of the words they write will probably not be spelled the way adults spell them, that problem should not prevent them from writing. Learning the correct spelling of words is something that occurs over time, and the ability to write is so important that children need to start writing even before they know how to spell all of the words they write.

Chapter 9

Learning to Read and Write Single-Syllable Words

This chapter focuses on (1) the phonics knowledge most important for reading and writing single-syllable words and (2) a few phonics activities you might want to use to help students acquire that knowledge. Before we move to that focus, however, let's try to place phonics instruction, once again, in proper perspective. The best way to describe the role of phonics in literacy development might be to go into a detailed discussion regarding the elements of effective literacy programs. However, since that is beyond the scope of this book, perhaps the next best thing would be to state a few literacy principles that would emerge from that detailed discussion. The following is not an exhaustive list; rather, it offers a few selected principles to be considered by those interested in providing meaningful phonics instruction in the classroom.

Principle 1: One of the best ways to improve children's reading and writing is to encourage them to read and write. Reading and writing are abilities that improve with use. Therefore, young children should have opportunities to read and write even before they are independent readers and writers.

Principle 2: If children can't read well, then use a research-based "assisted reading" strategy to help them read until they develop some reading independence. The Shared Book Experience (Eldredge, Reutzel, & Hollingsworth, 1996), and Group Assisted Reading (Eldredge, 1990; 1991) are only two of the many different ways teachers can assist children to read material they are unable to read by themselves.

Principle 3: Those children who have the ability to read books independently should be given opportunities to use that ability by reading books that are of interest to them.

Principle 4: Children should be provided with some "guided reading" experiences in text slightly more difficult than what they are reading independently so they can develop the reading strategies they need to become independent readers.

Principle 5: Children should be given opportunities to share their reading experiences with others.

Principle 6: Children should be encouraged to write. Two beginning writing approaches are the Language Experience Approach (LEA) and the writing process using invented spellings. Writing should be encouraged throughout the educational experience.

Principle 7: Children should be encouraged to write about topics that are relevant and of interest to them. They should be taught how to write both expositive and narrative text.

Principle 8: Reading and writing have both a form and a function. The function, or purpose, of reading and writing (to make and keep friends, to give and receive information, to find enjoyment, to express oneself creatively, etc.) is more important than its form (directionality of print, phoneme/grapheme relationships, etc.). However, form affects function. That is, we cannot function well with written language unless we understand its form.

Principle 9: Relevant phonemic awareness and phonics instruction can improve word recognition abilities, which in turn can improve reading comprehension. Relevant instruction on syntax, semantics, and style can improve writing.

Principle 10: Phonemic awareness, invented spellings, and phonics instruction should be brief, systematic, relevant, and linguistically sound, as should instruction regarding syntax, semantics, and style.

In sum, the ability to read and write is strongly affected by many factors. Children's schemata, self-confidence, motivation, language development, thinking ability, personal satisfaction and enjoyment derived from reading and writing, perceived relevance of reading and writing, plus the amount of time spent reading and writing, are just a few of those factors.

The focus of this book is phonemic awareness and phonics, topics of extreme importance. The cumulative research available to us today sends a strong message regarding their importance. As you study these topics, consider the total literacy development of children, and weave your phonemic awareness/phonics instruction into a well-balanced literacy program.

DEVELOPMENTAL SPELLING STAGES

As children are involved in independent writing, their spelling development seems to progress in predictable stages. Many different researchers have described these stages and given names to them. In this book we will refer to the model provided by Gentry and Gillet (1993). Children in the first stage, the *Precommunicative Stage,* are not phonemically aware and do not possess phonics knowledge. Their writing consists of scribbles, circles, lines, and a few letters randomly included that usually have no relationship to the words they are trying to write.

During the *Semiphonetic Stage* children are becoming phonemically aware and are developing some phonics knowledge. They represent words by a letter or two. For example, *mother* might be written *m* or *mr.*

Children in the *Phonetic Stage* of spelling begin to use vowels in their written words, even if those vowels are not always the right ones. Children in this stage possess phonemic awareness, so *almost* all of a word's sounds are represented, and most of what children write can be read. Children might write *bottom* as *botum* or *botm.*

Children in the *Transitional Stage* represent all of a word's sounds, but, again, the words are not always spelled correctly. For example, children might write *wisht* for *wished*, or *sertun* for *certain.*

Children in the last stage of spelling, the *Conventional Stage*, spell most of the words correctly for their age level, but we will still find misspellings in their writing. Spelling is an ability that many students continue to develop throughout their public school experience.

In Figure 11 we see a sample of David's writing. David is in the first grade, and he appears to be in the Phonetic Stage. David read his story to me: "I like dogs. Do you like dogs? Some dogs are nice and some are rude. Dogs are mammals and

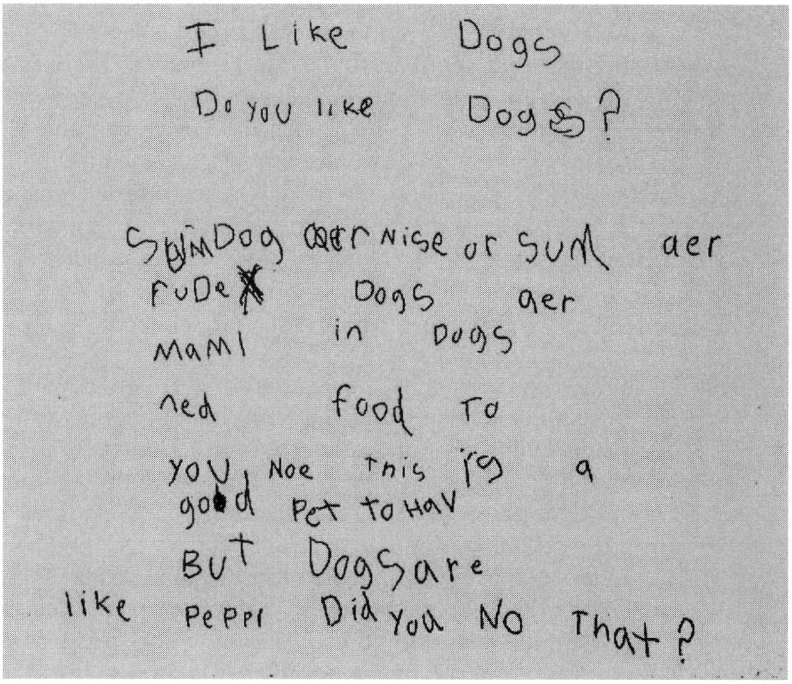

Figure 11

dogs need food too. You know this is a good pet to have, but dogs are like people. Did you know that?"

David has been encouraged to write on a regular basis. He enjoys writing, and he usually writes something every day. He was also taught phonics according to the principles discussed in the previous chapter.

You may have noticed how the developmental stages of decoding discussed in Chapter 7, the development of phonemic awareness, and the developmental spelling stages are all related. The phonemic awareness training and phonics strategies presented in Chapter 8 are designed to be compatible with children's development in phonemic awareness, decoding, and spelling. The strategies presented in this chapter and the next have also been designed in like manner. The important principles to remember are as follows:

1. Many students will not develop the phonics knowledge they need without explicit instruction.

2. Explicit phonics instruction should be brief, systematic, and based on sound linguistic principles.

3. Explicit phonics instruction should not interfere with relevant reading and writing activities in the classroom.

IMPORTANT PHONICS KNOWLEDGE

After children develop an understanding of basic letter/sound relationships, the most important phonics knowledge they need, perhaps, is a knowledge of (1) the syllable patterns used to help readers know when single vowel letters represent long or short vowel sounds, and (2) the vowel team patterns used to help readers know which vowel phoneme the vowel team represents. If we add to this important knowledge an understanding of consonant clusters (digraphs and blends), their ability to write and read single-syllable words increases.

Syllable Patterns

To say that phonics is the association of graphemes with phonemes is simplistic. Yet, this seems to be the popular definition of phonics among many reading teachers. Realistically speaking, phonics is much more than a simple association between the graphemes in written words and the phonemes in spoken words. Phonics also involves a study of written syllable patterns and how these patterns affect the grapheme/phoneme relationships.

The syllable is the smallest pronunciation unit in speech and is defined as the smallest part of the spoken word containing one vowel sound. In the American English language system, the way syllables are written reflects the way we pronounce them. The system is somewhat complicated because there are only five vowel letters, and these five vowel letters must be used in some way to represent 20 vowel phonemes. Some means had to be devised so vowel letters could predictably represent more than one sound. One of the ways this feat is accomplished is by writing the syllables differently so the same vowel letter could reflect different vowel sounds. For example, the words *mad* and *made* have (1) the same number of phonemes, (2) the same beginning and ending phonemes, and (3) the same vowel letter. The only difference in the two words when we pronounce them is the sound of the vowel phoneme. They are written differently to communicate to the reader that the vowel in the first word represents its short sound, and the vowel in the second word represents its long sound. The letter *e* added at the end of the word *made* helps us predict that the vowel letter in that word represents its long sound. This syllable pattern has been called the VCe pattern because the vowel letter is followed by one consonant letter plus the letter *e*.

When we speak of pronunciation units (syllables), those units end in either a vowel phoneme (for example: *me, so, ba con, ti ger, mu sic*) or a consonant phoneme (for example: *men, sod, bat, tip, mud,* or *eve, bone, bake, mine, fuse*). We call syllables ending in vowel phonemes open syllables, and the vowel phonemes in open syllables are generally long. When those syllables are written, they end in vowel letters; therefore, the syllable pattern helps us predict the vowel phoneme sound. However, when we speak syllables ending in consonant phonemes, the vowel phonemes can be either long or short (*sob, stone*). Therefore, we call written syllables ending in consonant phonemes closed syllables if there isn't an *e* after the single consonant, and VCe syllables if the letter *e* is written after the single consonant letter.

In summary then, vowel letters in open syllables (*me, so*) and VCe syllables (*mine, bake*) predictably represent long vowel sounds. Vowel letters in closed syllables (*end, cat, scratch, inch*) predictably represent short vowel sounds.

Vowel Team Patterns

A fourth syllable pattern is the vowel team pattern. A vowel team is a vowel letter teamed with another letter to represent a vowel phoneme. Sometimes the letter teamed with the vowel letter is another vowel (*soap*). At other times the vowel letter is teamed with the letter *y, w,* or *r* (*may, cow, burst*).

The following words contain vowel teams (*beach, bird, coin, boy, seen*), but the words are also syllables and it is the syllable pattern that is the object of focus here.

The activities presented in this unit are designed to help children (1) discover the syllable patterns that reliably predict vowel phonemes; (2) discover the vowel team patterns that reliably predict vowel phonemes; (3) learn to coarticulate (blend) single-consonant phonemes at the beginning of words with the vowel phonemes following them; (4) discover the difference between consonant digraphs and consonant blends; and (5) learn to coarticulate consonant clusters (digraphs and blends) at the beginning of words with the vowel phonemes following them. All of the activities are focused on helping children understand how words of one syllable are written so that they can remember their spellings and increase their word recognition vocabularies. The focus is on reading and writing single-syllable words.

DISCOVERING SYLLABLE PATTERNS

Write the following words on the chalkboard before beginning this discovery activity:

1	2	3
go	fin	fine
he	dim	dime
so	rid	ride
she	rip	ripe
we	rob	robe
be	hop	hope
me	hid	hide
no	not	note
lo	tap	tape
ye	cut	cute

This is a discovery activity in which children can be guided to discover some generalizations regarding syllable patterns. The first generalization is: The vowel letters in syllables ending with vowels usually represent their long sounds (column 1), and the vowel letters in syllables ending with consonants usually represent their short sounds (column 2).

To guide their discovery, do the following:

1. Review the concept of a syllable: A syllable is a word, or word part, containing one vowel sound.

2. Divide the students into dyad groups.

3. Provide the following directions: "Focus on the words in both columns 1 and 2. The words in those columns have only one vowel sound, but study them carefully to see how many differences you can find between the words in column 1 and the words in column 2."

4. Give the student dyads time to make their discoveries. Have a class discussion afterward.

5. Conclude with the following directions: "Write a statement that explains why the vowels in the words in column 1 are long, and the vowels in the words in column 2 are short." Share the students' statements.

The second generalization is: The vowel letters in syllables ending with one consonant followed by an *e* usually represent their long sounds (column 3).

To guide their discovery do the following:

1. Divide the students into dyad groups.
2. Provide the following directions: "Focus on the words in both columns 2 and 3. The words in those columns have only one vowel sound, but study them carefully to see how many differences you can find between the words in column 2 and the words in column 3."
3. Give the student dyads time to make their discoveries. Have a class discussion afterward.
4. Conclude with the following directions: "Write a statement that explains why the vowels in the words in column 3 are long." Share the students' statements.

SYLLABLE PATTERN ACTIVITY WITH SINGLE CONSONANTS

Prepare cards for the following phonics elements. Make them large enough for all of the children in the classroom to see, put masking tape on the back of each element, and stick each element on the chalkboard.

1	2
b*a*	ck
b*e*	d<u>e</u>
b*i*	d
b*o*	g
b*u*	k<u>e</u>
ba	n<u>e</u>
bi	p<u>e</u>
bo	s
c*a*	s<u>s</u>
c*o*	t
cu	t<u>e</u>
c*u*	x
ca	n
co	m<u>e</u>
da	c<u>e</u>
di	v<u>e</u>
d*i*	p

Key:
Italic (blue) = short vowel sound
Bold (green for "go") = long vowel sound
Underlined (red for "stop") = silent

Note: The vowel letters in the elements in the first column should be colored blue or green. All of the vowel letters italicized in the columns represent blue, and those bolded represent green. The vowel letters in the elements in the second column are colored red. The underlined vowel letters in the second column represent red. (You may want to underline the letters with either a blue, green, or red magic marker instead of writing the letters in those colors.) Green means "go" and red means "stop." Green suggests that children go ahead and say the letter's name (long sound), and red suggests they stop and not say anything. Vowel letters in blue represent their short sounds.

Procedures: Divide the class into dyad groups. The children in each group should have pencils and paper. They should be instructed to make two column headings on their papers: "1. Long Vowel Words" and "2. Short Vowel Words." The words they construct should be written under the appropriate column headings.

Instructions to the children: "Today we are going to see how many words we can read and write by taking word parts from the first column and combining them with word parts from the second column. The word parts in column 1 are the beginnings of words, and the word parts in column 2 are the endings. All of the vowel letters underlined in blue in column 1 represent short vowel sounds. All of the vowel letters underlined in green in column 1 represent long vowel sounds. All of the vowel letters underlined in red in column 2 do not represent any sound at all.

"Look at the first word beginning in column 1. The vowel represents /a/. The consonant and the vowel together represent /ba/. To make a word, I look for an ending in column 2 to go with /ba/. Since my vowel sound is short, I will look for an ending that ends in a consonant, rather than an ending that ends in a consonant followed by an *e*. [Take the *ba* beginning off the board and post it next to the *ck* ending.] The first ending in column 2 represents /k/. Those parts would go together to make the word /ba/ . . . /k/, and the letters *b-a-ck* correctly spell the word *back*. I will write that word on my paper under the heading Short Vowel Words.

"Look at the sixth word beginning in column 1. The vowel represents /ā/. The consonant and the vowel together represent /bā/. To make a word, I look for an ending in column 2 to go with /bā/. Since my vowel sound is long, I will look for an ending that ends in a consonant followed by an *e*, rather than a consonant without an *e*. [Take the *ba* beginning off the board and post it next to the *ke* ending.] The fifth ending in column 2 represents /k/. Those parts would go together to make the word /bā/ . . . /k/, and the letters *b-a-ke* correctly spell the word *bake*. I will write that word on my paper under the heading Long Vowel Words.

"Now I am going to give you _____ minutes [set a reasonable time limit] to see how many words you can make and spell correctly. At the end of our time, we will see which team has identified the most words. At this time each team should check with a dictionary to make sure all of the words identified are spelled correctly. You may begin now."

Option: You may elect to modify this activity by having the students copy the word parts on paper squares so they can actually move the word beginnings to the word endings as they experiment with the various combinations that make words.

This activity gives children the practice they need in blending single-consonant phonemes with vowels, and blending consonant endings to those units. They get this practice *without distorting phonemes*. For example, they do not pronounce *ba*, /bu/-/a/, but /ba/, and they do not blend the words' phonemes /bu/-/ak/, but /ba/-/k/. This activity also focuses children's attention on how the syllable pattern informs readers and writers about the sound of the vowel letter. Furthermore, since the activity is gamelike, challenging, and competitive, it keeps children involved long enough for this concept to take root. The activity also improves children's spelling. It is a significant step in helping those children who are in the alphabetic phase of decoding and spelling to begin the move into the orthographic phase.

Incidentally, the word parts in this activity can be used to make at least 64 words. I include only a portion of the words here so you can see how a child's paper might look at the conclusion of the activity:

1. Long Vowel Words	2. Short Vowel Words
bake	back
bike	bad
bite	bag
bone	bat
cake	bed
cane	beg
code	bet
coke	big
cone	bit
cove	boss
cute	cut
date	dig
dime	did
dive	dip

We used only three beginning consonants in this activity—the first three consonants of the alphabet. The activity may be repeated with all, or some, of the other consonants. There is value in giving children experience blending the other consonants with long and short vowel sounds. Their phonics knowledge grows, their spelling improves, and their word recognition is enhanced.

DISCOVERING CONSONANT DIGRAPHS

Write the following words on the chalkboard before beginning this discovery activity:

1	2	3	4	5
ch	sh	wh	th	t̲h̲
ch*o*p	sh*u*t	wh*i*p	th*i*n	th*a*t
ch*i*n	sh*i*p	wh*e*n	th*i*ck	th*a*n
cha*s̲e̲*	sha*k̲e̲*	wh*i*ch	th*u*d	th*e*m
cho*k̲e̲*	sha*m̲e̲*	wha*l̲e̲*	th*u*g	the*s̲e̲*

Divide the students into dyad groups. Explain to them that when there are two consonant letters in a word representing only one sound, those letters are a **digraph.** Call their attention to the letters *ch, sh, wh,* and *th* at the top of each column. Tell them their assignment is to identify the sounds represented by those letters and determine which of them are digraphs.

Read the words in all of the columns with the children. Then, give the dyad teams time to identify the beginning sounds of the words in each column and determine whether the letter teams representing those sounds are digraphs. (*Note:* Help the children understand that the beginning sound of *wh* is /hw/ and not /w/; the sound represented by *wh* is voiceless, while the sound represented by *w* is voiced.) The children should be able to determine that all of the letter teams in all of the columns are digraphs.

The words in columns 4 and 5 begin with the same digraph. Ask the children to touch their throats with a hand while they isolate the sound of /th/ in the word *thin* and the sound of /t̲h̲/ in the word *that.* They should feel a vibration on their hands when they say /t̲h̲/, but not when they say /th/. Ask them to determine which digraph is voiceless (the voice is not used when the sound is made), and which is voiced (the voice is used to make the sound). They should be able to discover that /t̲h̲/ represents the voiced sound and that /th/ represents the voiceless sound.

Refer them to the key words and pictures for rimes and ask them to locate the key words representing the digraphs *wh, ch,* and *sh.* They should locate the key words *whale, chain* (or *chick*), and *ship* and their corresponding pictures. Ask them to choose two familiar words they can use as reference words to help them remember the two sounds represented by the digraph *th.*

SYLLABLE PATTERN ACTIVITY WITH BEGINNING CONSONANT DIGRAPHS

The following cards are needed for the consonant digraphs activity:

1	2	Key:
cha	se	Italic (blue) = short vowel sound
che	se	Bold (green for "go") = long vowel sound
chi	p	Underlined (red for "stop") = silent
cho	ck	
cha	n	
chi	me	
cho	ke	
sha	de	
shi	pe	
sha	ve	
shu	ne	
sho	le	
wha	te	
whi	s	
whi	m	
whe	g	
tha	t	
the	ss	
the		
thi		
thu		

Procedures: Divide the class into dyad groups and distribute pencils and paper to the children in each group. Ask the children to make two column headings on their papers: "1. Long Vowel Words" and "2. Short Vowel Words." The words they construct should be written under the appropriate column headings.

Instructions to the children: "The instructions for this activity are similar to those you used with the single consonant letters, except that since you are working with consonant digraphs, you may need to give some additional explanations regarding the pronunciation key for word parts. The *th* represents the voiced sound heard in the word *the,* and the *th,* not underlined, represents the voiceless sound heard in the word *thing.* You may also have noticed that one of the *s*'s in *se* is italicized in the word endings column and the other is not. The italicized *s* represents /z/, and the *s* not italicized represents /s/.

Children should be encouraged to say the vowel sound in the beginning word part first and then coarticulate the digraph with the vowel sound to get the correct pronunciation of the beginning word element. Then they should search the word ending column for suitable endings—either an ending with a consonant, if the vowel sound is short, or an ending with a consonant followed by an *e,* if the vowel sound is long.

The dyad groups should be given a reasonable amount of time to make their word lists, and the competition between the dyad groups should be friendly and fun. At the end of the allotted time, each team should check with a dictionary to make sure all of the words they identified are spelled correctly.

In addition to the benefits of this type of activity already mentioned, this particular activity might help children resolve a problem common to many regarding the phonemes represented by *w* and *wh.* In fact, you may want to talk about these phonemes before children participate in the digraph activity. The word *whip* should be pronounced /hwip/ rather than /wip/ as many people pronounce it. In the speech patterns of many, the phonemes represented by the digraph *wh* and consonant letter *w* are the same, rather than different. Therefore, some of the children may try to make the word *wipe* from whi + pe or the word *wise* from whi + *se.* As children make these kinds of mistakes, you can turn them into meaningful learning experiences.

The word parts in this activity can be used to make at least 44 words. I include only a portion of the words here so you can see how a child's paper might look at the conclusion of the activity:

1. Short Vowel Words	2. Long Vowel Words
chat	chase
check	chime
chin	choke
chop	chose
shack	shame
shut	shape
that	these
hick	whale
shop	shave
whip	white
when	while
then	shine

DISCOVERING CONSONANT BLENDS

Write the following words on the chalkboard before beginning this discovery activity:

Blends	**Digraphs**
*st*ack	**sh**op
*sk*ill	**ch**eck
*sl*ap	**wh**y
*bl*ed	**th**in
*br*at	<u>**th**</u>em

Read the words in both columns with the children. Ask them to study the words in both columns carefully to see if they can tell you the difference between consonant blends and consonant digraphs. As they offer explanations, help them discover that a digraph represents only one sound, but each consonant letter in a blend represents its own sound. To help them with this discovery, ask them such questions as, "If we added the letter *s* to the word *tack*, what word would we make? (*stack*)" "What would the word *skill* be if we took away the letter *s*? (*kill*)" "If we added the letter *s* to the word *hop*, would we get the word /s/ /hop/? (no)" Help them see that we can separate, add, or delete the letters in a consonant blend, and the sounds represented by all of the individual consonants do not change. However, the letters in a consonant digraph, if separated, represent a different sound individually than they do when those letters are together.

ACTIVITIES WITH CONSONANT BLENDS

Making Consonant Blend Words

Write the following letters and words on the chalkboard or type them on an activity sheet for a dyad group activity:

Consonants: *s, b, p, c*

t*a*b	t*a*ck	t*a*g	t*i*ll	t*u*b
t*u*ck	ton*e*	k*i*ll	k*i*d	k*i*t
l*a*p	l*i*d	l*o*t	l*i*p	l*i*ck
lat*e*	lic*e*	lim*e*	l*a*ck	l*e*d
r*a*t	r*a*g	r*e*d	r*i*g	r*i*m
r*u*sh	rac*e*	rak*e*	rav*e*	l*u*ck
l*u*g	lac*e*	lan*e*	l*a*m	l*a*ss
l*o*ck	l*o*g	r*a*ck		

Ask the children to make new words with consonant blends by adding the consonant *s, b, p,* or *c* to the words listed.

The new words that could be made are *stab, stack, stag, still, stub, stuck, stone, skill, skid, skit, slap, sled, slid, slot, slack, slip, slick, slate, slice, slime, black, bled, block, blot, brat, brag, bred, brig, brim, brush, brace, brake, brave, plot, pled, pluck, plug, place, plane, clip, clack, clam, clap, class, click, clock, clog, cluck, crack, crag,* and *crush.*

Making New Words from Consonant Blends

Write the following words on the chalkboard or type them on an activity sheet for a dyad group activity:

cr*i*b	cr*o*ck	cr*a*sh	cr*e*st	cr*u*sh
crat*e*	crav*e*	gl*a*d	gl*o*ss	glob*e*
gr*i*p	gr*i*d	gr*i*m	gr*u*b	gr*u*ff
grac*e*	grop*e*	pric*e*	prid*e*	prob*e*
tr*o*t	tr*i*m	tr*i*p	tr*a*ck	tr*a*sh
trac*e*	fr*o*ck	dr*i*p	dr*a*g	dr*u*g
dr*u*b	fl*a*p	fl*e*d	fl*i*p	fl*o*ck
fl*o*g	flak*e*	flam*e*	smil*e*	sw*e*ll
sw*i*sh	sp*o*t	sp*a*n	sp*a*t	sp*e*ck
sp*i*ll	sp*i*n	sp*i*t	spac*e*	spin*e*
spok*e*	sc*a*b	sc*a*t	sc*a*n	str*a*p
str*i*p	thr*o*b	thr*u*sh	shr*u*b	shr*e*d
shr*u*g	tw*i*n	tw*i*g	tw*i*ll	twin*e*

Begin this activity by asking the children such questions as, "What would the word *crib* be without the *c?*" "What would the word *crock* be without the *c?*" "What would the word *crash* be without the *r?*" "What would the word *crash* be without the *c?*"

Ask the children to make new words from the previous list by deleting various consonant letters. The following words could be made: *rib, rock, rash, cash, rest, rush, rate, cave, rave, lad, loss, lobe, rip, rid, rim, rub, ruff, race, rope, rice, ride, robe, rot, tot, rim, Tim, rip, tip, tack, rack, rash, race, rock, dip, rip, rag, dug, rug, rub, lap, fed, led, lip, lock, fog, log, lake, fake, fame, lame, mile, sell, well, wish, pot, pan, sat, pat, peck, pill, sill, sin, pin, sit, pit, pace, pine, poke, cab, sat, cat, can, trap, rap, trip, rip, rob, rush, rub, shed, red, rug, tin, twin, wig, till, will,* and *wine.*

SYLLABLE PATTERN ACTIVITY WITH BEGINNING CONSONANT BLENDS

The following cards are needed for the consonant digraphs activity:

fli	v**e**
sto	p
sto	n**e**
sla	k**e**
sla	m**e**
bra	c**e**
bra	n
pla	g
pla	b
cri	z**e**
cri	d
gla	s**s**
gla	d**e**

Key:
Italic (blue) = short vowel sound
Bold (green for "go") = long vowel sound
Underlined (red for "stop") = silent

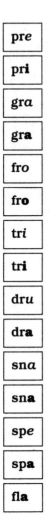

pre	pe̲
pri	be̲
gra	ck
gra	l̲l̲
fro	m
fro	
tri	
tri	
dru	
dra	
sna	
sna	
spe	
spa	
fla	

Procedures: Divide the class into dyad groups and give pencils and paper to the children in each group. Ask the children to make two column headings on their papers: "1. Long Vowel Words" and "2. Short Vowel Words." The words they construct should be written under the appropriate column headings.

Instructions to the children: The instructions for this activity are similar to those you used with single consonants and consonant digraphs. Children should be encouraged to say the vowel sound in the beginning word part first, then coarticulate the consonant next to the vowel with the vowel, and finally, coarticulate the first consonant with the second consonant and vowel to get the correct pronunciation of the beginning word element. Then they should search the word ending column for suitable endings—either an ending with a consonant, if the vowel sound is short, or an ending with a consonant followed by an *e*, if the vowel sound is long.

The dyad groups should be given a reasonable amount of time to make their word lists. At the end of the allotted time, each team should check with a dictionary to make sure all of the words they identified are spelled correctly.

The word parts in this activity can be used to make at least 64 words. I include only a portion of the words here so you can see how a child's paper might look at the conclusion of the activity:

1. Long Vowel Words	2. Short Vowel Words
stove	flip
stone	stop
slave	slap
brave	slam
brake	brag
brace	brass
plane	plan
crime	crib
glaze	glad
prize	press
pride	grab
grape	grass
froze	frog
tribe	trip
drape	drug
snake	snap
space	spell
flake	speck

DISCOVERING VOWEL TEAM PATTERNS

Vowel Digraphs and Diphthongs

Write the following words on the chalkboard:

1	2	3
oa	oi	ou
ro**a**d	oil	out
so**a**p	voice	loud
go**a**t	join	sound
to**a**st	point	count
bo**a**t	noise	house
lo**a**d	choice	scout
co**a**t	coin	mouse

Divide the students into dyad groups. Explain to them that when there are two vowel letters in a word representing only one sound, those letters are a **digraph.** Call their attention to the letters *oa* at the beginning of the first column of words. Ask them if the *oa* is a vowel digraph. Ask them to tell you the sound represented by the *oa* vowel digraph. Explain to them that you have underlined the *o* in these words with a green magic marker (I have bolded those letters) so they know that the long *o* vowel sound is heard. Also explain to them that you have underlined the *a* in these words with a red magic marker (I have underlined those letters), so they know that the letter *a* is silent. (Green means "go" and red means "stop." Green suggests to the children that they go ahead and say the name of the letter, and red suggests that they stop and don't try to say a sound for that letter.)

Explain to the children that the letters *oi* and *ou* represent gliding vowel sounds (these are vowel diphthongs, but you may not want to use that word with the children). Ask them to read all of the words in column 2 with you and listen to the vowel sound in each word. When you are finished, ask them to tell you the sound represented by the letters *oi*. Tell them that the vowel sound in these words is neither long nor short, so none of the letters have been underlined. However, if they remember the first word in the column (*oil*), they will be able to remember the sound represented by the letters *oi*. Ask them to say the word *oil* without saying the sound represented by the last letter (*l*), and they will be able to clearly hear the sound represented by the letters *oi*.

Ask the children to read all of the words in column 3 with you and listen to the vowel sound in each word. When you are finished, ask them to tell you the sound represented by the letters *ou*. Tell them that the vowel sound in these words is neither long nor short, so letters have not been underlined. However, if they remember the first word in the column (*out*), they will be able to remember the sound represented by the letters *ou*. Ask them to say the word *out* without saying *t*, and they will be able to clearly hear the sound represented by the letters *ou*.

You should continue this activity with other vowel digraphs: *ai (rain), ay (day), aw (lawn), au (sauce), ee (deep), ea (heat* and *head), oo (room* and *book), ew (blew), ue (blue)*, and *ow (show)*, and with other vowel diphthongs: *ow (cow)* and *oy (boy)*. Notice that *ow* represents either a diphthong sound or a long vowel sound. Children should also be helped to discover the sound represented by the vowel trigraph *igh (night)*.

Murmur Diphthong Vowel Teams

Write the following words on the chalkboard:

1	2	3	4	5
er	ir	ur	ar	or
her	first	burn	arm	for
herd	girl	curl	art	torn
verb	dirt	turn	car	storm
stern	third	nurse	dark	corn
term	bird	fur	shark	born
fern	shirt	purse	barn	short
germ	firm	hurt	farm	fork

Explain to the children that when there is a vowel letter followed by an *r*, the vowel and the *r* represent one murmuring vowel sound. (These sounds are called murmur diphthong sounds.) Ask them if the vowel-*r* teams at the top of the columns represent murmuring vowel sounds. Read the words in the first three columns with them. Ask them if the vowel sounds in these words are alike or different. They should conclude that all of these vowel teams represent the same sound, /ûr/.

Read the words in column 4 and help the children discover that the vowel team *ar* represents the phoneme /ar/. Read the words in column 5 and help the children discover that the vowel team *or* represents the phoneme /or/.

You may continue this activity with other murmur diphthongs: *are (care), air (chair), eer (deer), ear (year)*, and *ire (fire)*.

SYLLABLE PATTERN ACTIVITY INVOLVING OPEN, CLOSED, VCe, AND VOWEL TEAM SYLLABLES

Prepare cards for the following phonics elements. Make them large enough for all of the children in the classroom to see, put masking tape on the back of each element, and stick each element on the chalkboard:

1

ba
no
ba<u>i</u>
bo
bo<u>a</u>
pro
ma
me
ma<u>i</u>
she
mo<u>a</u>
mo
ra<u>i</u>
ra
ra
ba
bo
ma
mo

2

ck
d<u>e</u>
b
t
x
d
n<u>e</u>
n
k<u>e</u>
l<u>e</u>
g<u>e</u>
<u>d</u>g<u>e</u>
<u>t</u>ch

Key:
Italic (blue) = short vowel sound
Bold (green for "go") = long vowel sound
Underlined (red for "stop") = silent

Procedures: Divide the class into dyad groups and distribute pencils and paper to the children in each group. Ask the children to make four column headings on their papers: "1. Syllables Ending with Vowels," "2. Syllables Ending with Consonants," "3. Syllables Ending with Consonants Followed by an *e*," and "4. Vowel Team Syllables."

Instructions to the children: The instructions for this activity are similar to those you used with single consonants, consonant digraphs, and consonant blends. The task is to see how many words the dyad teams can read and write by taking the word parts from the first column and combining them with word parts from the second column. The word parts in column 1 are the beginnings of words, and the word parts in column 2 are the endings of words. The words the children construct should be written under the appropriate column headings.

All of the vowel letters underlined in blue (those I have italicized) in column 1 represent short vowel sounds. All of the vowel letters underlined in green (those I have bolded) in column 1 represent long vowel sounds. All of the letters in red (those I have underlined) in both columns 1 and 2 do not represent any sound at all.

You will need to help the children understand that when the phoneme /j/ occurs at the end of words, we spell that sound with the letters *ge*. So the *e* at the end of the *ge* helps the reader know that the vowel letter in that word is long and that the *g* represents /j/. Therefore, when we have a *dge* ending, the *d* lets the reader know that the vowel letter in that word is short, and the *ge* lets the reader know that the *g* represents /j/. The *tch* ending serves a similar function. The letter *t* lets the reader know that the vowel letter in the word is short, so it doesn't represent any sound at all, and the *ch* represents /ch/.

Children should be encouraged to say the vowel sound in the beginning word part first, then coarticulate the consonant next to the vowel with the vowel, and if there is another consonant unit in the word, coarticulate that unit with the second consonant and vowel to get the correct pronunciation of the beginning word element. Children should then search the word ending column for suitable endings. Some of the word parts in column 1 represent words by themselves and need no ending.

The dyad groups should be given a reasonable amount of time to make their word lists. At the end of the allotted time, each team should check with a dictionary to make sure all of the words they identified are spelled correctly.

The word parts in this activity can be used to make at least 47 words. I include only a portion of the words here so you can see how a child's paper might look at the conclusion of the activity:

1. Syllables Ending with Vowels	2. Syllables Ending with Consonants	3. Syllables Ending with Consonants + e	4. Vowel Team Syllables
no	badge	bake	bait
pro	box	bone	boat
me	match	make	maid
she	man	made	main
	mob	male	moan
	rat	rake	rain

Chapter 10

Learning to Read and Write Words of More Than One Syllable

The activities presented in this part of the book are designed to help children read and write multisyllabic words. Once again, one of the best ways to help children read and write is to engage them in reading and writing. In addition to children's independent writing discussed earlier, patterned writing activities might also be considered. An example of patterned writing is found in Figure 12.

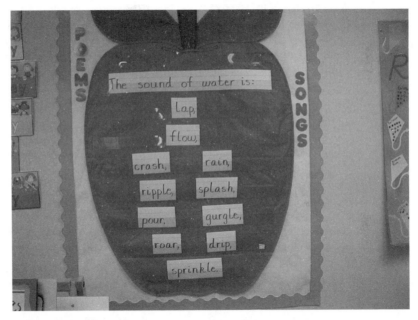

Figure 12
Patterned Writing

One formula for a patterned activity is:

Noun

Two action words (verbs)

Two describing words (adjectives)

Synonym

Examples of children's creations:

Frog
Leaping, Hopping
Green, Ugly
Amphibian

Mouse
Running, Hiding
Small, Cute
Rodent

Other writing patterns, such as the Adjective-Noun-Verb-Adverb pattern, involve alliteration. For example, write the names of some animals: *dogs, cats, pigs, cows.*

Everything else you write must begin with the same sound as the name of the animal. First, write something the animal does: *dogs defend; cats claw; pigs plod; cows climb.* Second, write something describing how the animal does it: *dogs defend dauntlessly; cats claw capriciously; pigs plod passively; cows climb cautiously.* Finally, write a description of the animal. The final product might look something like this:

Defiant dogs defend dauntlessly.

Cunning cats claw capriciously.

Paltry pigs plod passively.

Capable cows climb cautiously.

Animals are interesting.

The variations of patterned writing are legion, and its appeal to children's creativity is enormous. Furthermore, patterned writing also enhances children's vocabulary development as well as their reading and writing.

IMPORTANT PHONICS AND STRUCTURAL ANALYSIS KNOWLEDGE

The keys to reading and writing words of more than one syllable are (1) understanding morphemic units in multisyllabic words; (2) understanding the schwa sound in unaccented syllables of American English speech; (3) understanding how vowel sounds are predicted in written language by syllable and vowel team patterns; and (4) perceiving the syllable boundaries in multisyllabic words.

Morphemes

Morphemes are the smallest unit of meaning in a word. In the word *unable* there are two morphemes: *un* (meaning "not") and *able* (meaning "capable"). Another way of saying that someone is *unable* to walk, is to say that they are *not capable* of walking.

Many multisyllabic words contain more than one morpheme. Word variants contain a root word with an inflectional ending such as *s, es, er, est, ing,* and *ed.* Inflectional endings and root words are morphemes. Word derivatives contain a root word with either a prefix, a suffix, or both. Prefixes and suffixes are also morphemes, or units of meaning. When children recognize morphemes in written words, they can read those words more easily. The more children are knowledgeable about morphemic units, the more they will use that knowledge to write words containing them.

The Schwa Sound

When we pronounce two-syllable words, we usually accent (emphasize) one syllable and do not accent the other. For example, in the word *alone,* the unaccented syllable is *a* and the accented syllable is *lone.* In the word *pilot,* the accented syllable is *pi* and the unaccented syllable is *lot.* In the accented syllable, the vowel represents the sound predicted by the syllable pattern. However, in the unaccented syllable, the vowel represents the schwa sound, /u/. In words of more than two syllables, accented and unaccented syllables are often alternated. For example, in the word *communication,* the first syllable is unaccented, the second is accented, the third is unaccented, the fourth is accented, and the last syllable is unaccented. The schwa sound is the vowel sound we hear in all of the unaccented syllables in that word, and the vowels in the accented syllables are predicted by the syllable pattern. An awareness of the schwa sound helps improve children's spelling development and makes it easier for them to read and write words of more than one syllable.

Syllable Patterns and Vowel Team Patterns

All of the activities designed to help children read and write single-syllable words will also help them read and write words of more than one syllable. For example, the syllable and vowel team patterns you studied in single-syllable words also occur in multisyllabic words. Although these syllable patterns are more difficult for children to perceive in multisyllabic words, they provide some help for word identification.

A knowledge of open syllables (syllables ending with vowels) is particularly important when reading and writing words of more than one syllable. Although not many single-syllable words end in vowel sounds, multisyllabic words often contain a huge number of open syllables. For example, in the words *tiger, notice, fever, open,* and *bacon,* the first syllable in each word is open and accented, and the vowel letter in each syllable represents its long sound.

Perceiving Syllable Boundaries

Knowing when written syllables end and begin is particularly important for reading and writing words of more than one syllable. You learned about how to perceive these boundaries yourself in the first section of the book. Teaching children how to identify syllable boundaries in multisyllabic words helps them perceive the syllable patterns that are often difficult to perceive in such words, and provides an important key for word identification.

MORPHEMIC ANALYSIS

Morphemic Analysis activities are designed to help children become aware of morphemic units in multisyllabic words.

Word Variant Discovery Activity

Write the following words on the chalkboard, setting off the *ed* endings, before beginning this discovery activity:

1	2	3
smell**ed**	wish**ed**	land**ed**
chill**ed**	trick**ed**	act**ed**
yell**ed**	crush**ed**	plant**ed**
burn**ed**	march**ed**	melt**ed**
groan**ed**	wink**ed**	grad**ed**
join**ed**	park**ed**	hunt**ed**
long**ed**	stopp**ed**	shout**ed**
spell**ed**	yank**ed**	grant**ed**
snow**ed**	reach**ed**	mend**ed**

This is a discovery activity in which children can be guided to discover some generalizations regarding the *ed* inflectional ending. The first generalization is: The *ed* ending represents the phoneme /d/ when it follows voiced consonants (column 1), and the phoneme /t/ when it follows voiceless consonants (column 2).

To guide their discovery, do the following:

1. Review the concept of a word variant: A word variant is comprised of a root word and an inflectional ending.

2. Review the concept of voiced and voiceless consonants: The vocal cords are used when producing voiced consonants, but not when producing voiceless consonants.

3. Divide the students into dyad groups.

4. Provide the following directions: "Focus on the words in both columns 1 and 2. The words in those columns all end with the *ed* inflectional ending,

but study them carefully to see how many differences you can find between the words in column 1 and the words in column 2. As you study those differences, consider the consonant letter before the *ed* endings in each word. Is the consonant voiced or voiceless?"

5. Give the student dyads time to make their discoveries. Have a class discussion afterward.

6. Conclude with the following directions: "Write a statement that explains why the *ed* endings in the words in column 1 represent the phoneme /d/, and the *ed* endings in the words in column 2 represent the phoneme /t/." Share the students' statements.

The second generalization is: The *ed* ending is a separate syllable and represents /ud/ when it follows either the letter *t* or the letter *d*. To guide their discovery, do the following:

1. Divide the students into dyad groups.

2. Provide the following directions: "Focus on the words in column 3. The words in that column also end in *ed*. Identify the sound represented by the *ed* in the words. Notice the consonant letters before the *ed* ending in column 3. Then focus on the sounds of *ed* in the other two columns. Try to determine why the *ed* ending in column 3 represents the sound it represents.

3. Give the student dyads time to make their discoveries. Have a class discussion afterward.

4. Conclude with the following directions: "Write a statement that explains why all of the *ed* endings in column 3 represent the sound they represent." Share the students' statements.

Suffix Crossword Puzzles

Some suffixes, such as *tion, sion, tial,* and *ous,* occur so frequently in words that you may want to design instructional activities to help children become better acquainted with them. Crossword puzzles are challenging and interesting to most students, so we will use them as one potential activity.

The suffix *tion, sion,* or *ion* means "the condition" or "act" or "result of being." You may want to analyze the meanings of the following words: *selection, direction, invention, pollution, correction, protection, location, education, vacation, population, application, rejection, connection, celebration, television, division.*

Key to the solution of puzzle 1:

    1 Down: Provide a synonym for the word *eliminate.*

    2 Across: Provide a synonym for the word *attach.*

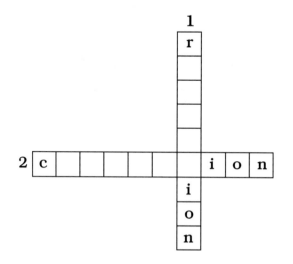

Answers: 1 Down: *reject;* 2 Across: *connect*

    The meaning of the suffix *ous* is "like" or "full of" or "having." You may want to analyze the meanings of the following words: *mysterious, famous, courageous, outrageous, dangerous, adventurous, poisonous, prosperous, vigorous, marvelous, religious, mountainous, continuous, humorous.*

Key to the solution of puzzle 2:

    1 Down: Provide a synonym for the word *bravery.*

    2 Across: Provide a synonym for the word *indignation.*

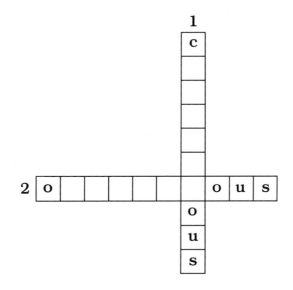

Answers: 1 Down: *courage;* 2 Across: *outrage*

Making Compound Words from Morphemes

Prepare cards for the following morphemes. Make them large enough for all of the children in the classroom to see, put masking tape on the back of each morpheme card, and stick each on the chalkboard.

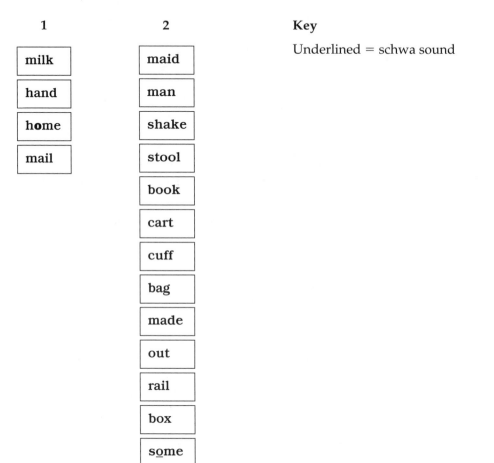

1	2	Key
milk	maid	Underlined = schwa sound
hand	man	
h**o**me	shake	
mail	stool	
	book	
	cart	
	cuff	
	bag	
	made	
	out	
	rail	
	box	
	s<u>o</u>me	

Procedures: Divide the class into dyad groups and distribute pencils and paper to the children in each group.

Instructions to the children: Instruct the children to see how many words their dyad teams can read and write by taking the root words from the first column and combining them with the root words from the second column.

   If children have difficulty reading the root words in the first column, encourage them to first say the vowel sound in the word, then coarticulate the consonant next to the vowel with the vowel, isolate the ending sound, and blend the sounds together to get the correct pronunciation of the word. After the children have iden-tified the words in the first column, they should then search the second column for a suitable ending, or endings.

The dyad groups should be given a reasonable amount of time to make words. At the end of the allotted time, each team should check with a dictionary to make sure all of the words they identified are spelled correctly.

The words the children could construct are *milkmaid, milkman, milkshake, milk-stool, handmaid, handshake, handbook, handcart, handcuff, handbag, handmade, hand-some, handout, handrail, homework, homemade, homesick, mailbox,* and *mailman.*

In order to construct words in this activity, the children need to be knowl-edgeable about both syllable and vowel team patterns. Furthermore, they need to be able to coarticulate phonemes to sound out words. Therefore, it is an effective tool to help reinforce and apply phonics knowledge.

Making Word Variants and Derivatives

Prepare cards for the following morphemes. Make them large enough for all of the children in the classroom to see, put masking tape on the back of each morpheme card, and stick each on the chalkboard.

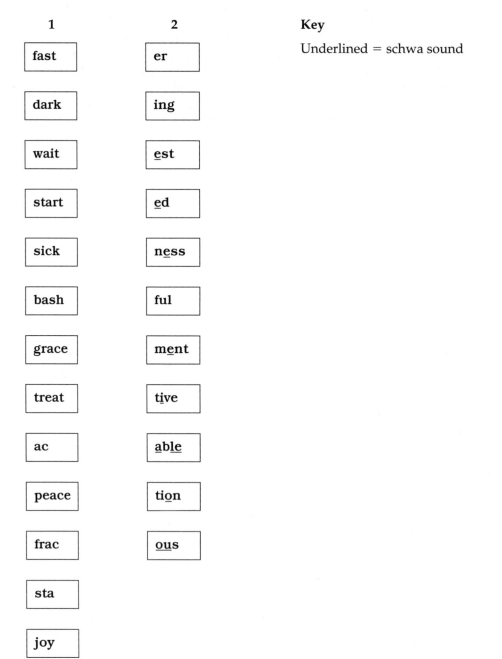

1	2	Key
		Underlined = schwa sound

1

fast

dark

wait

start

sick

bash

grace

treat

ac

peace

frac

sta

joy

2

er

ing

est

ed

ness

ful

ment

tive

able

tion

ous

Procedures: Divide the class into dyad groups and give pencils and paper to the children in each group.

Instructions to the children: Instruct the children to see how many words their dyad teams can read and write by taking the root words from the first column and combining them with the inflectional endings or suffixes from the second column. Help them understand that the underlined vowels in the inflectional endings or suffixes represent the schwa sound. You may need to help the children with the *tion* and *able* suffixes. Explain to them that the *ti* in the *tion* suffix represents /sh/ and the *o* represents the schwa sound. The *tion* suffix is therefore pronounced /shun/. The *le* at the end of multisyllabic words represents the /ul/ sound, and the *a* in the suffix *able* represents the schwa sound; therefore, the *able* suffix is pronounced with two schwa sounds: /u/-/bul/.

The dyad groups should be given a reasonable amount of time to make words. At the end of the allotted time, each team should check with a dictionary to make sure all of the words they identified are spelled correctly.

The words the children could construct are *faster, fastest, fasted, darker, darkest, waiting, waited, starting, started, sickness, bashful, graceful, treatment, active, treatable, peaceable, fraction, station, and joyous.*

This activity could be used many times, with different root words, inflectional endings, and suffixes.

SYLLABICATION AND PHONICS

Phonics is a study of the phoneme/grapheme relationships within a syllable. Therefore, phonics knowledge is not very useful to children when working with multisyllabic words unless they are taught how to perceive the open and closed syllables within those words. Furthermore, children encounter the schwa sound in multisyllabic words that they generally don't encounter in single-syllable words (the words *the* and *a* are the exception).

One way to help children become aware of the separate syllables within multisyllabic words would be to provide them with some reading activities similar to the following:

Ab.sence makes the heart grow fon.der.

Ap.pear.ances are de.cep.tive.

A.pril show.ers bring May flow.ers.

Ne.ces.si.ty is the moth.er of in.ven.tion.

In these familiar sayings, the words are broken into syllables for the children to see, and the vowels representing the schwa sound are underlined. In case you have forgotten, the schwa sound is similar to the /u/ sound you hear at the beginning of the word *up*.

Nursery rhymes and popular songs are also good for this kind of activity:

The bear went o.ver the moun.t<u>ai</u>n,

The bear went o.ver the moun.t<u>ai</u>n,

The bear went o.ver the moun.t<u>ai</u>n,

To see what he could see.

Syllable Riddles

Select several familiar sayings and arrange them as follows:

1. Op___ ___ ___ ___ ___ ___ knocks twice.
   (d<u>o</u>m, sel, ty, tu, n<u>i</u>, por)
2. An ___ ___ a day keeps the ___ ___ away.
   (ap, tor, doc, p<u>le</u>)
3. ___ ___ speak ___ ___ than words.
   (ti<u>o</u>ns, er, loud, Ac)

Task: Organize the syllables to form the words needed to complete the familiar sayings. (Notice that the letters representing the schwa sound are underlined.)

Answers: 1. *Opportunity, seldom*   2. *apple, doctor*   3. *Actions, louder*

Syllable riddles can also be used with nursery rhymes:

Lit.tle Boy Blue

Lit.tle boy blue, come blow your horn;

The sheep's in the ____ ___, the cow's in the corn.

Where is the ____ ____ boy who looks after the sheep?

He's ___ ____ the haystack fast _ ____.

Will you wake him? No, not I;

For if I do, he's sure to cry.

(sleep, <u>a</u>, der, un, t<u>le</u>, lit, ow, mead)

Answers: *meadow, little, under, asleep*

Syllable Crossword Puzzles

This activity is designed to help students become better acquainted with open and closed syllables in multisyllabic words. The activity can be used with multisyllabic words in which the first syllable is open: *April, baby, below, between, basic, became, beyond, climate, clover, crisis, data, driver, even, equal, fable, favor, female, famous, final, Friday, frozen, global, hero, hotel, human, idle, later, lazy, license, local, lotion, meter, music, moment, motion, nation, native, navy, notice, open, over, paper, racer, silence, solar, spider, station, table, tiger, tidy, total, unite, zebra.*

The activity can also be used with multisyllabic words in which the first syllable is closed: *basket, chicken, kitchen, costume, dentist, frozen, rocket, pocket, happen, problem, limit, hundred, market, kitten, jacket, ticket, model, secret, seven, travel, trumpet, tunnel, wagon, address, album, advice, athlete, attic, coffee, except, excite, finish, insect, magic, mascot, mistake, napkin, nonsense, picnic, plastic, punish, selfish, subject.*

Remember that open syllables predict long vowel sounds, while closed syllables predict short vowel sounds. Also remember that the vowel letters in syllables that are unaccented usually represent the schwa sound, unless those vowels are murmur diphthongs.

Puzzle 1 task: Write three open syllables in the blank spaces provided to make three familiar multisyllabic words.

Key to the solution of puzzle 1:

1 Across: A syllable that rhymes with *fly.*

2 Down: A syllable that rhymes with *fly.*

3 Down: A syllable that rhymes with *me.*

Answers: 1. Across: *ti;* 2. Down: *pi;* 3. Down: *fe*

Puzzle 2 task: Write three closed syllables in the blank spaces provided to make three familiar multisyllabic words.

Key to the solution of puzzle 2:

      1 Across: A syllable that rhymes with *ham*.

      2 Down: A syllable that rhymes with *pan*.

      3 Down: A syllable that rhymes with *red*.

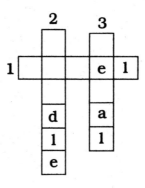

Answers: 1. Across: *cam;* 2. Down: *can;* 3. Down: *ped*

MAKING WORDS WITH SYLLABLES

Prepare cards for the following syllables. Make them large enough for all of the children in the classroom to see, put masking tape on the back of each syllable card, and stick each on the chalkboard.

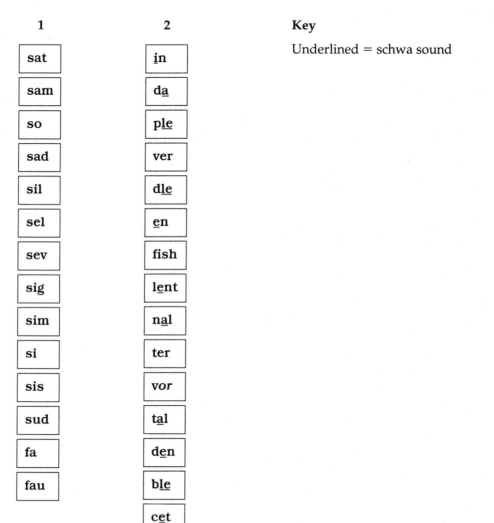

1	2	Key
sat	in	Underlined = schwa sound
sam	d<u>a</u>	
so	p<u>le</u>	
sad	ver	
sil	d<u>le</u>	
sel	<u>e</u>n	
sev	fish	
sig	l<u>e</u>nt	
sim	n<u>a</u>l	
si	ter	
sis	vor	
sud	t<u>a</u>l	
fa	d<u>e</u>n	
fau	b<u>le</u>	
	c<u>e</u>t	

Procedures: Divide the class into dyad groups and give pencils and paper to the children in each group.

Instructions to the children: Instruct the children to see how many words their dyad teams can read and write by taking the syllables from the first column and combining them with the syllables from the second column. The children are to use their knowledge of syllable patterns and vowel team patterns to determine the vowel sounds represented by the vowel letters in the syllables in the first column. The underlined vowels in the syllables in the second column represent the schwa sound.

This activity should help children become aware of the schwa sound in unaccented syllables. Furthermore, the activity should help them gain insights into syllable boundaries, as well as help them apply their knowledge of syllable patterns in determining the vowel sounds in syllables.

The dyad groups should be given a reasonable amount of time to make words. At the end of the allotted time, each team should check with a dictionary to make sure all of the words they identified are spelled correctly.

The words the children could construct are *satin, soda, sample, saddle, silver, selfish, seven, signal, simple, silent, sister, sudden, fatal, favor, fable, faucet.*

After the children have constructed words, they could organize them into the following groups:

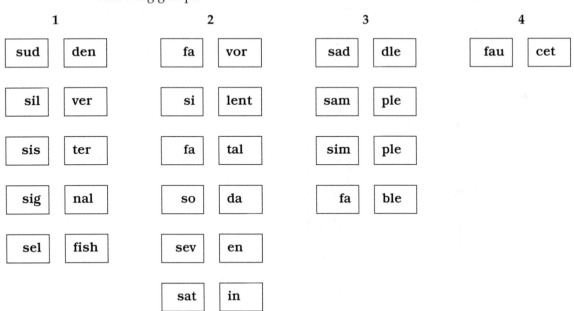

1		2		3		4	
sud	den	fa	vor	sad	dle	fau	cet
sil	ver	si	lent	sam	ple		
sis	ter	fa	tal	sim	ple		
sig	nal	so	da	fa	ble		
sel	fish	sev	en				
		sat	in				

With the words organized into these groups, you can help children discover the basic principles for identifying syllable boundaries that you learned in the first section of the book. **Principle one:** If two consonant units separate "sounding" vowels, the first unit ends after the first consonant unit (group 1). **Principle two:** If only one consonant unit separates "sounding" vowels, the first syllable will often end after the vowel; however, sometimes it ends after the consonant (group 2). **Principle three:** If a word ends in *le*, the last syllable begins with the consonant preceding *le* (group 3). The first syllable in the word *faucet* is accented and contains a vowel team; therefore, the vowel sound in the first syllable is determined by the vowel team pattern, and the vowel sound in the second syllable represents the schwa sound.

This activity may be used many times with different multisyllabic words. It is a very effective activity that helps children learn important concepts regarding multisyllabic words. The activity is challenging for children and provides them with considerable practice applying phonics knowledge for the identification of multisyllabic words.

Answers to Reviews and Self-Evaluation Tests

These reviews let you know how well you have mastered the content presented in this self-instruction program. If you seek to do well, you will realize your goal. Work to achieve 100% on each review. Good luck.

Review 1 **1.** receptive, written **2.** grapheme **3.** translating written words into speech **4.** the smallest unit of sound within a word. **5.** No. A grapheme is the unit of written text that represents a phoneme. Sometimes a grapheme is one letter and sometimes it is more than one letter. **6.** 45 **7.** five **8.** five: a th l e te

Review 2 **1.** *y* and *w* **2.** they begin words or syllables **3.** The letters *c, x,* and *q* have no sounds of their own. Other consonant letters predictably represent the phonemes these letters represent. **4.** *ch, sh, th, wh, ng* **5.** a two-letter grapheme representing one consonant phoneme

Review 3 **1.** lips, tongue, teeth, gums, palate, and vocal cords **2.** voiceless **3.** vibrating our vocal cords **4.** equivalent **5.** /b/ and /p/, /v/ and /f/, /z/ and /s/, /d/ and /t/, /g/ and /k/, /th/ and /th/, /w/ and /hw/, /zh/ and /sh/, /j/ and /ch/ **6.** Consonant phonemes are used in the initial and/or final position of syllables and single-syllable words.

Review 4 **1.** The letter *b* reliably predicts the phoneme /b/ in written words, the letter *d* reliably predicts the phoneme /d/ in written words, and the letter *f* reliably predicts the phoneme /f/ in written words. **2.** *m, t* (examples: *comb, subtle*) **3.** When the grapheme *c* is followed by an *e, i,* or *y*, it represents the phoneme /s/. All other times it represents the phoneme /k/. **4.** /k/ (76% of the time) **5.** /sh/ (examples: *ocean, social*) **6.** Unless *g* is followed by an *e, i,* or *y*, it represents its own sound. When *g* is followed by an *e, i,* or *y*, it usually represents /j/, but not always. However, when *ge* and *dge* occur at the end of words or syllables, they represent /j/. **7.** /g/ (70% of the time) **8.** is silent **9.** represents /g/ **10.** is silent (example: *gnat*), represents /g/ (examples: *guide, guess*)

Review 5   **1.** The graphemes *h, j, k, l,* and *m* reliably predict the phonemes /h/, /j/, /k/, /l/, and /m/, respectively.   **2.** represents a phoneme in the final position of a syllable or word   **3.** appears as the first letter of a word (examples: *honor, honest*), and when it follows the consonants *k, r,* and *g* at the beginning of words (examples: *khaki, rhine, ghost*)   **4.** *sh, th, wh, ch*   **5.** represents a phoneme in the final position of a syllable or word   **6.** is followed by an *n* at the beginning of words (examples: *know, knee*)   **7.** it precedes another consonant within a word or syllable (examples: *chalk, should*)

Review 6   **1.** The graphemes *n, p,* and *r* reliably predict the phonemes /n/, /p/, and /r/, respectively.   **2.** occurs in words more frequently   **3.** *ng* as in *sing, ph* as in *phone*   **4.** the letter *p* occurs at the beginning of words followed by an *s, t,* or *n* (examples: *psalm, ptomaine, pneumonia*)   **5.** at the beginning of words or syllables (examples: *run, already*)   **6.** a part of the vowel   **7.** *u*   **8.** /kw/ (examples: *quit, require*), /k/ (examples: *unique, opaque*)   **9.** /s/   **10.** at the end of words   **11.** /z/ (examples: *dogs, drums*), /s/ (examples: *sits, cups*)   **12.** /z/ (examples: *does, sues, flies, tubes*), /s/ (examples: *ropes, plates, makes*)

Review 7   **1.** *th*   **2.** /shun/ (example: *action*), /chun/ (example: *mention*)   **3.** silent (examples: *debut, listen*)   **4.** very reliable   **5.** it is never found at the end of words without an *e* after it   **6.** *r* (examples: *write, wrist*)   **7.** it follows the vowels *a, e,* or *o* (examples: *lawn, blew, town*)   **8.** /ks/ (example: *fix*), /gz/ (example: *exam*)   **9.** it is not used to begin words or syllables (examples: *myth, dry, rhyme*) and when it is preceded by a vowel (examples: *play, toy*)   **10.** /s/ as in *waltz,* /zh/ as in *azure*   **11.** *s* (example: *hounds*)

Review 8   **1.** *ng*   **2.** When a prefix ending with an *n* occurs before a root word beginning with a *g* (*ingest*), readers might think they see the *ng* digraph. When a *ge* or *gi* grapheme occurs at the ending of a word to represent /j/ and the letter before that ending is *n* (*range, changing*), readers might think they see the *ng* digraph. This situation, however, should not be confused with the situation in which vowel-beginning endings are added to root words ending in the *ng* digraph (*stronger, youngest*)   **3.** /th/, /t̲h̲/   **4.** When *th* is preceded by or follows another consonant letter (*tenth, three*), the *th* represents the voiceless /th/   **5.** /k/ (example: *chemical*), /sh/ (example: *machine*)   **6.** end, 100, short   **7.** The digraph *sh* consistently represents the phoneme /sh/ as in *shoe.*   **8.** The digraph *wh* represents the phoneme /hw/ (*white*) about 90% of the time, and it represents the phoneme /h/ (*whole*) about 10% of the time.   **9.** /ng+k/ (example: *sink*)

Review 9   **1.** Consonant digraphs are two letters representing one phoneme. Consonant blends are two or more consonant letters representing two or more consonant phonemes. The letters comprising consonant digraphs should never be separated when separating syllables or sounding out words because they represent one phoneme. However, the letters representing consonant blends can be separated because each letter represents a separate phoneme.   **2.** Any word containing *thr* or *shr* in the initial position (*three, shrub*), or any word containing *nch* or *ngth* in the final position (*lunch, length*) is acceptable.

Review 10 **1.** The letter *y* represents vowel phonemes by itself, and it is also used with other vowel letters to form vowel digraphs and vowel diphthongs. The letters *w, r,* and *gh* are also used as part of vowel teams (examples: *cow, bird, fight*).   **2.** the same phonemes the letter *i* represents when it occurs in words (examples: *myth, my, rhyme*)   **3.** either /e/ or /i/   **4.** When the letter *r* is preceded by vowel letters, the vowel letters and the *r* become one vowel grapheme (examples: *first, hair, bear, hurt*).

Review 11 **1.** voiceless   **2.** /a/ *at*; /ā/ *ate*; /e/ *edge*; /ē/ *eat*; /i/ *it*; /ī/ *ice*; /o/ *ox*; /ō/ *oat*; /u/ *up*; /ū/ *use*; /o͞o/ *moon*; /o͝o/ *book*; /oi/ *boy*; /ou/ *out*; /ûr/ *first*; /ar/ *car*; /or/ *for*; /âr/ *bear*; /ir/ *year*; /īr/ *fire*

Review 12 **1.** macron   **2.** the VCe pattern (examples: *bone, wine*) and the open syllable pattern (examples: *no, we*)   **3.** short vowel sounds   **4.** *e, ve*

Review 13 **1.** breve   **2.** short, long   **3.** The closed syllable pattern (*can, camp*) predicts that a single vowel grapheme will represent the short vowel phoneme. Closed syllables end in consonant phonemes.   **4.** are not (Murmur diphthongs end in vowel phonemes.)   **5.** *ost, old, oll, olt, ind, ild*   **6.** phonemes in the same way the letter *i* represents them. In closed syllables it represents the short sound of *i* (*myth*), and in VCe and open syllables it represents the long sound of *i* (*rhyme, my*).

Review 14 **1.** a vowel and some other letter representing one vowel phoneme   **2.** a vowel team syllable   **3.** murmur diphthong   **4.** /ûr/   **5.** *oi* (*coin*), *oy* (*boy*), *ou* (*out*), *ow* (*cow*)   **6.** *oi, oy, ou, ow*   **7.** /ō/(*show*), diphthong /ou/ (*how*)   **8.** The *ou* vowel team represents the /ou/ diphthong phoneme only about 60% of the time. It represents /u/ (*country*) about 18% of the time. It represents /ō/ (*soul*) about 10% of the time, and the remaining 12% of the time it represents /o͞o/ (*group*), /o/ (*sought*), and /o͝o/ (*should*).   **9.** two letters representing one vowel phoneme   **10.** *ai, ay, ee,* and *oa*   **11.** /ē/ (*meat*), /e/ (*bread*)   **12.** /o/ (*saw* and *sauce*)   **13.** /o͞o/ (*moon*), /o͝o/ (*book*)   **14.** /o͞o/ (*new, due*), /yo͞o/ (*few, cue*)   **15.** The digraph *ey* represents /ē/ only 70% of the time, and it represents /ā/ about 30% of the time. The digraph *ie* represents /ē/ (*piece*) only about 65% of the time, it represents /ī/ (*pie*) about 26% of the time, and it represents /e/ (*friend*) about 9% of the time. The digraph *ui* represents /o͞o/ (*fruit*) only 67% of the time, and it represents /i/ (*build*) about 33% of the time. The digraph *ei* is not too reliable. When *ei* and *eigh* are considered together, they represent /ā/ about 52% of the time (*vein, weigh*). About 32% of the time, *ei* represents /ē/ (*seize*), and the rest of the time it represents other phonemes (*heifer*, for example).

Review 15   1. are not   2. *sh, ine*   3. the onset   4. blends, digraphs   5. no
6. vowel   7. yes   8. they all contain one vowel sound   9. closed, VCe, vowel team

Review 16   1. A syllable is the smallest part of the word containing one vowel sound. It is the smallest unit of pronunciation.   2. the number of syllables in the word   3. we can feel the vibration of our vocal cords as we say syllables   4. We study syllabication so we can help young readers find the syllable patterns in multisyllabic words they don't recognize so they can use their phonics knowledge to identify them.   5. When we stress or emphasize a syllable in a multisyllabic word, that syllable is said to be accented. The phoneme represented by the vowel grapheme in an accented syllable is predicted by its syllable pattern. When we don't accent a syllable, the vowel in that syllable often represents the /u/ or schwa sound. However, the schwa sound is not used when unaccented syllables end in *c, y, ge,* or a murmur diphthong. Words of more than three syllables can have two accents—a primary accent and a secondary accent. These words generally follow the alternating principle; that is, if one syllable is accented, the next one will be unaccented, and so on.   6. /ī/ (*deny*), /ē/ (*baby*)   7. The accent usually falls on or within the first word of a compound word.   8. The accent usually falls on the root word.   9. In two-syllable words the accent is usually placed on the first syllable unless the word begins with a prefix.   10. The *ed* inflectional ending is a syllable when it is preceded by a *t* or a *d*.   11. In most multisyllabic words ending in *tion, sion, ic,* and *sive,* the primary accent falls on the syllable preceding these endings.   12. In most multisyllabic words ending in *ary, ist, ize, ism, fy, tude, y, ate,* and *tory,* the primary accent falls on the syllable before the syllable preceding these endings.   13. In most multisyllabic words ending in *al, an, ent/ant, ous, ar, ence/ance, able/ible, age, tive,* and *ency/ancy,* the primary accent falls on the syllable before the syllable preceding these endings *if* there is only one consonant before the suffix. If there are two consonants, the primary accent falls on the syllable preceding the ending.

Review 17   1. We begin the task of locating syllable boundaries by determining which vowel letters in a word represent vowel sounds.   2. We must know that vowel teams represent one phoneme; the *e* vowel in VCe syllables is silent; the *e* in *dge* and *ge* graphemes at the end of words is silent; the letter *y* represents a vowel phoneme when it isn't used to begin words or syllables; *le* at the end of multisyllabic words represents the syllable /ul/; the letters *ci* and *ti* when followed by vowels (*facial, direction*) represent vowel phonemes; and when the letters *gi* and *ge* are followed by vowels (*legion, pigeon*), those letters represent the phoneme /j/.   3. We look at the number of consonant units between the vowels representing phonemes. There will be either one or two consonant units. If there are two or more consonant units between vowels representing phonemes, the first syllable ends after the first consonant unit. If there is one consonant unit between vowels representing phonemes, divide the syllable after the first vowel and pronounce the word. If it doesn't make sense, divide the syllable after the consonant unit.

Answers to the Self-Evaluation Pretest

1. c	**2.** c	**3.** d	**4.** d	**5.** e	**6.** e	**7.** b	**8.** e	**9.** e	**10.** e
11. a	**12.** a	**13.** b	**14.** b	**15.** c	**16.** b	**17.** b	**18.** e	**19.** b	**20.** e
21. b	**22.** b	**23.** e	**24.** e	**25.** c	**26.** a	**27.** d	**28.** e	**29.** d	**30.** d
31. c	**32.** d	**33.** e	**34.** c	**35.** b	**36.** b	**37.** b	**38.** d	**39.** c	**40.** a
41. d	**42.** c	**43.** d*	**44.** d*	**45.** d*	**46.** a*	**47.** b	**48.** d	**49.** c	**50.** b

*Explanations of certain answers:

43. The grapheme *ti* represents /ch/ (*atten<u>ti</u>on*) as does the grapheme <u>ch</u> in the word <u>ch</u>in. The grapheme *ti* also represents /sh/ (*apprecia<u>ti</u>on*) just as the graphemes *sh* and *s* do in the words <u>sh</u>op and <u>s</u>ure.

44. The grapheme *ci* represents /sh/ (*fa<u>ci</u>al*) just as the graphemes *sh* and *s* do in the words <u>sh</u>oot and <u>s</u>ugar. The grapheme *ci* also represents /si/ (*<u>ci</u>ty*) just as the grapheme *si* does in the word <u>si</u>t.

45. The grapheme *ge* represents /ge/ (*<u>ge</u>t*) just as the grapheme *gue* represents that phoneme in the word <u>gue</u>st. The grapheme *ge* also represents /je/ (*<u>ge</u>m*) just as the grapheme *je* does in the word <u>je</u>t. The grapheme *ge* also represents /j/ (*ra<u>ge</u>*) just as the grapheme *di* does in the word sol<u>di</u>er.

46. The grapheme *ce* represents /s/ (*fen<u>ce</u>*) just as the grapheme *s* represents that sound in the word <u>s</u>ign.

Answers to the Self-Evaluation Posttest

1. e	**2.** c	**3.** c	**4.** c	**5.** d	**6.** d	**7.** e	**8.** e	**9.** b	**10.** e
11. a	**12.** a	**13.** b	**14.** a	**15.** e	**16.** b	**17.** b	**18.** e	**19.** b	**20.** d
21. b	**22.** b	**23.** e	**24.** e	**25.** c	**26.** a	**27.** d	**28.** e	**29.** d	**30.** b
31. c	**32.** d	**33.** e	**34.** b	**35.** c	**36.** b	**37.** c	**38.** d	**39.** e	**40.** a
41. d	**42.** e	**43.** d*	**44.** d*	**45.** d*	**46.** a*	**47.** b	**48.** c	**49.** c	**50.** b

*Explanations of certain answers:

43. The grapheme *ti* represents /ch/ (*men<u>ti</u>on*) as does the grapheme *ch* in the word <u>ch</u>oose. The grapheme *ti* also represents /sh/ (*no<u>ti</u>on*) just as the graphemes *sh* and *ch* do in the words wi<u>sh</u> and ma<u>ch</u>ine.

44. The grapheme *ci* represents /sh/ (*ra<u>ci</u>al*) just as the graphemes *sh* and *si* do in the words <u>sh</u>arp and ses<u>si</u>on. The grapheme *ci* also represents /si/ (*<u>ci</u>nder*) just as the grapheme *si* does in the word <u>si</u>p.

45. The grapheme *ge* represents /ge/ (*<u>ge</u>t*) just as the grapheme *gue* represents that phoneme in the word <u>gue</u>ss. The grapheme *ge* also represents /je/ (*<u>ge</u>ntle*) just as the grapheme *je* does in the word <u>je</u>llo. The grapheme *ge* also represents /j/ (*hu<u>ge</u>*) just as the grapheme *j* does in the word <u>j</u>ump.

46. The grapheme *ce* represents /s/ (*dan<u>ce</u>*) just as the grapheme *s* represents that sound in the word <u>s</u>ingle.

Appendix ▬▬▬▬▬▬▬▬▬▬

COMMON RIME WORD LIST

ab	cab, crab, dab, jab, scab, stab
ace	ace, brace, face, trace, space, race, place, lace, grace
ack	rack, pack, quack, lack, jack, crack, back, black, shack, smack, snack, stack, tack, track
ad	sad, pad, mad, lad, had, fad, dad, bad, glad
ade	fade, made, wade, blade, shade, spade, trade
ag	bag, gag, rag, sag, tag, wag, drag, flag, snag
age	age, cage, page, stage, sage
aid	aid, paid, laid, maid, braid
ail	ail, fail, hail, jail, mail, nail, pail, rail, sail, tail, wail, frail, quail, snail, trail
ain	gain, lain, main, pain, rain, brain, chain, drain, grain, plain, sprain, stain, train
aint	faint, paint, saint, quaint
air	air, fair, pair, hair, chair, stair
ake	cake, rake, bake, fake, lake, make, sake, take, wake, quake, brake, flake, shake, snake, stake
ale	ale, tale, sale, pale, male, bale, gale, scale, stale, whale
all	ball, wall, tall, hall, fall, call, small, stall
ame	came, dame, game, lame, name, same, tame, blame, flame, shame
amp	camp, damp, lamp, ramp, clamp, cramp, stamp, tramp
an	an, can, fan, man, pan, ran, tan, bran, plan, span, than
and	and, band, hand, land, sand, stand, brand, grand
ank	bank, sank, tank, blank, crank, drank, frank, plank, spank, thank
ap	cap, lap, map, nap, sap, tap, rap, chap, clap, gap, scrap, wrap, trap, snap
ar	bar, car, far, jar, mar, tar, scar, star
ard	card, hard, lard, yard, guard
are	care, dare, fare, bare, glare, scare, share, snare, square, stare
ark	ark, dark, bark, lark, mark, park, spark, shark

art	art, cart, part, tart, chart, smart, start
ash	ash, rash, sash, mash, hash, gash, dash, cash, clash, crash, flash, smash, splash, trash
ass	pass, lass, mass, brass, class, glass
ast	cast, fast, last, past, mast, blast
aste	haste, paste, taste, waste, baste
at	at, bat, cat, fat, hat, mat, pat, rat, sat, vat, chat, flat, that
atch	catch, hatch, latch, patch, batch, scratch, snatch
ate	ate, date, gate, hate, late, mate, rate, plate, skate, slate, state
ave	cave, gave, pave, rave, save, wave, brave, grave, shave
aw	jaw, law, paw, raw, caw, taw, claw, draw, flaw, gnaw, squaw, straw, thaw
ay	day, gay, hay, jay, lay, may, pay, ray, say, bay, bray, clay, gray, play, spray, stay, tray
ea	pea, sea, tea, flea
each	beach, each, reach, teach, bleach, preach
ead	dead, head, lead, read, thread, bread
eal	heal, meal, seal, veal, deal, squeal, steal
eam	beam, team, dream, gleam, scream, steam, stream
ean	bean, mean, wean, lean, clean
eap	heap, leap, reap, cheap
ear	ear, dear, fear, hear, near, rear, clear, smear, spear
eat	eat, beat, heat, meat, neat, seat, peat, cheat, treat, wheat
eck	deck, neck, peck, check, speck, wreck
ed	bed, fed, led, wed, shed, sled
ee	bee, see, free, tree, knee, three
eed	feed, need, seed, weed, deed, bleed, speed, tweed
eek	peek, seek, week, meek, cheek, creek
eel	eel, feel, heel, peel, reel, steel, wheel, kneel
een	seen, keen, green, queen, screen
eep	deep, keep, peep, weep, creep, sheep, sleep, sweep, steep
eer	beer, deer, steer, cheer
eet	beet, feet, meet, sleet, sheet
eeze	sneeze, freeze, breeze, squeeze, wheeze
ell	bell, cell, fell, sell, tell, well, yell, shell, smell, spell, swell
em	gem, hem, them, stem
en	hen, men, den, then, when, wren

end	end, bend, lend, mend, send, tend, blend, spend
ent	bent, dent, cent, lent, sent, vent, tent, spent, went
ept	wept, kept, crept, slept, swept
ess	mess, less, bless, chess, dress, guess, press
est	west, vest, test, rest, pest, nest, best, chest, guest
et	bet, get, yet, wet, set, pet, net, met, jet
ew	new, chew, flew, grew, knew, stew (few, mew, pew)
ice	ice, dice, lice, nice, rice, price, slice, spice, twice
ick	kick, lick, nick, pick, sick, wick, brick, chick, click, quick, stick, thick, trick
id	did, bid, hid, kid, lid, rid, skid, slid
ide	hide, ride, side, tide, wide, bride, glide, guide, pride, slide
ief	thief, grief, chief, brief
ife	life, wife, fife, knife
ift	gift, lift, sift, drift, swift
ig	wig, pig, fig, dig, big, twig
ight	night, might, light, fight, bright, flight, fright, knight
ike	hike, like, pike, spike, strike
ild	child, mild, wild
ill	ill, bill, dill, fill, hill, kill, mill, will, chill, drill, grill, skill, spill, still, thrill
im	him, dim, rim, skim, slim, trim
ime	dime, lime, time, chime, crime, grime, prime
in	in, bin, fin, gin, pin, sin, tin, win, chin, grin, skin, spin, thin, twin
ind	bind, find, kind, mind, hind, wind, grind
ine	dine, fine, line, mine, nine, pine, vine, wine, shine, spine, swine, twine, whine
ing	king, ding, ping, ring, sing, wing, bring, cling, sling, spring, sting, string, swing, thing, wring
ink	ink, link, pink, sink, wink, blink, brink, drink, kink, shrink, stink, think
int	hint, lint, mint, tint, flint, glint, print, splint, squint
ip	dip, hip, lip, nip, rip, sip, tip, chip, clip, drip, flip, grip, ship, skip, slip, snip, strip, trip, whip
ipe	wipe, ripe, pipe, snipe, stripe, swipe
ire	fire, wire, tire, hire
it	it, bit, fit, hit, kit, lit, mit, pit, sit, wit, grit, quit, slit, spit, knit, split
ite	bite, kite, spite, white, write, site
ive	dive, five, hive, live, strive, thrive

oat　oat, boat, coat, goat, float, gloat, throat

ob　sob, rob, mob, job, knob, cob

ock　dock, lock, rock, sock, block, clock, crock, flock, frock, knock, shock, smock, stock

og　dog, fog, hog, log, bog, cog, frog

oil　oil, boil, coil, foil, soil, toil, broil, spoil

oke　joke, poke, broke, choke, coke, smoke, spoke, stroke

old　cold, bold, fold, gold, hold, mold, sold, told

ook　book, hook, look, took, brook, crook, shook

ool　cool, fool, pool, spool, tool, school, drool

oom　boom, room, loom, broom, gloom, bloom, groom

oon　moon, noon, soon, croon, spoon

oop　hoop, loop, coop, droop, scoop, stoop, swoop, troop

oot　boot, hoot, loot, shoot, toot

op　hop, mop, pop, top, chop, crop, drop, flop, prop, shop, slop, stop

ore　tore, wore, bore, core, fore, score, shore, snore, sore, store, swore

orn　born, corn, horn, morn, scorn, thorn

ort　sort, fort, port, short, sport

ose　nose, rose, pose, those, chose, close

oss　boss, loss, moss, toss, cross

ot　cot, dot, got, hot, jot, lot, not, pot, rot, tot, blot, knot, plot, shot, trot

ouch　ouch, couch, pouch, slouch, crouch

ought　ought, bought, brought, fought, sought, thought, wrought

ound　bound, found, ground, hound, mound, pound, round, sound, wound

out　out, pout, scout, snout, spout, stout, trout

ow　bow, cow, how, mow, row, sow, vow, brow, plow, prow, scow

ow　blow, bow, crow, flow, glow, grow, know, low, mow, row, show, slow, snow, stow, throw

owl　owl, fowl, growl, howl, prowl, scowl

own　brown, clown, crown, down, drown, frown, town, gown

own　own, blown, flown, grown, mown, known, shown, sown

ox　ox, fox, box

oy　boy, coy, joy, toy

ub　cub, hub, tub, club, grub, scrub, shrub, stub

uck　duck, luck, puck, suck, tuck, chuck, cluck, stuck, shuck, truck

udge　budge, grudge, judge, nudge, smudge

uff   cuff, puff, bluff, gruff, snuff, stuff

ug   bug, dug, hug, jug, mug, rug, tug, drug, plug, smug, snug

um   gum, hum, rum, sum, drum, plum, scum, slum, strum

umb crumb, dumb, numb, plumb, thumb

ump bump, dump, hump, jump, lump, pump, rump, plump, slump, stump, thump, trump

un   bun, fun, gun, nun, pun, run, sun, spun, stun

unch bunch, hunch, lunch, munch, punch, crunch, scrunch

ung hung, lung, rung, sung, clung, flung, slung, sprung, strung, swung, stung

unk bunk, hunk, junk, punk, sunk, chunk, drunk, shrunk, skunk, spunk, trunk

unt bunt, hunt, punt, runt, stunt, grunt, blunt

up   up, cup, pup, sup

ush hush, gush, mush, rush, blush, brush, crush, flush, plush, slush, thrush

ust dust, bust, just, must, rust, trust, crust

ut   but, hut, nut, jut, rut, shut, smut

References

Adams, M. J. (1990). *Beginning to read: Thinking and learning about print.* Cambridge, MA: MIT Press.

Anderson, R. C., Hiebert, E. H., Scott, J. A., & Wilkinson, I. A. G. (1985). *Becoming a nation of readers.* Washington, DC: National Institute of Education.

Backman, J., Bruck, M., Herbert, M., & Seidenberg, M. S. (1984). Acquisition and use of spelling-sound correspondences in reading. *Journal of Experimental Child Psychology, 38,* 114–133.

Ball, E. W., & Blachman, B. A. (1991). Does phoneme segmentation training in kindergarten make a difference in early word recognition and developmental spelling? *Reading Research Quarterly, 26,* 49–66.

Barr, R. C. (1972). The influence of instructional conditions on word recognition errors. *Reading Research Quarterly, 7,* 509–529.

Beers, J., & Henderson, E. (1977). A study of developing orthographic concepts among first graders. *Research in Teaching English, 11,* 133–148.

Blachman, B. (1983). Are we assessing the linguistic factors critical in early reading? *Annals of Dyslexia, 33,* 91–109.

Blachman, B. (1984). Language analysis skills and early reading acquisition. In G. Wallach & K. Butler (Eds.), *Language learning disabilities in school-age children* (pp. 271–287). Baltimore: Williams and Wilkins.

Blachman, B. (1989). Phonological awareness and word recognition: Assessment and intervention. In A. G. Kamhi & H. W. Catts (Eds.), *Reading disabilities: A developmental language perspective* (pp. 133–158). Boston: College-Hill Press.

Blachman, B., & James, S. (1985). Metalinguistic abilities and reading achievement in first-grade children. In J. Niles & R. Lalik (Eds.), *Issues in literacy: A research perspective, Thirty-fourth yearbook of the Conference.*

Bradley, L., & Bryant , P. E. (1983). Categorizing sounds and learning to read: A causal connection. *Nature, 30,* 419–421.

Bradley, L., & Bryant, P. E. (1985). *Rhyme and reason in reading and spelling.* Ann Arbor: University of Michigan Press.

Calfee, R. C., Lindamood, P., & Lindamood, C. (1973). Acoustic-phonetic skill and reading—kindergarten through twelfth grade. *Journal of Educational Psychology, 64,* 293–298.

Chall, J. S. (1967). *Learning to read: The great debate.* New York: McGraw-Hill.

Chall, J. S. (1983). *Learning to read: The great debate* (2nd ed.). New York: McGraw-Hill.

Chall, J. S. (1996). *Learning to read: The great debate* (3rd ed.). New York: McGraw-Hill.

Cohen, A. S. (1974–1975). Oral reading errors of first-grade children taught by a code-emphasis approach. *Reading Research Quarterly, 10,* 616–650.

Ehri, L., & Wilce, L. (1983). Development of word identification speed in skilled and less skilled beginning readers. *Journal of Educational Psychology, 75,* 3–18.

Ehri, L., & Wilce, L. (1985). Movement into reading: Is the first stage of printed word learning visual or phonetic? *Reading Research Quarterly, 20,* 163–179.

Eldredge, J. L. (1990). Increasing the performance of poor readers in the third grade with a group-assisted strategy.

Journal of Educational Research, 84, 69–77.

Eldredge, J. L. (1991). An experiment with a modified whole language approach in first grade classrooms. *Reading Research and Instruction, 30,* 21–38.

Eldredge, J. L. (1995). *Teaching decoding in holistic classrooms.* Upper Saddle River, NJ: Merrill/Prentice Hall.

Eldredge, J. L., & Baird, J. E. (1996). Phonemic awareness training works better than whole language instruction for teaching first graders how to write. *Reading Research and Instruction, 35,* 193–208.

Eldredge, J. L., Quinn, D. W., & Butterfield, D. D. (1990). Causal relationships between phonics, reading comprehension, and vocabulary achievement in the second grade. *Journal of Educational Research, 83,* 201–214.

Eldredge, J. L., Reutzel, D. R., & Hollingsworth, P. M. (1996). Comparing the effectiveness of two oral reading practices: Round robin reading and the shared book experience. *Journal of Literacy Research, 28,* 201–225.

Fox, B., & Routh, D. K. (1975). Analyzing spoken language into words, syllables and phonemes: A developmental study. *Journal of Psycholinguistic Research, 4,* 331–342.

Fox, B., & Routh, D. K. (1980). Phonemic analysis and severe reading disability in children. *Journal of Psycholinguistic Research, 9,* 115–119.

Fox, B., & Routh, D. K. (1984). Phonemic analysis and synthesis as word attack skills: Revisited. *Journal of Educational Psychology, 76,* 1059–1061.

Gentry, J. R., & Gillet, J. W. (1993). *Teaching kids to spell.* Portsmouth, NH: Heineman.

Golinkoff, R. M. (1978). Phonemic awareness skills and reading achievement. In F. B. Murray & J. H. Pikulski (Eds.), *The acquisition of reading: Cognitive, linguistic, and perceptual prerequisites*

(pp. 23–41). Baltimore: University Park Press.

Helfgott, J. (1976). Phoneme segmentation and blending skills of kindergarten children: Implications for beginning reading acquisition. *Contemporary Educational Psychology, 1,* 157–169.

Hoover, W., & Gough, P. B. (1990). The simple view of reading. *Reading and Writing: An Interdisciplinary Journal, 2,* 127–160.

Johnson, D. D., & Bauman, J. F. (1984). Word identification. In P. D. Pearson (Ed.), *Handbook of reading research.* New York: Longman.

Jorm, A. F., Share, D. L., Maclean, R., & Matthews, R. (1984). Phonological recoding skills and learning to read: A longitudinal study. *Applied Psycholinguistics, 5,* 201–207.

Juel, C. (1988). Learning to read and write: A longitudinal study of 54 children from first through fourth grades. *Journal of Educational Psychology, 80,* 437–447.

Juel, C., Griffith, P., & Gough, P. B. (1986). Acquisition of literacy: A longitudinal study of children in first and second grade. *Journal of Educational Psychology, 78,* 243–255.

LaBerge, D., & Samuels, S. J. (1974). Toward a theory of automatic information processing in reading. *Cognitive Psychology, 6,* 293–323.

Leong, C. K., & Haines, C. F. (1978). Beginning readers' awareness of words and sentences. *Journal of Reading Behavior, 10,* 393–407.

Lesgold, A. M., Resnick, L. B., & Hammond, K. (1985). Learning to read: A longitudinal study of word skill development in two curricula. In G. E. Mackinnon & T. G. Waller (Eds.), *Reading research: Advances in theory and practice* (Vol. 4, pp. 107–138). San Diego, CA: Academic Press.

Liberman, I. Y. (1973). Segmentation of the spoken word and reading acquisition. *Bulletin of the Orton Society, 23,* 65–67.

Liberman, I. Y., & Shankweiler, D. (1979). Speech, the alphabet, and teaching to read. In L. Resnick & P. Weaver (Eds.), *Theory and practice of early reading* (Vol. 2). Hillsdale, NJ: Erlbaum.

Liberman, I. Y., Shankweiler, S. , Fischer, F. W., & Carter, B. (1974). Explicit syllable and phoneme segmentation in the young child. *Journal of Experimental Child Psychology, 18*, 201–212.

Lomax, R. G., & McGee, L. M. (1987). Young children's concepts about print and reading: Toward a model of word reading acquisition. *Reading Research Quarterly, 22*, 237–256.

Lundberg, I., Frost, J., & Peterson, O. (1988). Effects of an extensive program for stimulating phonological awareness in preshool children. *Reading Research Quarterly, 23*, 263–284.

Lundberg, I., Olofsson, A., & Wall, S. (1980). Reading and spelling skill in the first school years predicted from phonemic awareness skills in kindergarten. *Scandinavian Journal of Psychology, 21*, 159–173.

Manis, F. R., & Morrison, F. J. (1985). Reading disability: A deficit in rule learning? In L. S. Siegel & F. J. Morrison (Eds.), *Cognitive development in atypical children* (pp. 1–26). New York: Springer-Verlag.

Mann, V. (1984). Longitudinal prediction and prevention of early reading difficulty. *Annals of Dyslexia, 34*, 117–136.

Mann, V. A., & Liberman, I. Y. (1984). Phonological awareness and verbal short-term memory: Can they presage early reading problems? *Journal of Learning Disabilities, 17*, 592–599.

McNeill, D. (1968). Production and perception: The view from language. *Ontario Journal of Educational Research, 10*, 181–185.

Morais, J. (1991). Constraints on the development of phonemic awareness. In S. A. Brady & D. P. Shankweiler (Eds.), *Phonological processes in literacy* (pp. 5–27). Hillsdale, NJ: Erlbaum.

Morais, J., Cary, L., Alegria, J., & Bertelson, P. (1979). Does awareness of speech as a sequence of phonemes arise spontaneously? *Cognition, 7*, 323–331.

Morris, D. (1983). Concept of word and phoneme awareness in the beginning reader. *Research in the Teaching of Reading, 17*, 359–373.

Nathan, R. G., & Stanovich, K. E. (1991). The causes and consequences of differences in reading fluency. *Theory Into Practice, 30*, 176–184.

National Reading Panel. (2000). *Teaching children to read: An evidence-based assessment of the scientific research literature on reading and its implications for reading instruction.* Washington, DC: National Institute of Child Health and Human Development.

Olofsson, A., & Lundberg, I. (1985). Evaluation of long term effects of phonemic awareness training in kindergarten: Illustrations of some methodological problems in evaluation research. *Scandinavian Journal of Psychology, 26*, 21–34.

Pearson, P. D. (2000). Reading in the 20th century. In T. Good (Ed.), *American education: Yesterday, today, and tomorrow. Yearbook of the National Society for the Study of Education* (pp. 152–208). Chicago: University of Chicago Press.

Perfetti, C. A. (1985). *Reading ability.* New York: Oxford University Press.

Perfetti, C. A. (1986). Cognitive and linguistic components of reading ability. In B. R. Foorman & A. W. Siegel (Eds.), *Acquisition of reading skills: Cultural constraints and cognitive universals* (pp. 1–40). Hillsdale, NJ: Erlbaum.

Perfetti, C. A., & Lesgold, A. M. (1979). Coding and comprehension in skilled reading and implications for reading instruction. In L. B. Resnick & P. Weaver (Eds.), *Theory and practice in early reading* (Vol. 1). Hillsdale, NJ: Erlbaum.

Rayner, K., Foorman, B. R., Perfetti, C. A., Pesetsky, D., & Seidenberg, M. S. (2001). How psychological science informs the teaching of reading. *Psychological Science in the Public Interest, 2*, 31–74.

Rayner, K., Foorman, B. R., Perfetti, C. A., Pesetsky, D., & Seidenberg, M. S. (2002). How should reading be taught? *Scientific American, 286,* 85–91.

Read, C. (1971). Pre-school children's knowledge of English phonology. *Harvard Educational Review, 41,* 1–34.

Read, C., Zhang, Y., Nie, H., & Ding, B. (1986). The ability to manipulate speech sounds depends on knowing alphabetic writing. *Cognition, 24,* 31–44.

Rohl, M., & Tunmer, W. E. (1988). Phonemic segmentation skill and spelling acquisition. *Applied Psycholinguistics, 9,* 335–350.

Rozin, P., & Gleitman, L. (1977). The structure and acquisition of reading II: The reading process and the acquisition of the alphabetic principle. In A. Reber & D. Scarborough (Eds.), *Toward a psychology of reading* (pp. 55–141). Hillsdale, NJ: Erlbaum.

Share, D. J., Jorm, A. F., Maclean, R., & Mathews, R. (1984). Sources of individual differences in reading achievement. *Journal of Educational Psychology, 76,* 466–477.

Snow, C. E., Burns, M. S., & Griffin, P. (Eds.). (1998). *Preventing reading difficulties in young children.* Washington, DC: National Academy Press.

Snowling, M. (1980). The development of grapheme-phoneme correspondences in normal and dyslexic readers. *Journal of Experimental Child Psychology, 29,* 294–305.

Snowling, M. (1981). Phonemic deficits in developmental dyslexia. *Psychological Research, 43,* 219–234.

Stanovich, K. E. (1985). Explaining the variance in reading ability in terms of psychological processes: What have we learned? *Annals of Dyslexia, 35,* 67–96.

Stanovich, K. E., Cunningham, A. E., & Cramer, B. B. (1984). Assessing phonological awareness in kindergarten children: Issues of task comparability.

Journal of Experimental Child Psychology, 38, 175–190.

Stanovich, K. E., Cunningham, A. E., & Freeman, D. J. (1984). Intelligence, cognitive skills and early reading progress. *Reading Research Quarterly, 19,* 278–303.

Tangel, D. M., & Blachman, B. A. (1992). Effect of phoneme awareness instruction on kindergarten children's invented spelling. *Journal of Reading Behavior, 24,* 233–261.

Thompson, G. B. (1986). When nonsense is better than sense: Non-lexical errors to word reading tests. *British Journal of Educational Psychology, 56,* 216–219.

Tunmer, W. E. (1989). The role of language-related factors in reading disability. In D. Shankweiler & I. Y. Liberman (Eds.), *Phonology and reading disability: Solving the reading puzzle* (pp. 91–131). Ann Arbor: University of Michigan Press.

Tunmer, W. E., Herriman, M. L., & Nesdale, A. R. (1988). Metalinguistic abilities and beginning reading. *Reading Research Quarterly, 23,* 134–158.

Tunmer, W. E., & Nesdale, A. R. (1985). Phonemic segmentation skill and beginning reading. *Journal of Educational Psychology, 77,* 417–427.

Vellutino, F. R., & Scanlon, D. M. (1984). Converging perspectives in the study of the reading process: Reactions to the papers presented by Morrison, Siegel and Ryan, and Stanovich. *Remedial and Special Education, 5,* 39–44.

Vellutino, F. R., & Scanlon, D. M. (1987). Phonological coding, phonological awareness, and reading ability: Evidence from a longitudinal and experimental study. *Merrill-Palmer Quarterly, 33,* 321–363.

Wagner, R. (1986). Phonological processing abilities and reading: Implications for disabled readers. *Journal of Learning Disabilities, 19,* 623–630.

Wagner, R., & Torgesen, J. (1987). The nature of phonological processing and its causal role in the acquisition of reading skills. *Psychological Bulletin, 101,* 192–212.

Williams, J. (1986). The role of phonemic analysis in reading. In J. Torgesen & B. Wong (Eds.), *Psychological and educational perspectives on learning disabilities* (pp. 399–416). Orlando, FL: Academic Press.

Index

Accent, 102–104, 106
Alphabet books, 169–170
Alphabet sounds, 131–132, 165

Balanced literacy programs, 123
Beginning consonants, 58, 155–156
Blends
  consonant, 55–59, 128, 191–194
  discovery activity, 190
  onsets and rimes and, 92
Books, 130–134, 169–170
Breve, 74

Code, defined, 13
Compound words, 206–207
Consonants, 21–59
  b, 31
  blends, 55–59, 92, 190–194
  c, 22, 32–33
  ch, 52–53
  ci, 109
  d, 33
  digraphs, 24, 35, 50–55, 93, 128, 187–190
  f, 33
  g, 33–36
  ge, 109
  gh, 54
  gi, 109
  graphemes and, 21–22
  h, 37
  j, 38–39
  k, 39
  l, 39–40
  n, 41
  ng, 50–51
  onsets and rimes and, 144–149
  p, 41–42

phonemes, 26–30, 91, 144
  q, 23–26, 42–43
  r, 43
  s, 43–45
  self-evaluation, 21–22
  sh, 53
  single-letter, 31–49
  syllable division clues and, 109, 111
  syllable pattern activity and, 183–186
  t, 46
  th, 52
  ti, 109
  v, 46
  w, 47
  word cards and, 154–155
  x, 23, 47–48
  y, 48
  z, 48–49
Consonant-vowel-consonant (CVC)
    words, 128

Decoding
  by analogy, 127
  by context, 127
  CVC words, 128
  defined, 13
  by phonics, 124
  stages, 128–129
Derivatives, 208–209
Digraphs
  consonant, 24, 35, 50–55, 93
  discovery activity, 187–190
  vowel, 61, 86–90, 195–196
Diphthongs, 63, 64, 76, 79, 81–84,
    195–196

Ending consonants, 58, 160–164

Find the missing word activity, 135–136
"Foolers," 77

Graphemes, 16–19, 21, 31–49, 69–80,
103–104, 160–164

Hink Pink game, 144, 152–154

Inflectional endings, 105
Invented spellings, 173–176

Language
expressive, 12
receptive, 12
spoken, 13
written, 14
Language Experience Approach (LEA),
168–169
Literacy development, 11–12
Long vowels, 69–73, 186, 190, 194

Macron, 69, 74
Making words
compound, 206–207
consonant blends, 191–192
with ending consonant graphemes,
160–164
games, 149–152
with onsets and rimes, 144–149,
156–160
with syllables, 213–215
variants and derivatives, 208–209
Morphemes, 200–201, 206–207
Morphemic analysis activities, 202–205
Multisyllabic words, 101, 106–108, 110,
200–201
Murmur diphthongs, 63, 64, 76, 79, 81–84,
195–196

Nonrhyming words, 139

Onsets and rimes, 92–97
games, 156–157
making words with, 144–149, 157–158
phonemic awareness and, 101

Patterned writing, 199–200
Phonemes
consonant, 26–30, 91, 144
defined, 8
self-teaching about, 14–16

syllable division clues and, 109–110
voiced and voiceless, 26–29, 98
vowels, 65–69, 91
Phonemic awareness
activities for developing, 142–167
defined, 8
importance of, 8–9
onsets and rimes and, 96, 101
phonics knowledge and, 9–10
rhyming and, 95
Phonics
games, 167
instruction, 123–124, 177–178
"out of context" concept for, 124
as a process to use, 124–125
self-evaluation, 2–7, 115–120
structural analysis knowledge and,
200–202
syllabication and, 209–212
teaching sequence, 125–126
Phonics knowledge
activities for developing, 142–167
literacy development and, 11–12,
122–123
phonemic awareness and, 9–10
syllable patterns and, 180–181
vowel team patterns and, 181
Prefixes, 104–105, 112
Puzzles, 203–205, 210–212

Reading books, 10–11, 130–132, 168–169
Rhyme
activities for creating, 141–142
awareness, developing, 130–131,
139–142
phonemic awareness and, 95
Rimes, 77, 92–97
closed and VCe, 159–160
commonly used, 222–226
creating words with, 156–157
words and pictures for, 144

Schwa phoneme, 102–104
Schwa sound, 201
Self-evaluation tests, 2–7, 21–22, 60–64,
115–120, 217–221
Short vowels, 73–80, 165, 186, 190, 194
Single-syllable words, 143, 144
Skilled readers, 123

Sorting words, 136–139
Spelling(s)
    developmental stages, 178–180
    experiences, 170–172
    invented, 173–176
    phonics knowledge for remembering, 127
Suffixes, 104–105, 112–114, 203–205
Syllabication
    generalization, 111–112
    multisyllabic words, 106–108, 110
    phonics and, 209–212
Syllable(s)
    accented and unaccented, 102–104, 106
    boundaries, 202
    crossword puzzles, 210–212
    defined, 98–99
    division, 108–114
    making words with, 213–215
    riddles, 210
    vowel team, 81
    why to study, 99–101
Syllable patterns
    activity with beginning consonant
        blends, 192–194
    activity with beginning consonant
        digraphs, 188–190
    activity with single consonants, 183–186
    advance activity, 196–198
    closed, 75–76, 79, 100
    discovering, 182–183
    open, 72–73, 100
    phonics knowledge and, 180–181
    VCe, 70–73, 78, 86–87, 94
    vowel team patterns and, 201

Trigraph, 86

Unaccented syllables, 102–104, 106

Variants, 208–209
VCe pattern, 70–73, 196–198
Vowels, 60–91
    a, 65, 66
    ai, 65
    air, 67
    ar, 66
    are, 67
    au, 66
    aw, 66

ay, 65
digraphs, 61, 86–90, 195–196
diphthong, 63, 64, 84–86
e, 65
ea, 65
ear, 67
ee, 65
eer, 67
er, 66
ere, 67
ew, 66
graphemes, 103–104
i, 65
igh, 65
ir, 66
long, 69–73, 186, 190, 194
o, 66
oa, 66
oi, 66
oo, 66
or, 66
ou, 66
ow, 66
oy, 66
phonemes, 65–69, 91
self-evaluation, 60–64
short, 73–80, 165, 186, 190, 194
sounds, 166–167
u, 66
ue, 66
ur, 66
word cards and, 165–166
y, 65
Vowel team patterns
    discovery activity, 195–196
    phonics knowledge and, 181
    syllable patterns and, 201
Vowel teams, 80–89, 108–109, 196–198

Word awareness
    activities for building, 132–139
    defined, 130
Word cards
    alphabet sounds and, 132–139
    consonant letters and, 154–155
    onsets and rimes and, 144–149
    vowel letters and, 165–166
Word games. *See* Making words
Word matching (activity), 134–136

Word recognition, 127, 129
Word variant discovery activity, 202–203
Word walls
    for beginning consonant sounds, 155
    for ending consonant sounds, 164
    for phonics games, 167
    rhyming words, 141–142
    for vowel sounds, 166–167

Writing
    activities, 168–169
    alphabet books, 169–170
    with invented spellings, 173–176
    patterned, 199–200
    phonemically, 67–68
    with sentence starters, 172–173

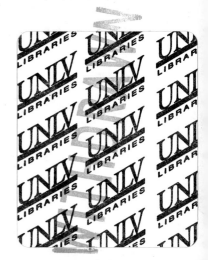